Language Contact

Trends in Linguistics

Studies and Monographs 60

Editor

Werner Winter

Mouton de Gruyter
Berlin · New York

Language Contact

Theoretical and Empirical Studies

Edited by
Ernst Håkon Jahr

Mouton de Gruyter
Berlin · New York 1992

Mouton de Gruyter (formerly Mouton, The Hague)
is a Division of Walter de Gruyter & Co., Berlin.

Library of Congress Cataloging-in-Publication Data

Language contact : theoretical and empirical studies / edited
by Ernst Håkon Jahr.
    p.   cm. — (Trends in linguistics. Studies and mono-
graphs: 60)
    Based on a symposium held Sept. 1989 at the University
of Tromsø. Includes bibliographical references and in-
dex.
    ISBN 3-11-012802-0 (acid-free paper) :
    1. Languages in contact-Congresses. 2. Sociolinguistics-
Congresses.   I. Jahr, Ernst Håkon, 1948– .   II. Series.
P130.5.L34   192
   306-4′4-dc20
                                  92-8084
                                    CIP

Die Deutsche Bibliothek — Cataloging-in-Publication Data

Language contact ; theoretical and empirical studies / ed. by
Ernst Håkon Jahr. — Berlin ; New York : Mouton de Gruyter,
1992
    (Trends in linguistics : Studies and monographs ; 60)
    ISBN 3-11-012802-0
NE: Jahr, Ernst Håkon [Hrsg.]; Trends in linguistics / Studies
and monographs

Preface

The present volume has grown out of the Fifth International Tromsø Symposium on Language held at the University of Tromsø in September 1989. The theme of the symposium was "Language Contact". Ten of the twelve papers included in this volume were first presented and discussed at the Tromsø symposium. (Peter Trudgill's paper was not presented at the symposium, and Peter Nelde presented a different paper from that included here.)

Thanks are due to the University of Tromsø, the School of Languages and Literature (University of Tromsø), and the Norwegian Research Council for the Humanities, all of which supported the symposium financially.

Ernst Håkon Jahr

Preface

Contents

Introduction

Since the publication of Uriel Weinreich's *Languages in Contact* (1953), the study of language contact has been extensive. However, we still lack an overall theory of language contact. Empirical data have been collected from many languages and language-contact situations around the world, but no one has as yet formulated a theory that can be said to account for all — or most of — the empirical data. This is unfortunate, since it is obvious that language-contact studies would make considerable progress if we were able to develop a more advanced framework of theoretical generalizations.

It would be a great help if we had a language laboratory where we could experiment with, and study the outcome of, various kinds of language contact situations. But, of course, we do not have and cannot get such laboratories. What we can do, however, is look for areas of the world where the conditions for mapping out the different important and, perhaps, decisive factors are better than in other regions. The papers in this volume suggest several such promising areas.

It is of great importance for the further development of language contact studies that fresh empirical data from "new" and typologically different languages and language contact areas are collected, described, and discussed. Such new data will contribute to broadening the basis for theoretical generalizations concerning linguistic and sociolinguistic effects of language contact. In that way, stimulating suggestions and new approaches may be brought forward, leading, hopefully, to new theoretical insights. By trying to generalize theoretically from specific case studies of language contact around the world, eventually we can hope to be able to formulate an overall theory of language contact.

The present volume is intended to be a contribution to this development. It contains twelve papers in which different languages from various parts of the world are described and discussed in a language-contact perspective. It covers a wide range of languages, societies, and language-contact situations, from North American Indian languages to the dialect-contact situation of Longyearbyen — the Norwegian town on Spitsbergen, situated right under the North Pole on the 78th parallel; from the

Pacific Ocean to continental Europe; from the Faroe Islands in the North Atlantic to the Indo-Chinese jungle between Thailand and Laos; from Belize in Central America to Alsace in France; and to the Scandinavian minority languages Sami and Romani.

In his paper "Language contacts between Southern Sami and Scandinavian", Knut Bergsland describes the amazing history and present situation of the Southern Sami language, which is spoken today by about five hundred people in Norway and Sweden. This language has been in intimate contact with Scandinavian (i.e., Norwegian and Swedish) for centuries, but in spite of having very few and scattered speakers, it exhibits no sign of language death. Bergsland shows that it has preserved a genuinely Finno-Ugric and Sami structure. Scandinavian influence is, however, clearly seen in lexical borrowings.

Tove Bull's paper, "A contact feature in the phonology of a northern Norwegian dialect", concentrates on a discussion of some rather unusual phonological developments found in a Norwegian dialect spoken in northern Norway, in a formerly Sami-speaking area. She explains the phonological varieties in question as being the result of the transmission of features through language shift (from Sami or Finnish to Norwegian), and views them as part of an "ethnolect" created by the speakers of this dialect in order not to be totally assimilated linguistically.

Ian Hancock ("The social and linguistic development of Scandoromani") surveys the history and present situation of the Romani language in Scandinavia and discusses its origin and development. A comparison of Scandoromani with Angloromani in Britain sheds light on the Scandinavian situation, and Hancock cautiously concludes that Scandoromani has not descended historically from inflected Romani via language attrition, but is based on Scandinavian sociolectal varieties.

In "Language contact in the Pacific: Samoan influence on Tokelauan", Even Hovdhaugen describes the linguistic influence from Samoan on the much smaller linguistic community of Tokelau over the past one hundred and fifty years. He shows that the influence is restricted mainly to lexical borrowings, and that the Samoan impact on Tokelauan is caused by the fact that Samoan has been the only language of church and school for the Tokelau people until quite recently, Tokelauan being, up till now, an oral language only.

Following up some of the ideas in his and Andrée Tabouret-Keller's book *Acts of identity* (1985), Robert B. Le Page discusses in his paper " 'You can never tell where a word comes from': language contact in a diffuse setting" what "languages in contact" means when you have a diffuse language situation like the one in Belize in Central America. Le Page objects to the view that contact-phenomena are the outcome of "contact" between "pairs" of discrete languages only, and argues instead in favor of a framework which focuses on evolutionary linguistic processes in language-contact situations.

Marianne Mithun ("The substratum in grammar and discourse") reports on some very subtle substratum effects from the Northern California Indian language Central Pomo, and shows how important grammatical features and discourse rules from this now almost extinct language have been transferred into the English spoken in Central Pomo communities. These communities are very small, and the substratum effects described by Mithun are fading today. The English variety spoken in Central Pomo communities is, thus, parallel to the Norwegian variety spoken in formerly Sami-speaking areas in northern Norway, described by Tove Bull in her paper.

Brit Mæhlum investigates the mixed dialect situation in the northernmost settlement in the world in her paper "Dialect socialization in Longyearbyen, Svalbard (Spitsbergen): a fruitful chaos". Longyearbyen's inhabitants originally came from all over Norway, and it is the only Norwegian town without its own indigenous dialect. The children who grow up there are exposed to many different Norwegian dialects. Mæhlum describes this quite unique situation of dialect mixing, and she maps the different social and linguistic factors that constitute the framework in which the children and adolescents of Longyearbyen form their personal language. In her discussion, Mæhlum draws considerably on Le Page's and Tabouret-Keller's "acts of identity" model.

In his paper "Ethnolinguistic minorities within the European community: migrants as ethnolinguistic minorities", Peter H. Nelde focusses on the language contacts and conflicts caused by the large groups of recent migrants in Europe which constitute new important language minorities. Nelde views these non-indigenous minority languages in a European multilingual perspective and compares them with traditional, indigenous minority languages in Europe. He raises and discusses various politically difficult questions of language planning concerning these new minority groups.

Jørgen Rischel ("Isolation, contact, and lexical variation in a tribal setting") reports on his study of Mlabri and Tin, two languages spoken on the border between Thailand and Laos, the first by a small elusive tribe, the second by hilltribe peasants. Contact features between these two languages are discussed, as well as their contact with Thai and other surrounding languages. In his discussion, Rischel emphasizes the importance of studying the communicative linguistic norms of "primitive" societies or communities in order to remedy the obvious bias caused by the fact that most linguistic and sociolinguistic theories are based on insights about languages from established civilizations.

In Andrée Tabouret-Keller's paper, "Language contact in focused situations", the language situation and the language history of the French province of Alsace, which is a Germanic dialect area, is described and discussed under the perspective of language contact and language focusing. The principal languages are French and German, with Alsatian as the local vernacular. Tabouret-Keller maps the linguistic history of some local families, and points to important factors that determine the degree of language focusing.

Is it possible to link different types of society to specific types of linguistic change? Peter Trudgill raises this question in his paper "Dialect typology and social structure". He concentrates his discussion on possible differences in linguistic history between smaller, isolated speech communities which have little contact with other languages, and larger, more central ones which have more extensive language contacts. His careful conclusion is that it is not totally futile to look for connections between the social structure of a given society and the linguistic history of that society. Different social structures seem to favor different linguistic developments. Data are drawn mostly from Faroese and Norwegian.

In "Borrowing and non-borrowing in Walapai", Werner Winter describes the history of loanwords in the Amerindian language Walapai, which is spoken in northwestern Arizona. He demonstrates how the Walapai up till the 1950s effectively resisted direct borrowings from English, and that most of the obvious Spanish and English loanwords one could find in Walapai at that time had entered into the language via neighboring Amerindian languages (Hopi and Mohave). The older generation's negative attitude towards English accounts for this puristic tradition. However, in the 1960s and 1970s, Walapai was reduced to a very marginal status among the younger generation, and English became the dominant language. Today, Walapai faces extinction unless there is a change in attitude towards the language among the youngest generation of Walapai.

Language contacts between Southern Sami and Scandinavian

Knut Bergsland

The Sami (Lapp) people are divided between four states — Norway, Sweden, Finland, and the Soviet Union. The national borders were drawn through the territories of many Sami groups — the one between Norway and Sweden-Finland (then united) in 1751 — and so to a large extent cut across the dialectal borders within Sami.

The dialectal differences within Sami are very great, and the dialectal groups are currently regarded as six or seven different Sami languages. One of them is Northern Sami (NS), spoken in Norwegian Finnmark (which means Sami country), in northern Finland, in northern Sweden and in the corresponding parts of Norway (Troms and northern Nordland). In the northwest, Sami borders on Norwegian, and in the southeast on Finnish, a closely-related language. The so-called Lule and Pite Sami spoken farther south, mostly on the Swedish side (see map 1), have more in common with Northern Sami than with the Sami dialects spoken south of them. South of Northern Sami, the Sami have Scandinavian neighbors both in the west (Norwegian) and in the east (Swedish).

Southern Sami in the broader sense is spoken southward from about 66° north, including the so-called Ume Sami dialects, which are spoken on the Swedish side down to the Ume River (Ume älv) but are now close to extinction. Southern Sami in the narrower sense (SS) is spoken southward to about 62° north, in the border area of Norway and Sweden, and includes several subdialects characteristic of the traditional local groups of reindeer-breeders. In our century, however, the dialectal picture has been complicated by administrative southward relocations of Northern Sami reindeer-breeders.

In the course of time, the Southern Sami — like many other Sami groups — have seen large parts of their territories occupied by Scandinavian settlers. A couple of centuries ago, the Southern Sami (in the narrower sense) numbered perhaps some twelve hundred people, and practically all of them were nomadic, living from hunting, fishing, and

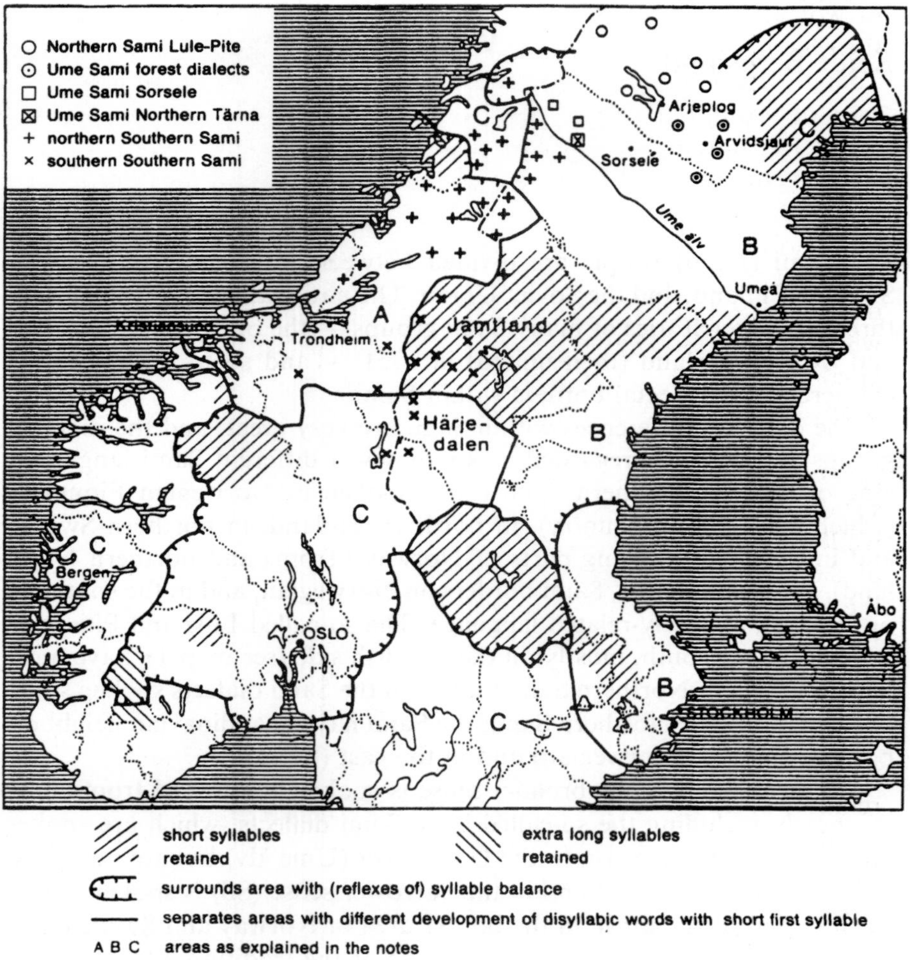

Map legend:

- ○ Northern Sami Lule-Pite
- ☉ Ume Sami forest dialects
- ☐ Ume Sami Sorsele
- ☒ Ume Sami Northern Tärna
- + northern Southern Sami
- × southern Southern Sami

short syllables retained

extra long syllables retained

surrounds area with (reflexes of) syllable balance

separates areas with different development of disyllabic words with short first syllable

A B C   areas as explained in the notes

Map 1.

reindeer-breeding: a way of life very different from that of their Scandinavian neighbors. Until quite recently, practically no Scandinavian man or woman married into a Sami family, while many Sami must have left their Sami society to become farmers or servants of Scandinavian settlers. Today (or a couple of decades ago) the Southern Sami number about two thousand, but only some eight hundred live from reindeer-breeding, about five hundred on the Swedish side and some three hundred on the Norwegian side of the national border of 1751. Without the reindeer-breeding, which in the Sami territories of Norway and Sweden is a Sami monopoly, the Southern Sami could hardly have survived as an ethnic entity, that is, as groups of perhaps twenty or thirty people living in different rural districts dominated by Scandinavian farmers (see map 1, where the crosses and x's indicate clusters of Sami homesteads, but their grazing lands are much more extensive, including state property and properties of Scandinavian farmers).

Until a few decades ago, practically all Southern Sami were active speakers of Sami. At least some of them, however, were also fluent speakers of the Scandinavian dialect of the respective neighborhoods, while very few (if any) of their Scandinavian neighbors had any command of Sami. The documents of the sixteenth and later centuries show that the local authorities dealt with the Sami in Norwegian or Swedish, and the same was probably true of the medieval agents and the Viking chieftains who collected taxes and carried on fur trade with the Sami.

Today, all the Southern Sami are fluent speakers of the respective Scandinavian dialects, while the active speakers of Southern Sami number perhaps some five or six hundred people, including about half of the reindeer-breeders. Sami is used predominantly in connection with the reindeer-breeding, and even the most competent speakers switch between their Sami and Scandinavian dialects, sometimes in the middle of a sentence.

The social dominance of Scandinavian is clearly reflected in the lexicon of the respective languages. In the neighboring Scandinavian dialects, there are practically no Sami loanwords other than, in some of them, a few words relating to Sami matters, whereas the number of Scandinavian loanwords in Southern Sami (as in other Sami languages) is very high, perhaps about two thousand. Some of them are fairly recent, others very old, some adopted perhaps about fifteen hundred years ago: for instance, the word for the edge of a knife or axe, which was taken into Sami in two forms, a southern form *aavtjoe* [àwčuo],[1] found in Ume and Southern Sami, and a northern form *ávju*, found in several variants in the other

Sami languages, both reflecting the Primitive Scandinavian accusative singular *aɣjō*, which in Old Norse and modern Scandinavian became *egg*.

Under these circumstances, one might perhaps expect a thorough-going Scandinavian influence on Southern Sami phonology and grammar as well, but this is not what one finds. In many details the Scandinavian influence is evident, but the overall structure of Southern Sami has remained surprisingly intact and is even more archaic than Northern Sami in certain important respects.

In addition to short and long vowels, Southern Sami — like the other Sami languages — has a number of opening diphthongs of a type also found in Finnish but foreign to Scandinavian: for instance, *giesie* 'summer', *guelie* 'fish', *gåetie* [gɔɛ-] 'house', *gïele* [gieɫə] 'language', *noere* [nuorə] 'young', *råahke* [rɔɑ-] 'male draught-reindeer', *bearkoe* [-uo] 'meat', *guapa* 'sock', *gåaroes* [gɔɒruos] 'empty'. All the vowels and diphthongs occur in an initial (stressed) syllable before a geminate consonant or a consonant cluster: for instance, *bissie* 'holy' vs. *biessie* 'birchbark'. In an open initial syllable, however, Ume and Southern Sami — unlike Northern Sami — have only long vowels and opening diphthongs, the short vowels either having been lengthened and diphthongized (to *ij*, *uv*, etc., in Northern Sami *i*, *u*) or having conditioned the gemination of a following single consonant, as in *bïssem* [bissəm] 'I wash', Northern Sami *basan*. This is reminiscent of the simplifications of the Old Norse quantity patterns in modern Scandinavian, where short stressed syllables have mostly been abolished by lengthening of the short vowel or gemination of the short consonant.[2] As shown in detail in Bergsland (1983), however, the Sami and Scandinavian innovations are rather different and the Sami one seems to be the older, some of the Scandinavian dialects in the immediate neighborhood having even retained the very prosodic feature abolished in Southern Sami. The Southern Sami innovation may reasonably be explained by an increased stress on the initial syllable, which also conditioned the reduction of the short vowels in the following unstressed syllable. The increased stress, actually stronger than in Northern Sami, could quite possibly be due to Scandinavian influence, but this is, of course, impossible to prove or disprove.

In all Sami languages, the vowels of an initial stressed syllable, or at least the opening diphthongs, were subject to metaphonic shifts. In Southern Sami, the metaphony is much more comprehensive than in Northern Sami, including labialization, and the phenomenon recalls the Scandinavian metaphony, which as a process is more than a thousand years old. The Southern Sami metaphony is probably of later date, and it is rather different in its details: for instance, imperative 2nd p. sing. *bissieh!* 'roast!', *bæssam* [b̌ässàm] 'I roast', *byssove* [b̌üssuwə] 'is roasted'; *giesieh!* 'drag!', *geasam* 'I drag', *geesim* 'I dragged', *gyösove* [g̍ōsuwə] 'is dragged'; *guedtieh!* [g̍uettieh] 'carry!', *guadtam* 'I carry', *göödtim* [g<ōttim] 'I carried'. An equally comprehensive metaphony is found in eastern Sami languages where Scandinavian influence is out of the question. But the most remarkable fact is that, in a Scandinavian neighborhood, the Southern Sami metaphony has conditioned a phonological feature foreign to Scandinavian, namely, the opposition of palatalized and velarized initial consonants, as in *gyösove* vs. *göödtim*; *byögki* [b̌ōkkiʲ] 'was exposed to wind' vs. *bööti* [b<ōtiʲ] 'he came'; *gillehtem* [g̍i-] 'I throw down' vs. *gîllehtem* [g<i-] 'I feed to satisfaction' (derived from *gallas* 'satisfied, full'). Rather than Scandinavian, this new opposition is reminiscent of Russian or Celtic, but there could, of course, be no historical connection.

Like the other Sami languages, Southern Sami has consonantal phonemes and clusters foreign to Scandinavian, for instance, affricates, as in *tjåetskeme* [čɔɛckəmə] 'cold (weather)', or a velar nasal in postconsonantal position, as in *gâsngese* [gɑsŋəsə] 'juniper'. An initial *h-*, however, was probably introduced through Scandinavian (or Finnish) loanwords, being absent from the older loans: for instance, SS *aejlege* 'holiday' from an older form of ON *heilag(r)* 'holy', but *hïejme* 'home' from ON *heim(r)* or later Norwegian *heim* 'home' (cf. Qvigstad 1946).

In a few loanwords, the Southern Sami *h-* also reflects the Old Norse voiceless fricative þ: for instance, *hovre-* [huwrə-] 'thunder' in *hovres-åektie* 'thunder-shower' from ON *þór-r* (the thunder god). More intriguingly, the southern *h-* also reflects a Uralic dental fricative which in the other Sami languages and in Baltic Finnish merged with the dental stop: for instance, Ume and Southern Sami *hipmie* 'fish glue', Lule Sami *tapmē*, gen. sing. *tamē*, Finnish *tymä*, Mari (Cheremiss) *lümə*, etc. Since the southern Sami dialects have been spoken in a Scandinavian neighborhood for more than a thousand years, it seems reasonable to think that the Uralic opposition of an initial dental fricative and a dental stop may have been supported by the Scandinavian opposition, which was lost only about 1400 A.D. (cf. Bergsland 1977: 7). Later on, however, probably before the seventeenth century, Southern Sami eliminated the fricative in its own way, with the passage to *h-* rather than to a dental stop as in modern Scandinavian.

In intervocalic and preconsonantal position the voiceless and voiced dental fricatives, preserved in Northern Sami, passed in Southern Sami to trills, respectively voiceless (written *hr*) and voiced (*r*), and in the southernmost dialect to stops: e. g., NS *muotta*, SS *muahra, muata* 'mother's younger sister'; NS *oðða* [ɔðða], SS *orre* [urrə], *odde* [uddə] 'new'. This is probably a later innovation, although the secondary *r* is attested as early as about 1700 A.D. and could easily be due to Scandinavian influence.

Like Finnish and other Finno-Ugric languages, Sami once had only single consonants in word-initial position, and clusters were introduced through Scandinavian loanwords. Most of the Sami languages have clusters with an initial sibilant, but in the south one also finds initial clusters of a stop plus a liquid, for instance in the very old loanword *kraevies* 'grey' (Lule Sami *rāvuk* with a Sami suffix) from Primitive Scandinavian **grāwaR*, Old Norse *grár*, modern Scandinavian *grå* (cf. Qvigstad 1945). From such loanwords, the pattern has been transferred to original Sami words as an expressive feature: for instance, SS *prïhtjege* 'bitter, coffee', NS *rihča*, gen. *rihččaga* 'bitter'; SS *pråetjkiestidh* 'to boil fast', as in *prïhtjege pråetjkestemienie* 'the coffee is boiling'. The same phenomenon is known from western Finnish dialects, in the neighborhood of Swedish (Rapola 1966: 19 – 24), whereas the eastern Finnish dialects have only single consonants in initial position, as do the easternmost Sami languages.

Some other instances of Scandinavian influence upon Southern Sami phonology could be adduced, but in general Southern Sami has stayed remarkably distinct from the Scandinavian dialects. Thus, even quite recent loanwords are processed to fit into the Sami patterns. The first name *Knut*, for instance, needs a final vowel, say *-a*, and with the obligatory metaphony it becomes *Knavhta*, a phonic product that is inconceivable in the Scandinavian dialect of the same speaker.

The morphology presents a similar picture. The inflection of Southern Sami nouns includes eight cases, fully operative, while the four cases of Old Norse have been drastically reduced in modern Scandinavian. The Sami postpositions are likewise preserved, whereas Scandinavian has only prepositions. However, the possessive suffixes, foreign to Scandinavian, are greatly reduced (as also is the case in modern dialects of Northern Sami). A suffixed form like *aahtje-me* 'my father' may be used as a term of address, but the common expression is the phrase *mov aehtjie*, with the genitive of the personal pronoun before the noun. Occasionally one may also hear *aehtjie mov*, which reflects the order of the Scandinavian *far min*.

Unlike modern Scandinavian, the Sami verb is inflected for person and number, although the dual is losing ground in the south, being replaced by the corresponding plural forms. Thus the subject pronouns, obligatory in modern Scandinavian, are used mostly for emphasis: e.g., *guarkam (gujt)* 'I understand', *manne (gujt) guarkam 'I* understand' (*gujt* is an affirmative particle, here optional). Negation, very different from the Scandinavian particles, is effected by a preposed verb inflected for two tenses and for the imperative, with the negated verb having in all cases a special suffix -*h*: for instance, *im daejrieh* 'I don't know', *idtjim daejrieh* 'I didn't know', *aellieh dam vaeltieh* 'don't take that' (*dam* is the accusative of *dïhte* 'that').

In addition to the indicative and the imperative moods, Northern Sami also has a conditional and a potential, like Finnish. In Southern Sami, these moods are greatly reduced, probably due to the influences of modern Scandinavian, where practically nothing is left of the Old Norse subjunctive. The conditional, found only in the southernmost dialects, is limited to the auxiliary verb *lea-* 'to be': e. g., 1st pers. sing. *luvnem*, a near equivalent of the Scandinavian *ville* 'would'. Farther north, where there are traces of the potential, one uses the preterite, as in dialectal Scandinavian: for instance, *Manne lim aaj bååteme, jis lim asteme* 'I too would have come if I had had time', literally "I had too come if I-had had-time."

Another interesting innovation of Southern Sami (and of Ume Sami, attested since the seventeenth century) is the auxiliary verb *edtje-* 'shall', as in *vaarrem, edtjem ohtsedidh* 'I run in order to look for (the reindeer)', literally "I-run, I-shall look-for", which corresponds to Scandinavian constructions such as *jeg springer og skal lete*, literally "I run and shall look for". The verb *edtje-* apparently reflects the suffix of the so-called supine, an infinitive form found in Pite and Lule Sami and farther north: e. g., Lule *vuolgijme stålpijt tjuoigati-ttjat* 'we took off in order to ski after wolves'. Occasionally, one may also hear the simple infinitive with a preceding *jïh* (or *jih*) 'and' in the same sense: e. g., (Røros 1941) *aehtjie vuelkiejæjja jih vaagka-sjïjjiem ohtjedijt* 'father took off in order to look for a place where the wolf had killed a reindeer'. This use of *jih* reflects the merger in modern Scandinavian of the conjunction *og* 'and' with the infinitive marker *å* 'to, in order to' (normal Sami has no infinitive marker other than the suffix).

In Southern Sami conversation, or in a story recorded on tape or dictated, one may sometimes observe expressions carried over from the speaker's Scandinavian dialect. More typical of Southern Sami, however, are constructions that are quite un-Scandinavian.

The most remarkable of these is perhaps the nominal sentence type, used most regularly in the southernmost dialects, that is, in the closest neighborhood of Scandinavian: for instance:

> *Laara   saemie.*
> Larry   Sami
> 'Larry is a Sami.'
> *Noere   dïhte.*
> young   that
> 'He is young.'
> *Dan jïjjen   dan tjåetskeme.*
> that night   so   cold
> 'It was so cold that night.'

The nominal sentence is a Uralic heritage, lost in the other Sami languages through the obligatory use of the auxiliary *lea-* 'to be', which is probably due to Finnish influence (*ole-* 'to be'), where it came in from Germanic at an early date (Korhonen 1981: 343). In this respect, Southern Sami actually agrees with the eastern Finno-Ugric languages and Samoyed, even though in their Scandinavian speech the speakers use the normal Germanic copula.

In a yes/no question, a speaker of Scandinavian uses inversion: e. g., *Kommer far?* 'Does father come?' In Northern Sami and in Finnish, one employs in addition an enclitic particle: e. g., *Boahtá-go áhčči? Tuleeko isä?* In Southern Sami, one uses an initial particle (a petrified plural of the interrogative pronoun *mij* 'what') without inversion: e. g., *Mah aehtjie båata?* This may be a southern innovation but differs strikingly from Scandinavian.

Like Finnish, the Sami languages are highly inflecting, and word order is relatively free. In Northern Sami and Finnish, the so-called neutral order is SVO, as in Scandinavian, but in Southern Sami SOV is preferred, apparently a Uralic heritage like the nominal sentence type: for instance:

> *Laara bustem   darjoeji.*
> Larry spoon-ACC   made
> 'Larry made a spoon.'
> *Aehtjie gåatan   bööti.*
> father   house-to   came
> 'Father came home.'

If the verb has two complements, for instance an object and a local term, the latter tends to come after the verb, but as many as three complements may precede the verb, as in the following sentence produced spontaneously by a perfectly bilingual speaker in the southernmost Sami area (Røros 1941):

> *Ruhtjeste   gaejpiem   aeksjene   tjuahpa.*
> jaw-from   chin-ACC   axe-with   cuts (when slaughtering)
> 'One cuts the chin from the jaw with an axe.'

In Norwegian the sentence is: *Man hugger hakestykket fra underkjeven med øks*, with an order just as in English. In this part of the world, the structural difference could hardly be greater.

People speaking two different languages perfectly is, of course, no unusual phenomenon. In the case of Southern Sami, however, the question is how the language could survive at all after more than a thousand years in a dominant Scandinavian neighborhood, and how the phonological and grammatical structure could remain quite un-Scandinavian together with the very large number of Scandinavian loanwords.

In the basic vocabulary of Southern Sami one finds, for example, loanwords such as *fihkedh* 'to get, receive' (beside *åadtjodh*), from the Scandinavian preterite *fikk* 'got'. On the other hand, the lexicon also includes striking archaisms, for example in the field of reindeer-breeding. The most remarkable feature from a social point of view is, perhaps, the kinship terminology, with its age distinctions for in-laws, for instance between a woman's husband's elder and younger brothers and male cousins. This system, reminiscent of eastern Finno-Ugric languages and Samoyed, is found also in the eastern Sami languages but is reduced in Northern Sami. Until recently, kinship terms, rather than first names, were obligatory terms of address among the Southern Sami, and certain terms were used also for addressing unrelated Sami, but never for addressing Scandinavian neighbors. Even when speaking Norwegian or Swedish, a Southern Sami would address his or her father and mother with the Sami terms *aehtjie* and *tjidtjie*, the last words of the language to be given up.

By contrast, the Northern Sami reindeer-breeders of northern Sweden in their daily life would use Finnish loanwords for their parents: *isá* and *eidde*, Finnish *isä* and *äiti*. Their second language has been Finnish for centuries, and the Finnish impact is evident, not only from the vast number of Finnish loanwords but also, for example, from the general merger of the phoneme *š* with *s*, Finnish having only one sibilant. The languages being closely related, quite distinct but largely congruent, the way is open for all sorts of structural influences and transpositions, not the least where Sami differs sharply from Scandinavian.

The difference between the two situations is not only linguistic, however. As mentioned at the beginning, until recently no Scandinavian man or woman married into Southern Sami society, while intermarriage between Northern Sami and Finns has been common, and many Northern Sami descend directly from Finnish immigrants into their territory.

The social function of the Southern Sami language has not only been for the Sami to communicate among themselves, but also to keep the Scandinavian neighbors out. Thus the language has been used also as a secret language, for example to prevent Scandinavian visitors from following business discussions in connection with slaughtering reindeer for sale. A reflex of this function is the Southern Sami word *tjahta* 'wedge' and 'kilo'. As a "cryptic calque",[3] the Sami equivalent of the Scandinavian word *kile* 'wedge' was used also to cover the Scandinavian *kilo* in order to prevent the visitors from grasping the gist of the discussion.

Another example is *guelie* 'fish' used for a sheriff, equivalent to Swedish *fiskal* which is associated by the Sami with *fisk* 'fish'. This calque may have a certain humorous flavor, although not in the deprecatory sense of the Scandinavian *fisk* applied to a person — to a Sami, fish are good things. But the real point is deadly serious, for the language has served to maintain the Sami identity, that is, to defend their way of life and the rights to their territories, in opposition to their Scandinavian neighbors. In the course of the last couple of decades, their rights have been strengthened legally and their language may face a friendlier future. It has become a literary language, with an official orthography introduced in 1978, and is taught in the Southern Sami schools, so it may possibly be revitalized in Sami homes as well.

Notes

1. Sami words are given in the respective official orthographies; for Southern Sami see Bergsland (1982). The forms in square brackets are rough phonetic transcriptions, the [à] being a half-long variant of the long *aa*.
2. The Scandinavian data were analyzed by Trygve Skomedal in Bergsland (1983). In the area marked A on map 1, the vowel is short and the consonant lengthened in practically all cases. In area B, there is a general lengthening of a medial stop but a geographically varying mixture of vowel and consonant

lengthening in other cases. In area C, there is mostly vowel lengthening even before stops.

3. A cryptic word in Southern Sami is called *jorth* or *jorth-baakoe* (NS *jurda* 'thought'), and to talk with such words is *jortegi soptsestidh*.

References

Bergsland, Knut
  1977   "Saamen kieli ja naapurikielet / The Lapp language and its neigh-
              bours", *Virittäjä* 1/1977: 1—10 (Helsinki: Kotikielen seura).
  1982   *Sydsamisk grammatikk* [Southern Sami grammar] (Oslo: Univer-
              sitetsforlaget).
  1983   "Southern Lapp and Scandinavian quantity patterns", *Suomalais-
              ugrilaisen Seuran Toimituksia* 185: 73—87.
Korhonen, Mikko
  1981   *Johdatus lapin kielen historiaan* [Introduction to the history of the
              Sami language] (Helsinki: Suomalaisen Kirjallisuuden Seura).
Qvigstad, Just
  1945   "Dobbeltkonsonant i forlyd i lappisk" [Initial consonant clusters
              in Sami], *Studia Septentrionalia* II: 193—212 (Oslo).
  1946   "Das anlautende *h* im Lappischen", *Finnisch-ugrische Forschungen*
              XXIX: 37—51.
Rapola, Martti
  1966   *Suomen kielen äännehistorian luennot* [Lectures on the phonolog-
              ical history of Finnish] (Helsinki: Suomalaisen Kirjallisuuden
              Seura).

A contact feature in the phonology of a northern Norwegian dialect

Tove Bull

1. Background

The corpus on which the present analysis is based was collected in a small bilingual Norwegian village. The village is situated in an originally Sami area in northern Norway, one hundred and twenty kilometers from the city of Tromsø. The name of the village is Furuflaten; its population is about three hundred and fifty.

Up to the beginning of the last century, this part of Norway was more or less monolingual Sami. The very first time we hear of an ethnically Norwegian person in Lyngen, the municipality in which Furuflaten is situated, is as late as 1789. That year the ethnicity of all males of more than nineteen years of age was registered in connection with military enlistment. Out of a total of three hundred and nineteen men, only one was registered as being Norwegian. A factor that broadens the basis of multilingualism in the area has to do with immigration from northern Finland and northern Sweden. About one hundred to one hundred and fifty years ago, quite a few Finnish-speaking immigrants moved into this part of Norway because of famine in the north of Finland and Sweden. As a result of this immigration, most of the families at Furuflaten have one or more Finnish-speaking ancestors.

In 1860, Professor J. A. Friis mapped the ethnographic state of affairs in northern Norway. According to his ethnographic maps, there were sixteen families in the village of Furuflaten at that time (Friis 1861). The village was then called Dalen or Lyngsdalen. At least one person in every family was trilingual according to Friis, i. e., able to speak Sami, Finnish and Norwegian. In most cases the trilingual persons probably were the adult males of the households. The first language of all the families was Sami. How thorough the Norwegian and Finnish competence of the male adults may have been is, of course, hard to tell, but it is highly unlikely that all grown-up men in the area were fluent in both Finnish and

Norwegian. The ethnographic information given by J. A. Friis' new and revised maps of 1890 coincides with that of 1861, though the exact number of families is not given on these newer maps.

This in no way means that bi- or trilingualism was a common phenomenon in the whole population at the turn of the century. Most of the women and children were probably more or less monolingual. It is reasonable to assume that, at the beginning of this century, the village consisted of Sami-speaking grown-ups with a slight competence in Norwegian and/or Finnish, the males probably mastering their second and/or third language better than the women. In all probability, most of the children were more or less monolingual Sami-speakers when they started school.

Today this has changed drastically. By now all the children growing up in the village are monolingual, having command only of Norwegian. The older generations are still bi- or trilingual, but not very many know Finnish. According to my oldest informants, those over seventy, most of them were bilingual when they started school at the age of seven. Only one states that she did not know Norwegian at that time. This might, of course, be the result of over-reporting their Norwegian competence at the time. Today most middle-aged people do not speak Sami (or Finnish), but quite a few have a passive Sami competence. Some of them are what Nancy C. Dorian (1982) calls semi-speakers, i.e., persons able to take part in conversations in Sami in spite of having a rather low grammatical competence. There is a saying used by this generation: "They cannot sell me in Sami", or "I cannot be sold", meaning: I understand enough not to be cheated. Those that do not know any Sami at all put it like this: "I could be sold in Sami".

Based on this background, I consider it reasonable to claim that the Norwegian linguistic varieties spoken in the kind of communities of which Furuflaten is a representative example are the youngest or most recently formed of the Norwegian dialects.

During the years 1988 and 1989, I did linguistic fieldwork in the village of Furuflaten. My purpose is to describe the Norwegian vernacular from a language-contact perspective. More particularly, I am trying to look into Sami (and potential Finnish) substratum features in everyday speech. So far, I have recorded the speech of thirty-two of the inhabitants in the village, aged from four to eighty-seven, the sampling being carried out according to a kind of social network principle. My data have been collected in informal interviews and by the technique of participant observation, i.e., some of my recordings consist of conversations between two or more of the local people while others are rather informal interviews with one of the locals at a time. My informants may be divided roughly into three age groups:

1. People aged from their late sixties upwards, the oldest being eighty-seven when he was interviewed
2. People aged between about thirty and fifty
3. Young persons, roughly between the ages of ten and twenty

2. Language contact: postalveolarization or clusters, an example from the phonology of Furuflaten

If we take as our starting point the simplest possible model of language contact, we can illustrate it as in figure 1.

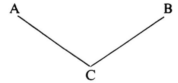

Figure 1.

Two languages A and B are in contact, this contact being the origin of the development of a new variety (a new language), language C, with a grammar and a lexicon that can be described as having originated from A or B, or both. The task of the contact linguist is, in this case, to show how it is possible to go from A and/or B to C.

The phonological system of Furuflaten is probably the result of language contact, though the variants used there do not in any way correspond directly to the Sami (or the Finnish) phonological system. An illustration corresponding to the model above is shown in figure 2.

Here the situation differs somewhat from Figure 1. My task is in this case, as I see it, to describe (and possibly explain) the development from N_1 to N_2, i.e., the history of the Norwegian language in a language-contact area, taking into consideration possible influences from Sami and maybe Finnish as well.

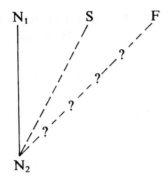

Figure 2.

In this paper, I am going to take a closer look at the realization of one phonological item only. My aim is to try to show how the phonological variants used at Furuflaten differ from the variants in the neighboring monolingual Norwegian area. To systematize the variation found in the contact area, we have to take morphology into account, as we will see later on. At the end of my paper, I will briefly touch upon a few other items for the purpose of comparison.

The item I have chosen concerns variation between the apico-postalveolars /tdn̩l̩/, often termed alveolar or retroflexed consonants, and consonant clusters consisting of a trill or flap followed by a lamino-alveolar (or apico-dental) phone /r + t, d, n, l/. In many Norwegian (and Swedish) dialects, these postalveolars are the result of an assimilation of retroflexion, postalveolarization or supradentilization, i. e., they represent a typical case of assimilation to an adjacent segment. Whether the products of the assimilation of /r/ and /t, d, n, l/ in fact are retroflexes or not is, of course, a matter open to discussion and a problem of definition. I will not discuss this matter further, and refrain from using the term. Instead I shall use the term postalveolar, naming the process of assimilation postalveolarization. In this connection I might also have considered the realization and distribution of the (lamino-) postalveolar voiceless fricative /ʃ/ versus /r/ + the (lamino-) alveolar voiceless fricative /s/, but this does not seem so straightforward as the other cases, and so far I have been unable to find any systematic or consistent pattern explaining the variatioin between the cluster /rs/ and /ʃ/.

These postalveolar consonants are found in eastern, central, and northern Norway, as well as in what might be considered a Norwegian standard. They are also used in the Swedish standard and in Swedish vernacular speech in central and northern Sweden. Exempt from the rule of postalveolarization are the western part of southern Norway as well as southern Sweden. Nor do postalveolars occur in standard Finland Swedish.

Sami has no postalveolar consonants like /tɖɳ ɭ/. In Northern Sami, the clusters /rt/ and /rd/ are found medially, whereas /rn/ and /rl/ do not occur in words of Sami origin, but can be found in words borrowed from, for instance, Norwegian. During the last few decades, some Sami dialects have been adopting Norwegian postalveolars, at least in some words, but this is a very recent and rare phenomenon.

In the Norwegian dialects in the monolingual vicinity of my research area, however, these original clusters have obligatorily and categorically been assimilated into postalveolar consonants. The mechanism behind postalveolarization is in itself very simple: a dental occurring after a postalveolar /r/ is assimilated into a postalveolar point of articulation, the phoneme /r/ thereby being absorbed by the general postalveolar pronunciation. There has been some discussion among linguists about whether the process proceeds in one or two steps or stages (cf. Eliasson 1986: 283 – 284). However, this problem will not be considered in the present paper.

The phenomenon of postalveolarisation has received the attention of several linguists investigating Scandinavian languages, e. g., Borgstrøm (1981 [1938] and 1958), Vogt (1981 [1939] and 1981 [1942]), Christiansen (1946 – 1948), Steblin-Kamenskij (1981 [1965]), Rinnan (1981 [1969]), Eliasson (1986), and others. Very little of this literature is suitable to serve as reference when dealing with vernacular speech in a Norwegian language-contact area, or to help explain the problems raised in the present paper. What has been of major interest to the linguists discussing postalveolarisation is first and foremost the structural status of the sounds in question. In connection with this question of phonological status, the distribution of the sounds has been documented, at least in some of the varieties in which they occur. The geographical distribution of the phenomenon has attracted dialectologists, e. g., Christiansen (1946 – 48). A closer phonetic analysis of the sounds in question and the potential historical development of postalveolarization constitute other domains of interest.

As for the question of structural status, different solutions have been suggested within the framework of traditional structuralism. Do the postalveolars function as independent phonemes or should they instead be considered allophones of clusters of /r/ + dental, i. e., merely phones?

Borgstrøm (1981 [1938]) considered them separate phonemes, although he doubts his own solution later on (cf. Borgstrøm 1958). His reasons for reconsidering this question are the following: a) the limited distribution of postalveolars in Norwegian (they occur only after vowels and never initially except in the case of external sandhi positions), and b) the fact that the use of postalveolars or clusters is subject to stylistic variations in many varieties of Norwegian: postalveolars prevail in ordinary colloquial speech (e. g., ['jæʈe]), while clusters are preferred in more formal styles (e. g., ['jærte]). In east Norwegian dialects and in the Norwegian standard, the quantity of clusters rises proportionally as the style becomes more formal and literary. According to Vogt (1981 [1939]: 191), the stylistic variation is rather free, even though some systematic patterns can be abstracted from this variation:

> The system varies from individual to individual, from style to style, but one fact remains: at one extreme, a careful pronunciation with a maximum of these clusters and a minimum of alveolars, at the other extreme, a careless pronunciation with a minimum of clusters and a maximum of alveolars. In practice the alveolars will hardly ever be totally absent, however literary the style, and in the most careless pronunciation some clusters will be kept unchanged. Between the two extremes, it is possible to define by the proportion of clusters and alveolars any intermediary pronunciation system.

The problem of structural phonological status is a marginal one in the perspective of the present paper. One should furthermore bear in mind that the rule of postalveolarization is a more general one in modern Northern Norwegian dialects than in many other varieties of Norwegian. In principle, this rule may now be considered general and compulsory in the Norwegian dialects spoken in the monolingual vicinity of the language-contact area in question. However, what is of some relevance to the present paper may be quoted from Vogt (1981 [1942]: 224 – 225):

> The outstanding fact is undoubtedly the increased importance of sandhi-phenomena — the word loses its rigid individuality by depending in its phonemic form on the surroundings. ... The form of the initial phoneme and cluster thus gets morphological significance — really a novel phenomenon in Norwegian morpho-phonemics. The problem of the alveolars can therefore only be solved on the basis of the word-groups and not of the isolated words.

What happens, then, when an originally Sami-speaking population is assimilated linguistically into the Norwegian community? In accordance with what is generally known from linguistic contact situations, one would expect to find a great deal of phonetic variation. And indeed this is the case. As all sociolinguistic experience tells us, however, linguistic variation is neither random nor arbitrary. Nor is this the case as regards the specific phonetic variation in question. Phonetic heterogeneity is an important patterned aspect of the linguistic variety in question. If I were to anticipate a result of my, so far incomplete, analysis, I would predict that a pattern of structured heterogeneity also characterizes the morphology and syntax of the variety.

As far as the variation of postalveolars and clusters is concerned, a very rough pattern can be shown co-varying with age. The members of age group 1 (the old people) realize what from a superficial point of view may be considered a mixture between the Sami and the north Norwegian system, exhibiting both the clusters and the postalveolars in their speech. Age groups 2 and 3 now seem to have adopted the north Norwegian system of postalveolarization completely.

In her cand.philol.-dissertation on place-name loans, Aud-Kirsti Pedersen (1988) has analysed the phonology of two north Norwegian dialects, one of them spoken just across the fjord from Furuflaten, the other spoken further north in the county. Her observations on the variation between clusters and postalveolars are worth quoting:

> When it comes to the use of these sounds (ṭ, ḍ, ṇ, ḷ, ṣ/ there is a difference between older and younger informants. The younger ones much more frequently than the older ones have a pronunciation with sublamino-alveolars [i. e., postalveolars in my terminology]. It is, however, never the case that any informant always prefers a sublamino-alveolar pronunciation. If a sublamino-alveolar pronunciation is not realized the pronunciation is /rt rd rn rl rs/. In front of the unvoiced sounds /t/ and /s/, /r/ is a distinct unvoiced fricative. One often notes that /r/ is deleted in front of /t/ and /s/. The words *sikkert* and *norsk* may be pronounced /'sik:eṭ/, /'sik:et/, /'sik:e/ and /'noṣk/, /'norsk/, /'nosk/. Among the sequences /rt rd rn rl rs/, r + plosives are most frequently pronuounced as clusters, while sublamino-alveolar pronunciation is very often used in stead of /rn rl rs/. (Pedersen 1988: 167−168, my translation.)

Pedersen's general observations on the differences between the older and the younger generations and on the high degree of variation seem to be valid for Furuflaten as well. Her last statement on the choice of postalveolars or clusters according to the quality of the original dental following the original /r/-sound does not hold for my material, however.

According to Eliasson (1986: 281), postalveolarization in Swedish and Norwegian is contingent on factors of three kinds: a) the phonetic nature of the input sequence, b) the immediate structural environment, notably grammatical boundaries, and c) wider, partly structure-external parameters. Vogt also takes the phonetic environment into consideration. In his own standard east Norwegian speech, the relation of /rt/ and /ṭ/ varies according to the phonetic structure of the word: "In the same style of natural speech rt instead of ṭ will hardly be heard after long vowels, but rt will often be pronounced after short vowels". (Vogt 1981 [1939]: 188)

On the other hand, the distribution of /rd/ and /ḍ/ is very different. Even in ordinary speech, the cluster is common after short vowels; /ḍ/ occurs only in a few simple words and in compounds, and is also common before a stressed syllable, i.e., mostly in words of foreign origin. In careful pronunciation, /ḍ/ may be almost completely replaced by /rd/. As for /ṇ/, it is common after long vowels, after /e:/, /i:/ and /y:/ apparently only as the result of internal or external sandhi. It is rare after short, stressed vowels. In all cases, /ṇ/ may be replaced by /rn/, though rarely after long vowels. /ḷ/ is frequent after long stressed vowels. After short stressed vowels, it occurs only in compounds. (Vogt 1981 [1939]: 189–190)

As has already been mentioned, the rule of postalveolarization has developed into a general rule in the northernmost dialects of Norway. In these vernaculars the system is much more simple than the complex one described by Vogt. This means that we would not expect rules like the ones formulated by Vogt to be operating in the Norwegian contact vernaculars in this area, either. As far as my analysis goes, the distribution of postalveolars is not sensitive to the phonetic environment except for boundary phenomena. That is, only b) and c) of Eliasson's factors are relevant in my data.

3. Morpho-phonemic interference: a development in three stages

Weinreich (1963: 18–19) distinguishes between four different types of phonemic interference stemming from language contact: (1) under-differentiation of phonemes, (2) over-differentiation of phonemes, (3) reinterpretation of distinctions, and (4) actual phone substitutions. Our case, in which north Norwegian postalveolars originally were realized as clusters, belongs to category 4 if these clusters are interpreted as Sami substratum elements. It might also be considered an example of under-differentiation of phonemes. As a matter of definition, it therefore is an example of "interference" as defined by Weinreich (1953: 14): "Interference arises when a bilingual identifies a phoneme of the secondary system with one in the primary system and, in reproducing it, subjects it to the phonetic rules of the primary language."

On the basis of this and of the potential development of other substratum phonological properties, I have postulated an abstract or potential pattern of development of the Norwegian dialect of Furuflaten in three stages, as in figure 3.

Stage 1
rt
rd   clusters, no assimilation
rl
rn

Stage 2
$[r(\#)\#/+t] \rightarrow [t]$
$[r(\#)\#/+d] \rightarrow [d]$
$[r(\#)\#/+n] \rightarrow [n]$
$[r(\#)\#/+l] \rightarrow (l]$
Clusters [rt rd rn rl] in all other positions.

Stage 3
$[rt] \rightarrow [t]$
$[rd] \rightarrow [d]$
$[rn] \rightarrow [n]$
$[rl] \rightarrow [l]$

Figure 3.

As it appears, my notation system is rather tentative. The point I want to illustrate is that the rule of postalveolarization at Stage 2 applies only across word and morpheme boundaries, that is, in internal and external sandhi structures, internal sandhi positions being represented by inflections, derivations, and compoundings.

What description or what linguistic model would be the most appropriate one to account for the linguistic change that undoubtedly has taken place? How can we describe and explain what has happened between the different stages? What processes have taken place? Had I written this paper ten years ago, I would probably have considered the rule of Stage 2 a variable rule. However, the concept of variable rule as described by Labov does not seem to have provided a fruitful basis for describing, explaining, and predicting linguistic variation. It has been criticized from different theoretical points of view, and now it seems to have been abandoned altogether by most linguists. I therefore see no point in trying to revitalize it in this context. On the other hand, the notion of lexical diffusion does not at all seem an appropriate concept to account for my data, except in the case of a few proper names, to which the rule postulated for Stage 2 does not apply. These are proper names always pronounced with a postalveolar, and sometimes quite contradictory to the rule, as for instance in ['asbjøɳ], ['jøɖis] and ['æ:[iŋ]. The spread of the postalveolar pronunciation may have started with these proper names and others of the same kind, but few other instances exist that can be interpreted as having been spread via lexical diffusion. "Grammatical diffusion" seems to be a much more appropriate concept, and this brings us back to the notion of variable grammatical rules. One should bear in mind, however, that trying to state the distribution of postalveolars and clusters in simple rules of a purely linguistic nature might be in vain.

As mentioned above, the rule of postalveolarization is by now a general rule in the monolingual neighborhood of Furuflaten. That is to say that postalveolarization occurs in all kinds of morpho-phonological positions. Figure 4 illustrates this (cf. Eliasson 1986: 278). The leftmost column lists the examples in conventional spelling and the morphological analysis when necessary, the second gives the English translation, the third and fourth provide rough phonetic transcriptions in two alternatives, both being possible at Furuflaten among age group 1, only the fourth among age groups 2 and 3.

What then do the data tell us? Since the variation in the data is largest in age group 1, I have made a close analysis of the speech of all the informants in this group, the analysis entailing the registering of all the tokens of these informants. All together there are thirteen informants, eight women and five men, the youngest born in 1926, the oldest in 1901. Except for the youngest one, all the informants were over the age of seventy when interviewed. Age groups 2 and 3 seem to have adopted the general rule of postalveolarization completely. As a spot check, I have registered all the tokens of two informants (a woman and a man) from age group 2 and three girls and one boy from age group 3.

Stage 1 (involving only clusters) is not realized by anyone living at Furuflaten today. In fact, it is not my intention to postulate that this stage has ever been realized by any observable speaker of Norwegian at Furuflaten. The main point is that Stage 1 represents the original /rt rd/

A. Morpheme-internally			
svart	'black'	[svart]	[svaṭ]
verden	'world'	[værdn̩]	[vædn̩]
garn	'yarn, net'	[ga:rn]	[ga:ɳ]
perle	'pearl'	[pæ:rle]	[pæ:ɭe]

B. Across inflectional boundaries			
hørt (hør + t)	'heard'	[hø(:)rt]	[hø(:)ṭ]
lærd (lær + d)	'learned'	[lærd]	[læḍ]
fjorden (fjord + en)	'the fjord'	[fju:rn̩]	[fju:ɳ]

C. Across derivational boundaries			
fortørna (for + tørna)	'angry'	[for'tø:rna]	[fo'tø:ɳa]
forderv (for + derv)	'destruction'	[for'dærv]	[fo'dærv]
fornuft (for + nuft)	'common sense'	[for'nʉft]	[fo'ɳʉft]
nordlig (nord + lig)	'northern'	['nu:rli]	['nu:ɭi]

D. In formal compounding			
fortid (for # tid)	'past'	['forti]	['foṭi]
fordel (for # del)	'advantage'	['fordel]	['foḍel]
fornavn (for # navn)	'first name'	['fornavn]	['foɳavn]
forledd (for # ledd)	'first element'	['forled]	['foɭed]

E. Across regular compound boundary			
stortå (stor # tå)	'big toe'	['stu:r‚to:]	['stu:‚ṭo:]
brordatter (bror # datter)	'brother's daughter'	['bru:r‚datr̩]	['bru:‚ḍatr̩]
gårnatt (går # natt)	'yesterday night'	['go:r‚nat]	['go:‚ɳat]
storlast (stor # last)	'big load'	['stu:r‚last]	['stu:‚ɭast]

F. Across word boundary			
har tatt (har # # tatt)	'have taken'	[har'tad]	[ha'ṭad]
har du (har # # du)	'have you'	['har‚dʉ:]	['ha‚ḍʉ:]
har nok (har # # nok)	'have enough'	[‚har'nok]	[‚ha'ɳok]
har litt (har # # litt)	'have a little'	[‚har'lit]	[‚ha'ɭit]

Figure 4.

and potential /rl rn/ Sami system of people who lost their Sami mother-
tongue in the process of Norwegianization.

Stage 2 seems to be realized by all the informants in age group 1. The
patterns below are based upon the analysis of the tokens of two of the
informants (a woman and a man).

The above formalizations may appear to be simplified versions of
Labov's variable rules which I just said I would refrain from using. I

have chosen, however, to formulate and quantify my findings in accordance with this convention solely for practical reasons. I consider my own "rules" purely pragmatic and descriptive devices which do not in any way imply a specific theoretical framework. Neither do the rules in themselves explain the mechanism of linguistic change. They just describe variation in linguistic data. The frequencies given in percentages thus imply no prediction of rule frequencies, as do orthodox variable rules. The percentages are the real frequencies found in the data, no more, no less. My problem has consistently been how to account for structural heterogeneity in a formal model, preferably one which is sensitive to variation. The type of "rules" used here reflect the conviction that language displays regular variation; they represent a rather simple and practical attempt to formalize and illustrate this regularity.

1. $[r(\#)\#/+t] \rightarrow \; <[t]> \; (85\%)$ [hat] (*hard + t*)
2. $[rt] \rightarrow \; <[rt]>/$in all other positions (i.e., word and   [svart] (*svart*)
   morpheme internally) (53%)
3. $[r(\#)\#/+d] \rightarrow \; <[d]> \; (74\%)$ ['bli:ɖe] (*blir + det*)
4. $[rd] \rightarrow \; <[rd]>/$in all other positions (100%)   ['orɖn̩] (*orden*)
5. $[r(\#)\#/+n] \rightarrow \; <[n]> \; (79\%)$ ['fju:n̩] (*fjord + en*)
6. $[rn] \rightarrow \; <[rn]>/$in all other positions (100%)   ['tørna] (*tørna*)
7. $[r(\#)\#/+l] \rightarrow \; <[ɭ]> \; (99\%)$ ['fa:ɭi] (*far + lig*)
8. $[rl] \rightarrow \; <[rl]>/$in all other positions?   no examples

Figure 5.

Before we turn to the whole corpus of data, I will comment on some of the proposed "rules". Rules 4 and 6 are proposed as simplified "variable rules" (as defined above), though all the tokens produced by the two informants fulfil the requirements of the rules. This is not the case with all the other informants; that is why I prefer not to consider rules 4 and 6 as categorial rules.

The quantification done on this basis seems in nearly all cases to justify the pragmatic notion of "variable rules". Exceptions to rule 1 are, for instance, ['staṭa], ['kufeṭ] and the proper name ['ed,vaṭ]. Rule 2 represents a problem; just a little more than half of the tokens analysed are sensitive to this "rule". Most of the exceptions, however, seem to fit into one grammatical category: they are past tenses (preterites and participles) of weak verbs, such as ['læ:rte], [læ:rt], ['hø(:)rte], [hø(:)rt]. Such forms are most frequently found in the data produced by the male informant. The speech of the female informant is in accordance with rule 2 in 83% of the total amount of tokens. A tendency for past tenses of weak verbs to be an exception to the suggested rule has also been noted in the data from other informants.

The exceptions to rule 3 are to a great extent found in the exclamation [du'vædn̩]. This exclamation mostly occurs in the speech of the female informant; her speech coincides with the rule only in 59% of all her tokens. As for all the other rules, there are no differences between the performance by the two informants. A frequent exception to rule 5 is [ba:ɳ] 'child' or compounds with [ba:ɳ]. As far as I can see, this is the only example besides proper names and perhaps some other simple words with a long /a:/ preceeding the postalveolar (like [ga:ɳ] 'yarn, net'), that can be explained by the notion of lexical diffusion.

As mentioned above, age groups 2 and 3 both realize Stage 3 in their speech, i. e., complete postalveolarization. Two minor exceptions are found in a large number of tokens from the female speaker representing age group 2: the proper name ['hæ:r̠lei:f] and the adjective ['ækstraor̠di,næ:ʈ]. Nevertheless, no firm conclusion can yet be made about age group 2; recorded speech from more people is required before a definite conclusion can be drawn. Age group 3, on the other hand, has definitely left the stage of linguistic development where clusters were used.

In 1960, the dialectologist Hallfrid Christiansen spent a fortnight in Lyngen collecting some data which unfortunately she did not analyse, as she died but a few years later. Her unanalysed material is filed in Norsk Målførearkiv at the University of Oslo. None of Christiansen's informants came from Furuflaten, but she wrote down vernacular speech produced by four persons from small villages in the vicinity. They were all in their sixties or seventies at the time when they were interviewed. In connection with a discussion of the quality of the /r/-sound, Christiansen also comments upon the phonetic phenomenon that has been the subject of this paper so far. She compares the rather strongly vibrating /r/-sound in Lyngen (an apico-alveolar trill) with the normal north Norwegian /r/ which has very little or no vibration at all (i. e., an apico-alveolar flap), saying:

> The distinct trilled r̠ may be a contribution from Sami, but may also have been spread from western Norway. Trilled r̠'s are not only heard from people who spoke Sami inn their childhood, but also from vernacular speakers who have grown up in a Norwegian home. On the other hand one can hear a less trilled and almost fricative r̠ among (older and younger) people who have for instance a Sami mother and a Swedish-Finnish father

or vice versa. A distinct trilled r̠ is not as easily assimilated into a following dental as is a slightly less trilled or untrilled r̠. (My translation.)

Thus Christiansen explains the tendency to assimilate these clusters in accordance with the quality of the /r/-phoneme, the trilled variant being a result of influence from Sami or from western Norwegian. A west-Norwegian influence is hardly possible, but there may be some connection between a strongly trilled /r/ and the avoidance of postalveolars, as seems to be the case in parts of western Norway. In most of Christiansen's examples, however, assimilation of the clusters occurs only at word and morpheme boundaries. That is to say that her data, too, can be taken as justifications for the postulated simplified "variable rules" proposed here, constituting Stage 2 of the potential development of the Norwegian variety at Furuflaten (and probably also of corresponding varieties of similar Sami-Norwegian villages in northern Troms).

At first glance, the patterned variation at Stage 2 seems indeed very astonishing and rather puzzling. The percentages indicate that the process of assimilation first takes place at word and morpheme boundaries, and not word- or morpheme-internally, which perhaps might be expected, and which also might be looked upon as a "natural" process of postalveolarization. Even if the neighboring dialects have a categorical rule of postalveolarization, one might expect that a varied norm would lead to more postalveolars word-internally than at word and morpheme boundaries, for the simple reason that there is a closer connection between /r/ + dentals within a morpheme than across a word or a morpheme boundary. As we have seen, it is exactly the other way around.

Let us now try to make a more complete morpho-phonological analysis of the whole corpus, using the system of classification in figure 4. The results are given in figure 6.

Distribution morpheme internally	
Postalveolars:	40.9% (160 tokens)
Clusters:	59.1% (231 tokens)

Distribution in inflected, derivated and compounded positions	
Postalveolars:	67.6% (492 tokens)
Clusters:	32.4% (236 tokens)

Distribution across word boundaries	
Postalveolars:	92.5% (173 tokens)
Clusters:	7.5% (14 tokens)

Figure 6.

There are no significant or marked differences between the distribution of postalveolars and clusters in inflectional forms, derivational forms and compound forms. That is why I have put all these categories together in one group in Figure 6.

There is a great deal of variation between the informants in the distribution of postalveolars and clusters respectively. The highest percentage of clusters is found in the speech of the youngest person in the group (a man born in 1926; that is why he is included in the oldest group). He has 83.3% clusters, and consequently postalveolarization in only 16.7% of all his tokens. The lowest percentage of clusters is found in the data of a woman; she follows the rule of postalveolarization in 95.3% of all her tokens. But in spite of this considerable variation, the patterns of postalveolarization seem to be the same for all the informants. In external sandhi position, i. e., across word boundaries, the tendency to postalveolarize is the strongest; the highest frequency of clusters is found word-internally, internal sandhi positions, i. e., inflections, derivations, and compounds, forming an intermediate stage.

If the connection between phonological elements is closer word- or morpheme-internally than across boundaries, the rule we have abstracted from the corpus may be formulated in this paradoxical way: the closer the connection between the elements in the clusters, the less the tendency to assimilate, and vice versa. Even if this is contradictory to what I just postulated as the most "natural" development, it perhaps does not seem so peculiar after all. First of all, the precise circumstances that led to the postalveolarization process remain obscure. The development of postalveolarization has not been studied in detail by historical linguists. Seip suggests that the rule may have arisen as early as the thirteenth century in Norway (Seip 1955: 177). For Swedish, Noreen assumes that the development started with the cluster /rt/ developing into /ʈ/ in the beginning of the fourteenth century, /rs/ assimilating into /ʃ/ from about 1500, /rn/ to /ɳ/ around 1700, /rd/ to /ɖ/ around 1800, and finally /rl/ to /ɭ/ not earlier than 1800 (Noreen 1903 – 1924 IV: 298 – 300).

My impression is that, though it has not been discussed explicitly, it has been taken for granted that the process starts lexically, i. e., within word boundaries at least, not to say within morpheme boundaries, before it expands to external sandhi positions. On the other hand, my own analysis of this recently-developed Norwegian dialect in a language-contact area shows that it might have been the other way around. Of course I cannot generalize from the quantitative distribution to a potential historical development, but there are reasons for claiming that the de-

velopment might have started postlexically and then expanded to the
lexicon as well, It is reasonable to assume that mother-tongue speakers
are more conscious of their pronunciation of individual lexical items than
of boundary phenomena. And that may explain why we have found that
the frequency of clusters is highest within morphemes, compared to
positions across boundaries.

Furthermore, according to Eliasson the process of postalveolarization
in external sandhi positions is typologically peculiar in that it stands
conspicuously apart from other sandhi-like features in Norwegian and
Swedish (Eliasson 1986: 271). He expresses the rule of postalveolarization
as it appears in Swedish informally as follows (1986: 285 – 286):

a) A dental (t d s n l) becomes postalveolar (ţ ḍ ṣ ṇ ḷ) after a short
postalveolar (including a single r) ... Postalveolarization is conditional
across word boundaries (# #) and, to some extent, word-internal
boundaries (+ or #). Postalveolarization of the cluster /rl/ is, however,
optional even within morphemes.

b) r is deleted before a secondary postalveolar, i. e. before ţ ḍ ṣ ṇ ḷ.

4. Suggested explanations

As has been shown in this paper, I postulate two homogeneous stages
with an intermediary heterogeneous stage, and my chosen three stage-
model does not in any way explain how Stage 2, which has been the
input to Stage 3, undergoes the change which produces the output of the
final stage. The development from Stage 1 to 2 is more easily explained
by reference to the contact between Sami and Norwegian, even though
the results of Stage 2 are hard to explain. Of course, linguistic change
always takes place by the gradual spread of a "new form" in a certain
domain, i. e., variant A is never replaced suddenly by variant B. But this
general tendency towards gradualness does not account for the particular
pattern of change found in my data.

A golden rule in linguistic research is that descriptions of statistical
co-occurrences do not say anything about causes. Trying to explain the
morpho-phonological distributions of postalveolars and clusters I have
described in this paper is to take a qualitatively different point of view.
This part of my paper is merely an attempt to suggest some tentative
ways of explanation.

One model of explanation may perhaps be sought in a type of socio-psychological accommodation theory. But then, why does accommodation have to undergo such a three-stage process to reach a pattern similar to that of the neighboring monolingual surroundings? As we have seen, from a linguistic point of view Stage 2 is more complex than Stages 1 and 3. So why, then, does this stage seem to function as an intermediary between the other two? As far as I can see, there is no social stigma attached to either the postalveolars or the clusters in northern Norway, even though this is not the case in eastern Norwegian dialects, where we have seen that clusters in many cases are preferred in formal speech. In fact, strict prescriptive language counsellors tend to conclude that clusters should be preferred to postalveolars in the standard variety.

One might consider this development to be a process of maintaining or creating a type of unmarked linguistic code in a particular social setting, or a search for neutrality, a neutrality strategy. Stages 1 and 2 may also be considered as a way of maintaining some kind of ethnic identity by establishing particular "ethnolectic" linguistic forms. As to the preference for clusters morpheme-internally, a potential explanation might be that the speakers of the variety constituting Stage 2 more or less consciously wish to give their linguistic variety some kind of ethnolectic marking to express a neutrality strategy. Thus they cannot abandon clusters altogether. And since they are more conscious of their pronunciation of individual lexical items than of boundary phenomena, clusters are preferred in such positions.

Robert Le Page's and Andrée Tabouret-Keller's concepts "diffused" and "focused" might be useful in understanding the development described above. In a language-contact situation, the speakers of the varieties in question, particularly of the minority language, lack social mechanisms whereby a highly focused set of vernacular norms can be consistently maintained against the constant pressure of competing sets of vernacular or institutionalized norms, and so they tend to drift away from a potential consistent norm. In Le Page's and Tabouret-Keller's terms, the language of these speakers becomes more diffuse (Le Page – Tabouret-Keller 1985). On the other hand, the output at Stage 3 might be considered a result of linguistic focusing.

5. Conclusion

As I have already mentioned, I consider these north Norwegian varieties, developed on a Sami or Finnish substratum, to be the youngest dialects of Norwegian. They have developed as Norwegian dialects partly during the very last part of the nineteenth century, but mostly during the twentieth century. After World War II, a process of homogenization with the neighboring Norwegian dialects has taken place. A language shift towards a general northern Norwegian norm has taken place or is taking place, with the Norwegian variety of Furuflaten undergoing a process of regionalization. The point I would like to make is that one could postulate that, if Stage 2 had been more stable and had not immediately been transformed into Stage 3 in the space of a single generation, another quite different variety of Norwegian might have existed.

The rather rapid change described in the present paper is not exlucive to the specific phonological items examined here. Variation between the Norwegian and the Sami stop systems could be studied in the same way, showing how Sami unaspirated, unvoiced stops initially, and preaspirated stops medially can be found at Stage 2, but more or less seem to disappear at Stage 3. The distribution of [ʃ] versus [s] in front of [l] appears to be patterned in the same way. Affricates also seem to vanish at Stage 3. Accommodation to the northern Norwegian palatal plosives, palatal nasals, and palatal laterals probably follows a similar pattern, though the rules of palatalization are more general at Stage 3 than in the monolingual vicinity. Changes in the vowel system may be studied within the same framework. The proposed three-stage model is probably applicable to changes in morphology and syntax, too, coalescence and variation in the Norwegian gender and species systems being characteristic of Stage 2 and, to a considerably lesser degree, of Stage 3. Development of prosodic patterns may also be analyzed in accordance with this three-stage model, the situation being that Sami substratum features seem to survive particularly well in the prosodic system of the Norwegian vernacular of Furuflaten and in other villages with a similar linguistic background. This finding concurs with data from English-speaking Polish and Italian immigrants in the United States. Carlock (1979) and Carlock — Wölck (1981) have shown that especially prosodic features are very important in identifying English-speaking people of Polish and Italian extraction, maintenance of the original accent characterizing the English speech even of third-generation immigrants (Appel — Muysken 1987: 132). According to

Appel — Muysken (1987), the maintenance of the accent of L1 also in L2 is part of a process of creating an "ethnolect", and as such it is a successful strategy of neutrality deployed by immigrant groups. As the Furuflaten corpus shows, it also appears to be a successful strategy for an indigenous ethnic group which has been forced to assimilate to the Norwegian majority and to adopt the majority language.

References

Appel, René — Pieter Muysken
    1987   *Language contact and bilingualism* (London: Edward Arnold).
Borgstrøm, Carl Hjalmar
    1981 [1938] "Om det norske skriftsprogs fonologi (efter østnorsk uttale)", in: Jahr — Lorentz (eds.). 170 — 186.
    1958   *Innføring i sprogvidenskap* (Oslo — Bergen: Universitetsforlaget).
Carlock, Elisabeth
    1979   "Prosodic analysis of two varieties of Buffalo English", *The fifth LACUS forum* (Congress Series), Columbia S.C., 377 — 382.
Carlock, Elisabeth — Wolfgang Wölck
    1981   "A method for isolating diagnostic linguistic variables: the Buffalo ethnolects experiment", in: David Sankoff — Henriette Cedergren (eds.), *Variation omnibus* (Edmonton), 17 — 24.
Christiansen, Hallfrid
    1946 — 1948 *Norske dialekter I — III* (Oslo: Johan Grundt Tanum).
Dorian, Nancy C.
    1982   "Defining the speech community to include its working margins", in: Suzanne Romaine (ed.), *Sociolinguistic variation in speech communities* (London: Edward Arnold), 25 — 33.
Eliasson, Stig
    1986   "Sandhi in Peninsular Scandinavian", in: Henning Andersen (ed.), *Sandhi phenomena in the languages of Europe* (Berlin, New York, Amsterdam: Mouton de Gruyter), 271 — 300.
Friis, Jens Andreas
    1861   *Ethnografisk kart over Finmarken* 1 — 5, 10 bl., (Videnskabsselskabet i Christiania).
    1890   *Ethnografisk kart over Tromsø Amt samt Ofotens Præstegjeld af Nordlands Amt*, 6 bl. (Christiania).
Jahr, Ernst Håkon — Ove Lorentz (eds.)
    1981   *Fonologi/phonologi* (Oslo: Novus).
Kelly, John — John Local
    1989   *Doing phonology* (Manchester — New York: Manchester University Press).

36   Tove Bull

Labov, William
1969   "Contraction, deletion, and inherent variability of the English
             copula", *Language* 45: 715—762.
Le Page, Robert—Andrée Tabouret-Keller
1985   *Acts of identity* (Cambridge: Cambridge University Press).
Noreen, Adolf
1903—1924   *Vårt språk. Nysvensk grammatik i utförlig framställning, I—IV,
             VII, IX* (Lund: C. W. K. Gleerups Förlag).
Pedersen, Aud-Kirsti
1988   *Stadnamnlån. Fonologi og ortografi i lydlig lånte stadnamn med eit
             oversyn over fonologien i norsk på Skibotn og i Kvenangsbotn*
             (unpublished cand. philol. thesis, University of Tromsø, School
             of Languages and Literature).
Rinnan, Gyda Dahm
1981 [1969] "Nok en gang om alveolarene", in: Jahr—Lorentz (eds.),
             273—277.
Seip, Didrik Arup
1955   *Norsk språkhistorie til omkring* 1370 (2nd ed.) (Oslo: Aschehoug).
Steblin-Kamenskij, Michail I.
1981 [1965] "Om alveolarer og kakuminaler i norsk og svensk", in:
             Jahr—Lorentz (eds.), 249—258.
Vogt, Hans
1981 [1939] "Some remarks on Norwegian phonemics", in: Jahr—Lorentz
             (eds.), 187—195.
1981 [1942] "The structure of the Norwegian monosyllables", in:
             Jahr—Lorentz (eds.), 208—231.
Weinreich, Uriel
1953   *Languages in contact* (2nd ed. 1963) (The Hague: Mouton).

The social and linguistic development of Scandoromani

Ian Hancock

In his review of Iversen's *Secret languages of Norway* Einar Haugen concludes that in that country, Romani is "just a dialect of Norwegian", yet goes on to say that the core of its vocabulary goes back to India (1949: 391). There is an evident anomaly here; being of North Germanic descent, no Scandinavian dialect can be shown to have a core of direct lexical retention of Indic origin, yet when we examine Scandoromani, it does indeed appear to have just that. In the normal course of linguistic evolution, we cannot expect a language to start as (in this case, for example) Indo-Aryan, spoken in Asia, to become Germanic and spoken in northern Europe. This apparent shift in genetic affiliation is itself sufficiently aberrant to warrant closer investigation.

Romani itself is an Indic language today having between six and ten million speakers throughout the world, principally in Europe, North Africa, the Americas, Australia, and South Africa. These are the Roma, commonly, though incorrectly, called Gypsies. In order to understand the Scandinavian linguistic situation, it will first be necessary to say something about the origin and spread of Romani in a world context.

Although the Indian roots of the language have been known to western scholarship for over two centuries, two questions still lack definitive answers: (a) to which people and language in India is it most closely related, and (b) what led to the exodus of the original population out of India, and when did it take place? In the Scandinavian case, a third may be added: (c) what linguistic process can account for its shift in genetic affiliation from Indic to Germanic, if this is indeed what has happened?

During the nineteenth century, and for much of the twentieth, speculation in this regard has been clouded by reliance upon vague and usually unsubstantiated hypotheses. A connection between the Roma and the lowest of the four Indian castes was made as early as 1783 by Grellmann, continuing to be supported by Leland and others a century later, and by Sampson in the 1920s. Grellmann's rationale was that the Romani populations in Europe have traditionally been employed in professions similar to those characteristic of the Śudra caste; later, a connection was made between the word *ḍom*, referring to members of a menial class in India, and the Gypsies' self-designation *Rom*. Supporting this hypothesis, and also providing a date for the departure from India, was the claim that Firdausi's epic poem the *Shah Nameh* was in fact an account of the first Gypsy migration out of the subcontinent. This Persian poem, written in the eleventh century, told of ten thousand Indian musicians being given as a gift by the Indian emperor to the ruler of Persia in A. D. 439. The story relates that after a year, the musicians had all vanished, presumably having migrated toward the West. What they were doing during the intervening eight centuries before entering Europe, and where they were located geographically, is not explained by Firdausi.

There are solid reasons for rejecting this explanation, both linguistic and historical. Phonological and morphological development within the neo-Indic languages, including Romani, cannot place separation as early as the fifth century A. D. Furthermore, the almost total absence of Arabic-derived items in Romani argues strongly against centuries of settlement in the Middle East. Persian and Byzantine Greek items on the other hand, are plentiful.

We must also re-evaluate the idea that the ancestors of the Roma were untouchables, doing the same jobs in India that typify them in Europe today. Nor can we dismiss the likelihood that it has been racial and social prejudice among western scholars which has helped to sustain this notion; in late 1930 for example, the Norwegian sociologist J. Scharffenberg published a series of articles demanding that Gypsies throughout Norway should be sterilized as a means of achieving the eventual permanent eradication of the population (Scharffenberg 1930; Bartels – Brun 1943; Johansen 1989); Unn Jørstadt, Director of the then Norwegian School for Gypsies concluded her 1972 report entitled "Norway's Gypsy minority" with the observation that "all of them are just like children. One thing is certain: they need help" (1972: 137). An early Swedish commentary on the nature of the Romani language by the Reverend Christfrid Ganander in 1780 claimed that the Gypsy's

> ... mouth and lips are big, wide and thick, convenient for the pronunciation of their language, which is rather aspirated and full of "schz" or "Sclawoniska" words, which call for a strong aspiration and a lot of spittle before they can be pronounced. Their pronunciation or sounds and voices are peculiar, loud, sharp, rough and harsh, and also demand twitches of the body and gestures with the hands, before they can be articulated.

These are prejudices originating outside of the Romani population; when we examine the Romani vocabulary itself, however, it becomes apparent that practically all of the words for concepts most stereotypically associated with Gypsies were not brought from India at all, but were acquired after reaching the Byzantine Empire — that is, it has been contact with European and other foreign societies which has brought about the Gypsies' contemporary social situation. Thus words for metals such as steel, copper, brass, lead, zinc, tin, the words for nail, pliers, chisel, furnace, bellows, forge, smelt, solder, horseshoe, hammer, file, anvil; and even the words for horse, hoof, donkey, mule, saddle, bridle, bit, reins, whip, waggon, wheel and road, are not Indian, but items acquired before reaching the gates of Europe at the time that five centuries of enslavement of the Romani people were just beginning.

The hypothesis which has gained ground most recently is the result of research undertaken by Indian scholars themselves. In the mid-1970s, interest in the Roma among academics in India led to the establishment of the Indian Institute of Romani Studies and the appearance of its journal *Roma*, devoted wholly to all aspects of the Romani experience (Rishi 1975). This hypothesis maintains that the ancestors of the Roma were a composite people consisting of high-caste Rajput warriors together with their camp followers who were drawn from the lowest caste. According to Watson in his *Concise history of India* (1981: 88), the Rajputs were "welded out of different non-Aryan material into a martial society of interrelated families, and rewarded with kśattriya status and certificates of descent from the sun and the moon" in the tenth century to fight against Islamic incursions into north-western India by the armies of Mohammed Ghaznavid. Watson also mentions the Rajputs' "facility for assimilating foreigners" (1981: 88), characteristic also of the modern Romani population. A remnant of the symbolic association of the Rajput warriors with the sun and the moon, as well as with the stars, is found among some central European Romani groups today (Chatard — Bernard 1959: 93 — 94; Sutherland 1975: 125). The Rajputs and their camp followers, presumably of mainly Dravidian descent, moved westwards into Persia, becoming embroiled in a succession of Middle Eastern battles against Islam; as they became more and more remote from their homeland, their shared Indian identity, we can hypothesize, overcame whatever caste distinctions might have divided them socially, and in time the population became one. This would account for the character of the Romani language, which demonstrates Central Indic, Northwestern Indic, and Dardic linguistic characteristics. A 1987 medical report in the *The*

Lancet August 15th issue determined that "Analysis of blood groups, haptoglobin phenotypes, and HLA types establishes the Gypsies as a distinct racial group with origins in the Panjab region of India."

While the original Romani language brought into Europe seven centuries ago exists today only in some sixty widely scattered dialectal forms, it has been possible to describe the proto-language using the techniques of linguistic reconstruction (Higgie 1984; see also Hancock 1988). Despite the fragmentation of the language, its dialects fall nevertheless into a number of well-defined subgroups, and it is easily possible to speak of a "Common Romani" core shared by all of them. Differences are, in the main, lexical and phonological, although calquing on local non-Romani idiom and morphosyntax is also everywhere apparent.

In a chapter which appears in a study of ethnic minority languages in Britain (Edwards—Alladina 1991) I proposed that all contemporary Romani populations have a non-Indic genetic component, because

> ... wherever Roma have migrated, they have encountered, and sometimes formed permanent alliances with, other, non-Romani peoples. This has given rise to newer, syncretic populations which, because of the pervasiveness of the core culture and language, have remained essentially Romani in terms of their own perceived identity; non-Romani groups have usually adjusted to the Roma rather than the reverse, although sufficient non-Romani elements have also been incorporated to affect the broader cultural and linguistic characteristics of each individual group ... In some instances, the Indic element has not been sufficient to keep the overall identity of the group Romani, so that while Romani elements are discernible in the speech of such peoples as the Jenisch in Germany or Switzerland, for example, or the Quinquis in Spain, other factors, both genetic and cultural, are insufficient either for them to think of themselves as Romani, or for them to be regarded as such by members of coexisting populations who do.

In Scandinavia, as elsewhere in Europe, the Romani populations consist of both first diaspora and second diaspora immigrants. The first European Romani diaspora began in the mid- or late thirteenth century, when the first Roma crossed the Dardanelles into the Balkans and subsequently fanned out into northern and western Europe. Perhaps half of those arriving from Asia Minor at that time, however, were held in slavery in the principalities of Moldavia and Wallachia (Hancock 1987), a situation which was not fully abolished until the middle of the 19th century. The flight of the ex-slaves out of Rumania from the 1860s onwards constituted the second diaspora, and descendants of these Roma, who are usually referred to as the *Vlax* (*Vlach, Wallachian*, sometimes also called *Danubian*), have settled everywhere that first-diaspora populations are also found. Because of the very different historical situations distinguishing the two migratory waves, and the resulting linguistic divergence, Vlax and non-Vlax Gypsies today share little social interaction, even when they inhabit the same environment. Vlax Roma in Norway numbered less than one hundred according to Unn Jørstad when she published her report seventeen years ago, a number which has at least tripled since that time; nevertheless pedagogical materials have been produced here to teach literacy in Vlax Romani (e. g., Jansen – Heltveit 1979; Syverud – Heltveit – Gaardner 1979). Such publications in Sweden, with its larger Vlax population, are more numerous, and have been mainly produced by Skolöverstyrelsen in Stockholm. This discussion is concerned not with the Vlax Romani minority in Scandinavia, but with the descendants of the first diaspora, the population generally, though incorrectly, referred to as *Tattare*.

Norbert Boretzky has recently drawn attention to the fact that in the Romani lexicon, the indigenous (i. e., Indic) and the non-indigenous items adhere tenaciously to their respective grammatical paradigms, a characteristic "hardly found in any other language" (1989: 357). While the majority of dialects do indeed retain their basically Indian structure, there are a number of varieties of the language which have survived lexically, but which demonstrate no, or almost no, indigenous grammar and phonology. These include Lomavren, the speech of the Armenian Gypsies (Finck 1903), Caló, spoken in Spain (Tudela 1985), Angloromani in England (Acton – Kenrick 1984; Hancock 1984a, 1984b), Hellenoromani in Greece (Triandaphyllidis 1923 – 24), Tent Gypsy in Yugoslavia (Uhlik 1941 – 43) and others. This phenomenon is not restricted simply to Romani; such languages as Mbugu (Goodman 1971), and Shelta (Hancock 1984c) also appear to consist of lexicons couched in the framework of other languages. It is to this category that Scandoromani also belongs.

Documentation on the various Romani populations in Scandinavia is extensive; a selection of references appears in the bibliography following this paper. The question most frequently addressed in connection with the Tattare is their ultimate origins, and the extent to which they are in fact ethnic Gypsies, if at all. Little has appeared on the linguistic classification of their speech, which has traditionally been viewed merely as a kind of slang consisting of cryptolectal vocabulary of mainly Romani origin in an entirely Scandinavian grammatical matrix.

Such languages have more relevance to linguistic theory, perhaps, than is at once apparent; first of all, they challenge the traditioinal genetic approach to language classification. Secondly, they provide useful insights into the maintenance of ethnic identity, as well as into contact phenomena and language attrition, both the focus of scholarly interest at the present time. The variety of Romani belonging to this category for which most theoretical work has been undertaken is Angloromani, which originated in England and which has subsequently spread to other parts of the English-speaking world (Hancock, 1986). It is in fact possible that the origins of Scandoromani may also be traced to Britain, in the light of early contact between the British Isles and Scandinavia, although the processes yielding each possibly differ.

While Gypsies may have entered Britain from southern Scandinavia in the first place, as the Jutes had done a thousand years before, the first record of their presence in Denmark indicates that they had been transported to that country by James IV of Scotland, in July, 1505. Their arrival in Sweden via Denmark is dated 1512, and they were being abandoned on the coast of Norway from British ships from 1544 onwards. According to Bergman (1964: 13),

> ... the Scottish and the Swedish Gypsies kept in touch during the 16th century ... in the Swedish National Archives there are two passports for the Tattare, or as he is also called the Egyptian, Anders Faa ... the name Faa is well-known in Scotland, and has been so (among Gypsies) for a long time. John Faa was the name of perhaps the most romantic Gypsy leader in Scotland, and he even had a poem written in his honour by our Swedish poet Orvar Odd.

Bergman (1964: 16) continues:

> Nowadays, a distinction is made between *Tattare* and *Zigenare*. This last term is used to refer to descendants of the Gypsies who immigrated in the latter part of the 19th century, mainly between 1860 and 1880, and later. They are bilingual, and speak both a pure European Gypsy dialect, and Swedish ... The term Tattare is reserved for a less well-defined group of people who live in the same way as the Gypsies, and who no doubt in certain cases are descendants of Gypsies who have mixed with Swedes, but who otherwise, and probably mainly, are descendants of the loose people from whom have come the (contemporary, non-Gypsy) significant group of loiterers.

Lastly, Bergman says (1964: 22)

> Just as the Spanish Gypsies, after having settled down, mixed their language with the Spanish of the lower classes, with the *germanía* of the criminals, etc., so the Swedish Gypsies have also mixed their language with Swedish. Today's Tattare speak a mixture (rotvälska) in which, to be sure, the basis is old Romani, but where the inflectional system of the Gypsy language has been lost.

The language of the Swedish Zigenare, as referred to here, has been superbly described by Gjerdman — Ljungberg (1963); while no comparable grammar yet exists for the same language in Norway, that dialect is closely related to the one described for Sweden, and work on a linguistic description of Norwegian Vlax (which is the Lovari rather than the Kalderash or Churari dialect spoken in Sweden) is in progress by Lars Gjerde under the supervision of Dr. Knut Kristiansen at Oslo University's Indo-Iranian Institute. The speech of the Swedish Tattare has been recently dealt with in a book by Johansson (1977), while for the Norwegian situation, Iversen's three volume *Secret languages in Norway* (1944 — 1950) remains the most comprehensive treatment. I am not dealing with Finland in this paper, but a number of linguistic works describing Fennoromani also exist, e. g., by Valtonen, Thesleff, and others.

While Bergman refers to the "mixing" of the Romani and the white populations, and of their languages, he makes no attempt to explain why such mixing should have taken place. No scholars seem yet to have attempted this from a linguistic perspective, although a number of ethnographic studies have been written such as those by Ethler, Heymowski, Bartels — Brun, Hansen, Takman, etc., which examine the ancestries of the Scandinavian Traveller population.

The parallel situation in Britain has received more attention in this regard, and it is likely that what we have learned about this may equally apply in Scandinavia. There are two principal hypotheses for the British situation: firstly, that contemporary Angloromani is the result of progressive language attrition or decay — a position favored by Romanologist Donald Kenrick, and secondly, that it is a deliberately contrived cryptolect dating from the sixteenth century, this being my own belief. I reject the possibility of language attrition because dying Romani dialects, such as that spoken in Wales today, are not restructuring themselves; Welsh Romani is not slowly becoming Angloromani. Nor, in fact, is Angloromani dying, but appears to be spreading, numerically and geographically. I favor a sixteenth century origin for Angloromani because we have numerous references to a "secret language" in use among the Gypsy population from that time. The fact that no samples of Angloromani occur in print until the nineteenth century attests only to its secret nature, although it has been used to support the attrition hypothesis; but absence of evidence is not evidence of absence; Shelta (cf. Hancock 1984 c) remained hidden from the outside world until the nineteenth century.

I will not repeat arguments supporting my position here, since they have appeared in print elsewhere. But to summarize, it would seem that the newly-arrived Roma found themselves thrown into the same social milieu as the British outlaws, and were obliged to interact with them for survival. The British outlaws already had a cryptolect of their own, known as Cant, evidence of which may be found in the still surviving speech of the Scottish Travellers (see Hancock 1986), and, of course, the Roma had Romani as a means of private communication. Cant, which seems to date from the eleventh century, consists of cryptolectal items in an all-English grammatical and phonological framework. It has been used for poetry in the past, and some words, such as *booze, gear, hooker*, etc., have passed into general English slang. The Roma were not opposed to allowing Romani items to be incorporated into Cant, and no doubt learnt the speech themselves; but withheld inflected Romani from the non-Gypsy community, in order to be able to maintain their separateness within the larger separate population. The inflected language survived in England until the early twentieth century, and may perhaps still survive; by the mid-nineteenth century, Smart—Crofton were able to transcribe stories from British Gypsies told first in inflected Romani and then in Angloromani. As noted earlier, in Wales it still survives.

The restructured language in Scandinavia appears to exist in several regional dialects; Johansson discusses two for Sweden, a Northern and a Skånish dialect, the differences between which appear to be mainly lexical. Phonologically and structurally, Scandoromani, or Tattarespråk, approximates almost completely to the Scandinavian host languages in the midst of which it exists. It is in its lexicon that it remains distinctively a Gypsy tongue. As with Angloromani, native morphology has undergone a process of collapse — taking the attritionist argument — or never existed in the first place, if Romani items were inserted into a co-existing Cant. We might still speak of reduction, however. For example, in Angloromani, the first-person personal pronominal forms all derive from the historical prepositional case *mande*, used following various prepositions (e. g., *mandi* 'I, me', *mandi's* 'my', etc.). The Scandoromani forms on the other hand have generalized equivalents based on the possessive singular masculine nominative in the inflected language, viz., *miro*, thus *miro* 'I, me', *miros* 'my', etc. Nearly all other morphology seems to be attributable to vernacular Scandinavian, for example reflecting their three-gender system rather than the two genders of the standard languages. Inflected forms appear to be frozen, e. g., *dakkri* 'mother', a genitive in historical Romani. Derivational morphemes are in the main non-productive, with the exception of the historical genitive, typically used in the inflected northern dialects such as Sinti or Welsh Romani as a means of lexical expansion.

Examples from Scandoromani include *däkkaskiro* 'soldier', from *däkka* 'sword', *minnsjeskre* 'gonnorhea', from *minnsja* 'vulva', *bängerske* 'hell', from *bäng* 'devil', *dikkopaskro* 'mirror', from *dikka* 'to see', and so on. Calques on Scandinavian languages also account for some forms. Examples include *sapp-jakkad* 'wicked', literally 'snake-eyed', from *ormøgd*, ditto, or *ali-jakkar* 'spectacles, glasses', literally 'glass-eyes', cf. *glasøgon*, ditto. Other lexical items have been created by a process of incoining, i. e. combining existing morphemes into new lexical combinations. Examples include *krajjo-dikklo* 'flag', literally 'king cloth', *starrto-mossj* 'policeman', literally 'capture person', *randrar-mossj* 'secretary', literally 'write person', and *båssjar-mossj* 'musician', literally 'play person', *pilo-dukht* 'having a hangover', literally 'drunk-pained', *rubb-smitto* 'silversmith', is an example of a Romani and a Scandinavian derived morpheme in combination. Items from Scandinavian and Scandinavian Cant are also common in Scandoromani, usually in disguised form. Thus *fimmpus* 'five', *dustus* 'flour', *vårsnos* 'our', *ersnos* 'your', *alonum* 'alone', (from *fem*, *dust*, *vår*, *er* and *alones*). This can even extend to Indian-derived items, e. g., *jekkum* 'one' (from *jekh*) or *nakkus* 'nose' (from *nakh*).

Following are three sentences in Swedish Scandoromani with their Angloromani, inflected Romani, English, and Swedish equivalents:

Scandoromani:	*miro honkar alonum; mander honkar alonum*
English:	'I am alone'
Swedish:	*jag är ensam*
Angloromani:	*mandi's alonus; mandi's akonya*
Romani:	*me šom kokoro*

Scandoromani:	*vi tradrar to fåron en vaver divus*
English:	'we('ll) go to town another day'
Swedish:	*vi åker till stan en annan dag*
Angloromani:	*we'll tradder to the forus a wavver divvus*
Romani:	*džasa ka o foros vaver dives*

Scandoromani:	*ska vi puttja dålle mossj om han vill suta palla i ratti?*
English:	'shall we ask that fellow if he'll stay and sleep tonight?'
Swedish:	*ska vi fråga den där karlen om han vill ligga kvar i natt?*
Angloromani:	*will we putch the mush if he'll atch and suti to-rati?*
Romani:	*phučas i muršeste te ačel te sovel akarat?*

Conclusion

The question has arisen whether languages of this type may be said to have undergone processes of pidginization or creolization (discussed in Hancock 1971). Although Arnbjørnsdottír — Smith (1986) attempt an argument against this in their discussion of Russenorsk, there is in fact no incontrovertibly attested case of the kind of linguistic restructuring typifying these processes which has arisen from the contact of just two languages; nor has what Whinnom called "tertiary hybridization" occurred, i. e., when the speakers of the language supplying the lexicon subsequently withdraw from the contact environment, the pidgin then having to expand using its own internal grammaticalizing and lexicalizing resources rather than drawing upon its lexifier for these components. When two language communities come into contact, speakers of one usually just learn that of the other (e. g., Sami and Norwegian in Norway, Spanish and English in Texas) with cross-interference, but generating no extensive structural or semantic innovations having no outside source. These processes have been discussed by the Scandinavian linguists Jespersen (1922) and Hjelmslev (1939); Reinecke (1937) tabulated at least ten social contexts which can yield contact languages, whether pidginized or not (discussed in Hancock 1990 b), those of the Scandoromani type being most like his category of "foreigners' mixed speech", although he discusses restructured Romani in particular under the heading "dying minor languages" (Reinecke 1937: 76 — 79), thereby adhering to the attrition hypothesis.

Scandoromani, like Angloromani and probably other such varieties, does not appear, then, to have evolved in direct descent from historical inflected Romani by a process of linguistic decay, but instead is based upon sociolectal varieties of Scandinavian — Norwegian in Norway, Swedish in Sweden, Danish in Denmark, whose speakers drew upon a (now extinct) coexistent inflected Romani which served as a lexical reservoir for maintaining and enriching it as a cryptolectal register. In light of claims which have been made for both Angloromani and for Caló or Hispanoromani (Hancock 1990 a: 96 — 97), however, regarding the nature of the Romani element in each, this explanation may require elaboration.

Whatever its ultimate origins, in the course of time, Scandoromani came to replace inflected Romani as the ethnic language of the community, we might guess because of increasing intermarriage with non-Gypsies, but surviving because of the continuing identity of the group as

Gypsy, and the resulting need for a linguistic means of reinforcing that identity, and to provide a protective insulation from the establishment — in this context functioning as an antilanguage (Halliday 1968). Language maintenance and choice as a factor of ethnic identity is discussed in Le Page — Tabouret-Keller (1985). For these reasons, as long as the Scandoromani population remains a distinct segment of the Scandinavian population, it is likely that their speech will survive in some form also.

References

Acton, Thomas — Morgan Dalphinis (eds.)
  1990   *Language, Blacks and Gypsies* (London: Karia Publications),
            17 — 31.
Acton, Thomas — Donald Kenrick (eds.)
  1984   *Romani rokkeripen to-divvus* ["Speaking Romani today"] (London:
            Romanestan Publications).
Andersen, Kirsten G.
  1971   *Sigøynere* [Gypsies] (Copenhagen: Munksgaard).
Arnbjørnsdottír, Birna — Connie Sherwood Smith
  1986   "Russenorsk." Unpublished paper, Creole Studies Seminar, The
            University of Texas at Austin.
Bartels, Erik — Gudrun Brun
  1943   *Gypsies in Denmark* (Copenhagen: Munksgaard).
Bergman, Gösta
  1964   *Slang och hemlige språk: Rommani* (Stockholm: Prisma Books).
Bergstrands, Carl-Martin
  1943   *Tattarplagan: Tattarna i svenskt folkliv* ["Tattare" in Swedish folk-
            life](Uppsala).
Boretzky, Norbert
  1989   "Zum Interferenzverhalten des Romani", *Zeitschrift für Phono-
            logie, Sprachwissenschaft und Kommunikationsforschung* 42:
            357 — 374.
Brynjolfsson, Bjarna — Bjarni
  1987   "Villtir, villtir, villtir: Sigauna i Bretland" [The free ones: Gypsies
            in Britain], *Mannlif:* 105 — 120.
Chatard, Jean — Michel Bernard
  1959   *Zanko, chef tribal* (Paris: La Colombe).
Dorpb, N. V.
  1837   *De judske Zigeunere og en rotvelsk Ordbog* [The Jutland Gypsies
            and a rotwelsh dictionary] (Copenhagen: Gleerup) [republished in
            1975 by Rosenkilde & Bagger, Copenhagen].

48   *Ian Hancock*

Edwards, Vivian – Safder Alladina (eds.)
1991   *Multilingualism in the British Isles* (London: Longman).
Ehrenborg, Harald
1928   "Djos Per Andersson's vocabulary", *Journal of the Gypsy Lore Society* 7(2): 7 – 18.
Etzler, Allan
1944   *Zigenare och deras avkomlingar i Sverige* [Gypsies and their descendants in Sweden] (Stockholm: Hugo Gebers Vörlag).
1959   "Svenskt tattarspråk" [Swedish "Tattare" language], *Svenska Landsmål och Svenskt Folkliv* 17(3): 130 – 151.
Finck, Franz Nikolaus
1907   *Die Sprache der armenischen Zigeuner* (St. Petersburg: Imperial Academy of Sciences).
Ganander, Christfrid
1780   *Undersökning om de så kallade Tattare eller Zigeuner* [An examination of the so-called "Tattare" or Gypsies] (Stockholm: Kongl. Svenska Vitterhetsakademien).
Gjerdman, Olof
1945   "Tattarna och deras språk", *Svenska Landsmål och Svenskt Folkliv* 3(4): 1 – 55.
Gjerdman, Olof – Eric Ljungberg
1963   *The dialect of the Swedish Coppersmith Gypsy Johan Dimitri Taikon* (Uppsala: Lundqvista).
Goodman, Morris
1971   "The strange case of Mbugu", in: Dell Hymes (ed.), 243 – 254.
Grellmann, Heinrich
1783   *Die Zigeuner: Ein historischer Versuch über die Lebensart und Verfassung, Sitten und Schicksale dieses Volkes in Europa, nebst ihrem Ursprunge.* (Dessau).
Halliday, M. A. K.
1969   "Antilanguages", *Language and social structure.* Chapter 9, 164 – 182.
Hancock, Ian
1971   "Is Angloromani a creole?", *Journal of the Gypsy Lore Society*, 3rd series, 49(1): 41 – 44.
1984 a   "The social and linguistic development of Angloromani", in: Thomas Acton – Donald Kenrick (eds.), 89 – 122.
1984 b   "Romani and Angloromani", in: Peter Trudgill (ed.), 367 – 383.
1984 c   "Shelta and Polari", in: Peter Trudgill (ed.), 384 – 403.
1986   "The cryptolectal speech of the American roads: Traveler Cant and Angloromani", *American Speech* 61(3): 206 – 220.
1988   "The development of Romani linguistics", in: Mohammed Jazayery – Werner Winter (eds.), 183 – 223.

1990 a   "The Romani speech community", in: Vivian Edwards – Safder Alladina (eds.), 89 – 106.

1990 b   "Creolization and language change", in: Edgar C. Polomé (ed.), 507 – 525.

Hansen, Hans Per

1917   Chapter entitled "Kjaeltringsproget", *Festskrift til Evald Kristensen*, 70 – 94.

1952   *Jyske skøyere og rakkere* [Jutlandish tramps and vagabunds] (Copenhagen: Hansens Bogtrykkeri).

Haugen, Einar

1949   "A note on the Romany 'language' ", *Norsk Tidsskrift for Sprogvidenskap* 15: 388 – 391.

Heymowski, Adam

1987   "Resende eller 'Tattare': En gammal minoritet på väg att försvinna" ["Travellers or 'Tattare': An ancient minority on the way to extinction"], in: Ingvar Svanberg (ed.), 13 – 22.

Higgie, Brenda Boerger

1984   A reconstruction of Proto-Western-Romani. Unpublished doctoral dissertation, Department of Linguistics, The University of Texas at Austin.

Hjelmslev, Louis

1939   "Études sur la notion de parenté linguistique: Relations de parenté des languages créoles", *Revue des Études Indo-Européennes* 2: 271 – 286.

Hymes, Dell (ed.)

1971   *Pidginization and creolization of languages* (Cambridge: Cambridge University Press).

Huttunen, Kari

1972   *Raportti suomen mustalaisista* [A report on Finnish Gypies] (Jyväskylä: Gummerus Publishers).

1976   *Gypsies in Finland, past and present* (Helsinki: Privately-circulated monograph).

Iversen, Ragnvald

1944   *The secret languages in Norway: Vol. 1, Romany* (Oslo: Dybwad).

1945   *The secret languages in Norway: Vol. 2, Rotwelsch* (Oslo: Dybwad).

1950   *The secret languages in Norway: Vol. 3, Mansing* (Oslo: Dybwad).

Jansen, R. – B. L. Heltveit

1979   *Gadi i rakli kaj bušol Mimi* [This is the girl called Mimi] (Oslo: Undervisningen av Fremmedspråklige Elever, Oslo Kommune-Skolesjefen).

Jazayery Mohammed – Werner Winter (eds.)

1988   *Languages and cultures, Papers in honor of Edgar C. Polomé* (Berlin – New York: Mouton de Gruyter).

Jespersen, Otto
1922   *Language, its nature, development and origin* (London: George Allen & Unwin).

Johansen, Jahn Otto
1989   *Sigøynernes holocaust* (Oslo: Cappelen).

Johansson, Roger
1977   *Svenskt Rommani* [Swedish Romani] (Uppsala: Acta Acad. Reg. Gustavi Adolphi LV).

Jørstad, Unn
1972   "Norway's Gypsy minority", *American Scandinavian Review* 58(2): 129–137.

Kumm, Evert
1965   *Zigenare och vanlige Svenskar* [Gypsies and the general [Swedish] population] (Örebro: Quintus Tryckeri).

Leland, Charles G.
1882   *The Gypsies* (Boston: Houghton Mifflin & Co.).

Le Page, Robert B. – Andrée Tabouret-Keller
1985   *Acts of identity* (Cambridge: Cambridge University Press).

Miskow, Johan
1904   "Rejsende" [Travellers], *Danske Studier* 129–140.
1909   "Mere om Romanier og Rejsende" [More on Gypsies and Travellers], *Danske Studier* 104–108.

Miskow, Johan – Viggo Brøndal
1923   "Sigøynersprog i Danmark", *Danske Studier* 99–145.

Nyrop, K.
1914   "Natmaendene og deres sprog" ["Nightmen" (i. e. Gypsies) and their language], *Politiken*, January 1st, 4, 6, 8.

Polomé, Edgar C. (ed.)
1990   *Research guide on language change* (Berlin – New York: Mouton de Gruyter).

Refsum, Helge
1945   "Tatermål i Norge" ['Tattare' language in Norway], *Maal og Minne*, 1/2: 83–92.

Reinecke, John
1937   Marginal languages: A sociological survey of the creole languages and trade jargons (Yale University: Doctoral dissertation, available from University Microfilms, Ann Arbor, order number 68–546).

Ribsskog, Øyvin
1941   "Sjargong, forbryterspråk og rommani", *Maal og Minne*, 142–146.

Rishi, Weer Rajendra
1975   *Roma: The Punjabi emigrants in Europe, Central and Middle Asia, the USSR and the Americas* (Patiala: The Punjab Press).

Sampson, John
1926   *The dialect of the Gypsies of Wales* (Oxford University Press).
Scharffenberg, Johan
1930   "Omstreiferondet" [The "Vagants" problem], *Arbeiderbladet* (Oslo), October 31st, and November 11th, 19th, 24th and 25th.
Scherp, Lambert – K. Wiming
1980   *Min bok om Zigenarna* (Stockholm: Skolöverstyrelsen).
Smart, Bath C. – Henry T. Crofton
1875   *The dialect of the English Gypsies* (London: Asher & Co.).
Smith, Hubert
1873   *Tent life with English Gypsies in Norway* (London: King & Co.).
Sundt, Eilert
1852   *Beretning om Fante eller landstrygerfolket i Norge* [An account of the Fante or Travellers in Norway] (Christiania).
Sutherland, Anne
1975   *Gypsies, the hidden Americans* (London: Macmillan).
Svanberg, Ingvar (ed.)
1987   *I samhällats utkanter om 'Tattare' i Sverige* [In the fringe society of 'Tattare' in Sweden] (Uppsala Multiethnic Papers, No. 11). (Uppsala: University).
Syverud, A.-M. – B. L. Heltveit – Jan Gaardner
1979   *Me ğinavav Romanes* [I read Romani], Parts I & II (Oslo: Undervisningen av Fremmedspråklige Elever, Oslo Kommune-Skolesjefen).
Takman, John
1976   *The Gypsies in Sweden* (Stockholm: Liber Vörlag).
Thesleff, Arthur
1901   *Wörterbuch des Dialekts der finnländischen Zigeuner* (Helsinki: Drukerei der Finnischen Literatur-Gesellschaft).
Triandaphyllidis, M. A.
1923 – 24   "Eine zigeunerisch-griechische Geheimsprache", *Zeitschrift für Vergleichende Sprachforschung* 52: 1 – 42.
Trudgill, Peter (ed.)
1984   *Languages in the British Isles* (Cambridge: Cambridge University Press).
Tudela, Jean-Louis
1985   *Trejiní e Caló: Cours de Caló* (Montferrand: Chez l'auteur).
Uhlik, Rade
1941 – 43   "Bosnian Romani", *Journal of the Gypsy Lore Society*, 3rd series, 20: 100 – 141, 21: 24 – 55, 22: 110 – 141.
Valtonen, Pertti
1972   *Suomen Mustalaikielen etymologinen sanakirja* [Etymological dictionary of Finnish Romani] (Helsinki: Suomolaisen Kirjallisuuden Seura).

Watson, Francis
    1981   *A concise history of India* (London: Thames & Hudson).
Whinnom, Keith
    1971   "Linguistic hybridization and the 'special case' of pidgins and creoles", in: Dell Hymes (ed.), 91 – 115.

Language contact in the Pacific: Samoan influence on Tokelauan

Even Hovdhaugen

1. Introduction[1]

The Pacific seems to be the closest the humanities can come to the experimental laboratories of natural sciences. In this vast area, we have a large number of small, isolated islands, and it has generally been assumed that these islands had very little mutual contact before the arrival of the Europeans. Their settlement was generally attributed to more or less casual drift voyages, and each island was seen as an isolated universe. For linguistics, this would mean that here we would have the ideal laboratory for testing, for example, the comparative method or glottochronology, because disturbing factors like lexical borrowings or other types of interference between the languages involved would be reduced to a minimum.

Today we know that this picture is a bit simplified. It has become clear that we must assume that there was more extensive contact between Pacific communities before the Europeans arrived than was thought earlier, and that the native legends about numerous and far-reaching sea voyages are much closer to the truth than generally supposed. Examples of identifiable loanwords or foreign elements in the vocabulary, for example, are turning up in an increasing number in many Polynesian languages (cf., e. g., Biggs 1980; Clark 1980; Elbert 1982; Ranby 1982), and the mixture of languages and dialects due to immigration and contact has resulted in a complicated set of phonological correspondences no less chaotic than in other parts of the world.

On many of the inhabited Pacific islands, the population has never been more than about a hundred people, and until recently it was quite rare to find islands with more than a few thousand people. In such small communities, which until about a hundred and fifty years ago were also illiterate, the impact of an otherwise superficial contact, consisting, for example, of a foreign missionary living there or of a boatload of five to fifteen foreigners arriving and staying for some time, could have profound effects. The linguistic contact between Samoan and Tokelauan is accordingly of some interest for understanding what happens when a small linguistic community like Tokelau is subjected to influence from another language.

2. Samoan and Tokelauan

Samoan and Tokelauan are two closely related but not immediately mutually-intelligible languages of the Samoic-Outlier group of the Polynesian group of languages.[2] Samoan is spoken by about 300,000 people today. 160,000 of them live in the independent state of Western Samoa, which consists of two large and two small inhabited islands. The rest (many of them probably more fluent in English than in Samoan) live in American Samoa, New Zealand, Australia, Hawaii, and the US West Coast. Samoan has been a written language for more than one hundred years.

Tokelauan is spoken by about 1,600 persons on the three Tokelau atolls of Atafu, Fakaofo, and Nukunonu, which are situated about 480 kilometers north of Samoa and constitute a non-self-governing territory under New Zealand administration. In addition, there are about 3000 Tokelauans living in New Zealand. Until quite recently, Tokelauan was exclusively an oral language, Samoan being used as the written language as well as the language of the church. This has been the case since Christianity was introduced in Tokelau (mainly from Samoa) in about 1860 and is to some extent still going on today, although the post-war period has witnessed a slow but steady increase in the use of Tokelauan as a church language. In the last ten to fifteen years, a few publications have appeared in Tokelauan. Recently, Tokelauan has been introduced in the schools as a separate subject and has also become the main language of instruction, replacing Samoan and, to some extent, English.

While the impact of Samoan on Tokelauan is significant, there are practically no traces of influence from Tokelauan in Samoan. This is not surprising. Although Samoans had for centuries, if not millennia, had extensive contacts with other powerful and culturally significant nations like Fiji and Tonga, this contact has resulted in only a few and mostly questionable cases of loanwords. Like the rest of Samoan culture, the language seems to have been very closed to influence from abroad. On the other hand, Samoan seems to have no inhibitions about allowing loanwords from English and other European languages; the majority of Polynesian and Oceanic loanwords in Samoan (mainly from Tongan, Tahitian and Fijian) were introduced by the missionaries!

Contact between Samoans and Tokelauans over the last one hundred and twenty years has not encouraged linguistic influence from Tokelauan on Samoan. The few Samoans going to Tokelau were mostly pastors who were persons of status and thus were people influencing, rather than being influenced by, the local language. In most cases, these Samoans did not (want to) learn to speak Tokelauan. The Tokelauans staying in Samoa are usually concentrated in certain areas close to the capital, Apia, and have hardly ever numbered more than a few hundred. In general, Samoans seem to have mixed feelings towards Tokelauans, and the Tokelau language is sometimes the topic of jokes and ridicule among Samoans. From the point of view of Tokelauan, the situation is quite different. Since about 1860, Samoan has been the language Tokelauans first learned to read and, in most cases, the only language they could read. Church services as well as most contacts with visitors and officials were carried out in Samoan, the teachers in Tokelau were mostly educated in Samoa, and a number of Tokelauans could, and still can, speak Samoan more or less fluently. And those who do not speak it (mainly younger people) can usually understand Samoan. The facts mentioned above, which clearly indicate that Samoan was a language of high prestige among the Tokelauans (to some extent it is still so today), easily explain the significant impact Samoan has had on Tokelauan.

3. Samoan influence on Tokelauan

The influence from Samoan on Tokelauan is twofold.

a. A number of Samoan loanwords

The extent of this borrowing is hard to determine since the phonology and morphology of the two languages are almost identical. Only when the two languages have different regular correspondences of Proto-Polynesian (PPN) phonemes is it possible to locate borrowings through forms showing deviations from these correspondences. An example is the treatment of PPN *k*. It is represented as *k* in Tokelauan and as ˋ in Samoan, cf. Tok. *kupu* 'word' = Sam. *ˋupu*.[3] Tokelauan has no glottal stop and, accordingly, when we find cases like Tok. *auala* 'road' = Sam. *ˋauala*, we can safely assume that the Tokelauan word is borrowed from Samoan. By these and a number of other similar criteria, we can state that we have about one hundred and ten words in Tokelauan which we can say with certainty are borrowed from Samoan, about twenty words that most likely are borrowings, and an unknown (but probably significant) number of undetectable borrowings.

b. Sporadic use of Samoan words and phrases

Such Samoan elements are found in all kinds of conversations and indicate various aspects of meaning ranging from joking and irony to politeness and solemnity. In traditional stories, the use of Samoan words and phrases is usually confined to quotations of direct utterances, and often such words are considered to be examples of old Tokelauan or pure Tokelauan. Mostly we find a mixture of Tokelauan and Samoan in such cases, the Samoan part consisting of a few typical (i. e., divergent from the point of view of Tokelauan) Samoan lexemes, the use of the Samoan singular specific article *le* and negation marker *lē* instead of Tokelauan *te* and *hē*, and a Samoan pronunciation of certain phonemes, see below. It is possible that this hybrid language reflects an earlier attempt by Tokelauans to speak Samoan in contact with Samoans. Most probably this attempt to speak Samoan or to Samoanize Tokelauan took place in connection with the arrival of the Samoan missionaries and was due to their attempts to introduce Samoan as the official language in Tokelau; but, as we shall see below, we cannot completely rule out the possibility that there was some contact between Samoans and Tokelauans before the missionaries arrived. Another sphere where the use of Samoan is very popular is when playing cards (and probably also dominoes and other games which I am not familiar with).

Such Samoan words and phrases within a Tokelauan discourse are marked by a more or less pure Samoan pronunciation both segmentally (e. g., by /f/ being pronounced [f] and not [hʷ] as in Tokelauan, and by using Samoan /s/ instead of Tokelauan /h/) as well as intonationally. This is in marked contrast to the loanwords, which are completely adapted to Tokelauan phonology.

On the other hand, I have found no traces of Samoan interference in Tokelauan morphology and syntax. The style of the traditional Tokelauan literary forms like fairy tales (*kakai*), songs, and speeches is markedly different from the corresponding genres in Samoan.

4. Some diachronic aspects

A problem which we can hope to solve only to a very limited degree, concerns the question of when the contact between the two language communities started. We have it very well documented since the arrival of the missionaries in Tokelau in the 1860s, but to what extent did these two language communities have contact before that time, and to what extent did this contact result in linguistic borrowings? To both questions our answers must be very tentative. As far as contact is concerned, we must, because of our knowledge of similar Polynesian societies and traditions, assume that there has been more contact than formerly imagined. The sea was no serious obstacle, and the Polynesians' ability to use their small canoes for far-reaching sea travel was almost unbelievable.

When a U. S. expedition visited Tokelau in 1841, the linguist Horatio Hale made some observations on the Tokelauan language and also compiled a short word list. Hale's material shows many traces of influence from Samoan, but it is hard to determine if this is due to Samoan interference in Tokelauan or to his informants trying to speak Samoan to him. There are some typical Samoanisms which are rarely found today and which may favor the latter interpretation. The /s/ is used instead of /h/ frequently, but not always (cf. Hale 1846: 258), something which is a favorite way of indicating Samoan word forms in Tokelauan today. For the pronouns, both Tokelauan and Samoan word forms are given (e. g., *koe* (Tok.) and *'oe* (Sam.) 'you (sg.)'), and this may be the reason for Hale's generalization, which is not supported by the rest of his data that "It is one peculiarity of this dialect that the *k* at the beginning of many words is often dropped, apparently at the mere pleasure of the speaker" (Hale 1846: 258). In Hale's vocabulary, we find Samoan forms like *alu* (instead of *fano*) 'go', *iti* (instead of *taigole*) 'small', and *fanua/faŋua*[4] (instead of *fenua*) 'country'. It is hard to draw definite conclusions from this material, but it seems likely that there were people on Fakaofo, and probably also on Atafu, in 1841 who had a fairly extensive knowledge of Samoan.

Hale also mentions a certain confusion of *t* and *k*[5] which may come from a mixing of the *tautala leaga* and the *tautala lelei* pronunciation of Samoan (see below). Note also that for "country" he gives both *fanua* and *faŋua* besides Tok. *fenua*. In the speech of an old man from Atafu I have, however, observed a tendency to mix *t* and *k*, and Hale's observation may accordingly also reflect an earlier specific trait of the Atafu dialect.[6]

5. The situation today

Probably in connection with the efforts to introduce Tokelauan in the schools and to create a literary Tokelauan language, there are today clear indications of a growing Tokelauan linguistic nationalism resulting in a conscious effort to avoid or Tokelauanize Samoan loanwords (e. g., by replacing *āoga* 'school' [cf. Sam. *ā'oga*] by the restored form *ākoga* or *leva* 'long ago' [= Sam. *leva*] with the synonymous word *mataloa*). But this purism has not affected the use of Samoan words and phrases (cf. 3 b above) as stylistic indicators or the use of Samoan pronunciation in certain situations.

There are also interesting differences between the three islands. On the Catholic island of Nukunonu, the impact of Samoan has been the least. The majority of people on Nukunonu do not speak Samoan well, and Samoan words and phrases are little used and partly frowned upon. It also seems that people on Nukunonu have the strongest and most out-spoken view about what are Samoan loanwords. The influence from Samoan seems to be strongest on Fakaofo, and there most people (es-pecially men) above school age are able to speak Samoan fairly well. The use of Samoan words and phrases is quite extensive even when people on Fakaofo speak in Tokelauan; they seem to have very little awareness of a word being Samoan or Tokelauan, and Samoan loanwords are definitely not stigmatized. Atafu is in this respect more similar to Fakaofo, but the position of Samoan seems to be less prominent there.

6. A formal classification of Samoan loanwords in Tokelauan

As already mentioned, we have few cases of phonological criteria for identifying Samoan loanwords in Tokelauan.

The best criterion is the dropping of a Samoan glottal stop (corresponding to $*k$ in PPN) in Tokelauan (Tokelauan has no glottal stop phoneme):

$$\text{Sam. } {}^\varsigma = \text{Tok. } 0^7 = \text{PPN } *k$$

A majority of the identifiable loanwords show this correspondence; see the following items in the appendix: 1, 2, 4−9, 11, 12, 14, 15, 17, 18, 23−38, 40, 41, 43−51, 55, 66, 67, 69, 71, 72, 76, 82, 85−87, 89, 90, 92, 95, 97, 98, 100, 101, 103, 106−108, 116, 118−120, 126, 127, 131, 135, 136.

Identical vowels are contracted when an intervening glottal stop disappears:

$$\text{Sam. } V_i{}^\varsigma V_i = \text{Tok. } \bar{V}_i{}^8 = \text{PPN } *V_i k V_i$$

The following examples illustrate this development (in some cases the same word can show both varieties of dropping of intervocalic glottal stop; see, e. g., 58 and 129): 21, 51, 52, 54, 57−59, 62−65,[9] 83, 84, 91, 96, 104, 109, 111−113, 115, 121−124, 129, 130.

But even these examples are far from certain in all cases, and a few of the examples referred to above can also be interpreted in another way. Especially interesting are those containing the suffix *-aga* = Sam. *-ʻaga* (e. g., 65, 72, 92, 95, 135) where we do not have a contraction of two identical vowels. Historically, the Tokelauan suffix *-aga* has been a productive variant of PPN *-(C)aga*, just as in Samoan *-ʻaga* has been the productive allomorph. Furthermore, Samoan has a few cases of etymologically unexplainable glottal stops, e. g., in the dual pronouns *māʻua* 1. exc. du., *tāʻua* 1. inc. du., and *lāʻua* 3. du., cf. Tokelauan *māua*, *tāua*, and *lāua*, where the other Polynesian languages mostly correspond to the Tokelauan forms. Cases like Tokelauan *io* 'yes' = Sam. *ʻio* 'yes' can also be ruled out, because utterance-initial vowels frequently get an unetymological glottal stop in Samoan (interjections are notoriously utterance initial).

In some cases, we find forms both with and without *k* in Tokelauan corresponding to PPN *k* and Sam. *ʻ*: 3, 10, 16, 29, 42, 56, 78, 102, 105, 113. The forms with *k* may be genuine old Tokelauan forms (that is probably the case in 42 where the *k*-form also has different vowel quantity). But in other cases, the *k*-forms are most likely new, restored formations, i. e., Tokelauanized versions of Samoan borrowings. This is especially clear in the case of words for concepts that belong to the "Christian" post-contact culture, e. g., 3, 56, and 105. There are also two other stems (e. g., 93 and 134) which are etymologically "correct", but where many Tokelauans assume borrowing (and a following Tokelauan-ization).

Another phonological criterion is related to the difference between the two main sociolects of Samoan, where one (*tautala leaga*) shows a different representation of the dental stop and nasal from what we have in the other, socially more prestigious variant (*tautala lelei*):

Proto-Polynesian	Samoan		Tokelauan
	tautala		
	lelei	*leaga*	
*t	t	k	t
*n	n	g	n

When we find Tok. *k* and *g* corresponding to PPN *t* and *n*, we can assume that these words are borrowed from the *tautala leaga* variant of Samoan.[10] The examples are, however, very few: 22, 39, and 73. An example of a hypercorrect form in Samoan as the source of borrowing is 74. Moreover, we find one example of *n* > *g* in a word where a *k* is retained, cf. *konā* > *kogā* in 42.

In one word we have an unsystematic phonological difference between Samoan and Tokelauan: tok. *fenua* — Sam. *fanua* 'land'. When we find Tokelauan words with *-fanua* (53 and 60), we can safely assume them to be borrowings, especially since one of them (53) also shows other phonological evidence of being a loanword.

Before turning to non-phonological criteria for determining borrowing, I shall briefly mention another phonological feature of Samoan loanwords in Tokelauan. A short vowel in an antepenultimate or preantepenultimate syllable of a Samoan word is frequently, but not consistently. lengthened in Tokelauan: e. g., *āuivi* 'skeleton' < Sam. *'auivi*,[11] *fāiaina* 'defeated' < Sam. *faia'ina*, *tamāitai* 'lady' < Sam *tama'ita'i*, and *lēaga* 'evil, bad' < Sam. *leaga*. In such prestressed syllables, both languages have a very weak phonological opposition between long and short vowels and great phonetic variation in the quantity of the vowels. But as the tendency towards phonological lengthening is more prominent in Tokelauan than in Samoan, this may explain the more or less haphazard choice in selecting a basic phonological representation of the lexemes involved.

Morphological criteria for determining borrowing are few and consist mainly of words containing affixes which are productive or common in Samoan, but which are restricted to one or a few loanwords in Tokelauan, e. g., 13 and 125. Similar examples are 117, where the root in Tokelauan (but not in Samoan) is only found with the suffix -*ga*, and 61, where a morpheme meaning 'hit' is only attested in one compound.

A possible semantic criterion for borrowing is the location of a word with a restricted meaning or sphere of use beside another and non-borrowed lexeme with the same core meaning but usually with a wider semantic or pragmatic range. Similar semantic specialization can be observed elsewhere, see 84 for a good example. Other examples are 77 (cf. also 10 and 20) and 75 (cf. 128 and 133). In other cases, we have just two synonymous words, one of which is a possible Samoan borrowing,[12] e. g., 79 and 88.

Some words are considered to be Samoan loanwords by speakers of Tokelauan without the classification being based on phonological or morphological criteria (70, 81, 93), and others (68, 94, 99, 110, 132, 134, 137) are classified as Samoan loanwords in the *Tokelau Dictionary* (TD) without the classification being based on phonological or morphological criteria.

Due to the genetic closeness of the two languages and the minimal phonological differences existing between them, most loanwords would not be recognisable. The list of recognisable or assumed borrowings given here most likely represents only a subset of the actual number of Samoan loanwords in Tokelauan. But I see no reason to assume that this subset is not representative of the semantic and grammatical distribution of these borrowings within Tokelauan.

7. A semantic classification of Samoan loanwords in Tokelauan

First of all, we have a large number of words referring to concepts that were not originally part of Tokelauan culture (new institutions, new animals, plants, instruments, house utensils, etc.) including aspects of Samoan culture they were exposed to, e. g., *agiagi* 'onion', *oti* 'goat', *fāili* '(music) band', *fāfanua* 'map', *fāmalū* 'mattress', *fōmai* 'doctor', cf. also 3, 12, 14, 44, 45, 48, 51, 52, 53, 55, 56, 59, 60, 76, 84, 88, 91, 105, 109, 114, 118, 122, 124, and 129.

Similarily we have a number of words connected with concepts of Christianity, including some terms for favorite themes of Christian preaching: *onohai* 'patience', *lēaga* 'evil', *paia* 'holiness', *pulelā* 'pulpit', *hō* 'disciple', and *vālohaga* 'prophecy'.

Other and less obvious semantic clusters consist of words relating to physical appearance, parts of the body, and illnesses: *āuivi* 'skeleton', *aulēaga* 'ugliness', *aulelei* 'handsomeness', *ava* 'beard', *avilu* 'midget, dwarflike', *ioimata* 'eyeball', *fāiai* 'brain', cf. also 77, 89, 96, 101, 131; or to the age group and sex of people: *lōmatua* 'old lady', *taulelea* 'mature man', *tamāitai* 'lady', *toeaina* 'old man'.

Furthermore, we have not only terms for a variety of common concrete and abstract concepts, such as *oa* 'wealth', *olo* 'fortress', *fālī* 'anger', *gātaaga* 'end of the world', *lāhaga* 'step', *lio* 'circle', *mutaaga* 'end', *puā* 'pig', cf. also 15, 16, 21, 23, 29, 35, 37, 41, 54, 106, 107, 115, 117, and 130, and for similarly common verbs, such as *aunoa* 'be without', *inohia* 'be hated', *uma* 'be finished', *gauai* 'yield', *paepae* 'be white', cf. also 2, 17, 24, 27, 50, 61, 66, 69, 79, 86, 96, 103, 107, 116, 123, 126, 128, 132, and 136, but also a number of interjections, grammatical words and verbs functioning to some extent as grammatical words, such as *aua* 'don't', *auā* 'because', *ātonu* 'perhaps', *oe* 'acknowledge a call by name', cf. also 1, 39, 42, 64, 111, and 112.

As we see, many of the Samoan loanwords in Tokelauan belong to the central core of the vocabulary. Frequently they exist as synonyms for old Tokelauan words or with a more narrow or specified meaning than the original terms. Due to the tendency towards linguistic purism in the more or less organized language planning which for the moment is going on in Tokelau, some of these loanwords may be stigmatized, but in most cases there is no awareness of a word's status as a borrowing or not. Or rather, there is such a strong awareness when and only when we have pairs of synonyms where one word is identical to a corresponding Samoan word. But where we have no phonological or morphological criteria to support this classification it may as well be based on folk linguistics. And some of the borrowings, like *toeaina* 'old man', belong to the basic cultural vocabulary and would hardly be accepted as being a loanword by Tokelauans.

7. Conclusion

The contact between Samoan and Tokelauan has mainly taken place in the last one hundred and fifty years. During this period, most of the contact has taken place in Tokelau, where all Tokelauans have acquired a fluent, passive command and a more or less good active command of

Samoan through reading the Samoan Bible, singing Samoan psalms and songs, and listening to Samoan pastors. The result of this contact with Samoan is that many Tokelauans on certain occasions use Samoan words and phrases as a stylistic device (sometimes in a Samoan-Tokelauan mixed language which is considered by many to represent old Tokelauan) and that a number of Samoan loanwords have entered the Tokelauan vocabulary. Some of these loanwords represent additions to the vocabulary by designating new cultural or technical concepts, but a number of them are replacements of lexical and grammatical words of the core vocabulary of Tokelauan. Since the main sphere of contact was the church and the schools, and since the contact was more literary than oral, it is interesting to find among the borrowings a number of interjections, grammatical words, terms designating physical appearance, age groups, and other semantically basic nouns and verbs. This is not exactly what we should expect, especially since there are hardly any indications of Samoan interference in Tokelauan morphology and syntax.

The position of Samoan in Tokelau bears some resemblance to, for example, the position Latin earlier had in Catholic communities or to the position Arabic still has in the Muslim world. The influence from Samoan in the Tokelauan vocabulary is certainly more basic and significant than that of Latin in most Catholic countries[13] and is closer to the influence of Arabic on, for example, Turkish. Since the amount of exposure to spoken or written Samoan in Tokelau was not significantly greater than the exposure to Latin in the Catholic countries of Europe in the middle ages, the strong Samoan influence on Tokelauan can perhaps be connected with the high degree of linguistic similarity between the two languages and the small size of the Tokelauan population.

Appendix

An alphabetic[14] list of some Samoan loanwords in Tokelauan

1. *ailoga* 'it is doubtful whether' < Sam. *'ailoga.*[15]
2. *aihiga* 'entertaining to receive something' < Sam. *'aisiga.*
3. *āoga* 'school', cf. Sam. *ā'oga.* Tok. *ākoga* is either a restored form or a new derivation from the verb *ako* 'learn', cf. Sam. *a'o.* Cf. also *faiāoga* and *faiākoga* 'teacher' (Sam. *faiā'oga*) and *fakaāoga, fakaakoga* or *fakaākoga* 'give education' (Sam. *fa'aā'oga*).
4. *aua* 'don't' < Sam. *'aua.* Observe that Sam. *'aua* is a verb while Tok. *aua* is an interjection.
5. *auā* 'because' < Sam. *'auā.*

6. *auala* 'road' < Sam. *'auala*.
7. *āuivi* 'skeleton' < Sam. *'auivi*.
8. *aufai* 'bunch of bananas' < Sam. *'aufa'i*.
9. *auleaga* 'ugliness' < Sam. *'auleaga*. (cf. *leaga*).
10. *aulelei* 'handsomeness' < Sam. *'aulelei*. We also find the (restored?) variant *kaulelei*, cf. Tok. *gali* 'beautiful, decent'.
11. *aulualua* 'small bunch of bananas' < Sam. *'aulualua*.
12. *āumāga* 'group of all able-bodied men' < Sam. *'aumāga*.
13. *aunoa* 'be without' < Sam. *aunoa*. Observe that we do not have a prefix *au-* in Tokelauan.
14. *aute* 'hibiscus' < Sam. *'aute*.
15. *autu* 'ditch' < Sam. *'autū*.
16. *autū* 'main theme' < Sam. *'autū*. We also find the form *kautū* in Tokelauan.
17. *afihi* 'carry under the arm' < Sam. *'afisi*. Cf. Tok. *kopi* id.
18. *āgai* 'towards' < Sam. *aga'i*.
19. *agaleaga* 'unkindness', cf. Sam. *agaleaga* and *leaga* below.
20. *agalelei* 'kindness', cf. Sam. *agalelei*. There is no phonetic evidence for borrowing or influence, but the word is quite parallel to the preceding one.
21. *agavā* 'ability, competence' < Sam. *agava'a*.
22. *agiagi* or *aniani* 'onion' < Sam. *aniani* [aniani, aŋiaŋi] < Eng. *onion*.
23. *alou* 'pus' < Sam. *'alou*, and *aloua* 'contain pus' < Sam. *'aloua*.
24. *aha* 'be unsuccessful' < Sam. *'asa*.
25. *ātonu* 'perhaps' < Sam. *'ātonu*.
26. *ava* 'beard' < Sam. *'ava*.
27. *āvau* or *avau* 'bawl, shout' < Sam. *'avau*.
28. *āvilu* 'midget, dwarflike' < Sam. *'āvilu*.
29. *ele* 'clay, earth' < Sam. *'ele*, cf. Tok. *kelekele*, Sam. *'ele'ele* 'soil, earth' and *faguele* below.
30. *io* 'tuber' < Sam. *'i'o*.
31. *ioimata* 'eyeball' < Sam. *'i'oimata*.
32. *ili* 'saw' < Sam. *'ili*.
33. *inohia* 'hated, disliked' < Sam. *'inosia*.
34. *oa* 'wealth' < Sam. *'oa*.
35. *oa* 'lather, soapfroth' < Sam. *'oa*, and *oā* 'soapy' < Sam. *'oā*.
36. *oe* 'acknowledge a call by name' < Sam. *'oe*.
37. *ōō* 'hollowness' < Sam. *'ō'ō*.
38. *ogāumu* 'stove, oven' < Sam. *'ogāumu*.
39. *oka* or *okaoka* 'sign of surprise < Sam. *ota* [ota, oka] and *otaota* [otaota, okaoka]. The original Tokelauan word is probably *ola* or *olaola*.
40. *olo* 'fortress' < Sam. *'olo*.
41. *omo* 'hollow, depression' < Sam. *'omo*.
42. *ona* 'because' < Sam. *'ona*, cf. Tok. *kogā* and *konā* id.
43. *onohai* 'patience' < Sam. *'onosa'i*.

44. *oti* 'goat' < Sam. *'oti.*
45. *ulo* 'pan, pot' < Sam. *'ulo.*
46. *ulu* 'breadfruit' < Sam. *'ulu.*
47. *uma* 'be finished' < Sam. *'uma.*
48. *fai* 'banana' < Sam. *fa'i.*
49. *fāiai* 'brain' < Sam. *fāi'ai.*
50. *fāiaina* 'be defeated' < Sam. *faia'ina.*
51. *fāili* 'band' < Sam. *fa'aili.*
52. *fāipoipo* 'marry' < Sam. *fa'aipoipo.* Tok. *fakaipoipo* is probably a modern Tokelauanized form since the Samoan word is a borrowing from Tahitian or Rarotongan, introduced into Samoan by the missionaries.
53. *fāfanua* 'map' < Sam. *fa'afanua,* cf. Tok. *fenua* 'land' = Sam. *fanua.*
54. *fāfia* 'pride' < Sam. *fa'afia.*
55. *faguele* 'earthware pot' < Sam. *fagu'ele,* cf. *ele* above.
56. *falemai* 'hospital' < Sam. *falema'i*; a restored form is *falemaki,* cf. also *fāmai, fōmai,* and *maimāliu.*
57. *fālī* 'anger, displeasure', cf. Sam. *fa'ali'i* 'rage'.
58. *fāmai* 'epidemic' < Sam. *fa'ama'i,* cf. *mai.*
59. *fāmalū* 'mattress' < Sam. *fa'amalū.*
60. *fanafanua* 'naval gun, field gun' < Sam. *fanafanua,* cf. *fāfanua* above.
61. *fahioti* 'kill' < Sam. *fasioti.* Observe that *fahi* (= Sam. *fasi* 'hit') is not attested elsewhere in Tokelauan.
62. *fātele* 'multiplication' < Sam. *fa'atele.*
63. *fā(telo)* 'stick the tongue out', cf. Sam. *fa'a(eto).*
64. *fātoā* 'just' < Sam. *fa'ato'ā.*
65. *fātoaga* 'garden' < Sam. *fa'ato'aga.*
66. *feitagai* 'hate one another' < Sam. *feitaga'i.*
67. *fōmai* 'doctor' < Sam. *fōma'i,* cf. *falemai.*
68. *fuhu* 'fight with fist', according to TD from Sam. *fusu.*
69. *gae* 'heavy breathing' < Sam. *ga'ega'e* 'pant'.
70. *gaoi* 'thief, steal', cf. Sam. *gaoi.* The only indication of borrowing is the widespread feeling among Tokelauans that this is a Samoan word and that the original Tokelauan term is *kaihohoa* id.
71. *gauai* 'yield' < Sam. *gaua'i.*
72. *gātaaga* 'end of the world' < Sam. *gata'aga.*
73. *gila* and *nila* 'needle' < Sam *nila* [ní:la, ŋí:la] < Eng. *needle.*
74. *kēni* and *kēgi* 'gang' < English *gang,* but with the Samoan hypercorrect pronunciation of [ŋ] as [n].
75. *lauiti* 'narrowness', pl. *lāuiti* or *lauitiiti,* cf. Sam. *lauititi. Iti/itiiti* are only found in loanwords from Samoan in Tokelauan; otherwise we find *taigole/ tainole/taikole* 'little, small' in Tokelauan.
76. *lauulu* 'leaf of breadfruit tree' < Sam. *lau'ulu.*

77. *lālelei* 'be attractive (of women)', cf. Sam. *lālelei*. The original Tokelauan word seems to have been *gali* 'attractive, beautiful, decent' (cf. also *aulelei* above).
78. *lāhaga* 'step' < Sam. *la'asaga*, cf. also Tok. *lakahaga*.
79. *lata* 'be close', cf. Sam. *lata*. The original Tokelauan word seems to be *pili* id.
80. *lēaga* 'evil, bad', cf. Sam. *leaga*. The original Tokelauan word seems to be *kino* id.
81. *leva* 'be long ago', cf. Sam. *leva*. This is a doubtful example, but some Tokelauans consider *leva* to be a loanword in contrast to Tok. *mataloa*.
82. *lio* 'circle, ring' < Sam. *li'o*.
83. *lōmatua*, pl. *lōmātutua* 'old lady' < Sam. *lo'omatua*, pl. *lo'omātutua*. The now obsolete Tokelauan equivalent is *nuafafine*.
84. *mā* 'battery, made of stone, monument' < Sam. *ma'a* 'stone, battery'. The Tokelauan word for 'stone' is *fatu*.
85. *māea* 'finished' < Sam. *māe'a* and *māeaea* 'thorough' < Sam. *māe'ae'a*.
86. *māelegā* 'zealous, industrious' < Sam. *mā'elegā*.
87. *mai* 'ill' < Sam. *ma'i*. We also find *maki* sometimes in Tokelauan, also in traditional songs and stories, but the normal term for 'ill' is *tauale* in Tokelauan, cf. also *falemai*, *fāmai*, *fōmai*, and *maimāliu*.
88. *maile* 'dog' < Sam. *maile*, cf. Tok. *kulī*[16] id.
89. *maimāliu* 'epilepsy' < Sam. *ma'imāliu*.
90. *māfuie* 'earthquake' < Sam. *mafui'e*.
91. *māmōlī* 'battery' < Sam. *ma'amōlī*.
92. *mātaaga* 'interesting sight' < Sam. *māta'aga*.
93. *manako* 'wish, desire', cf. Sam. *mana'o*, and *manakomia* 'be needed, required, desire, want'', cf. Sam. *mana'omia* are words that many Tokelauans feel to be loanwords but which then must be examples of restored forms which sometimes are used instead of Tok. *fofou* id.
94. *matai* 'master, male head', cf. Sam. *matai*, according to TD borrowed from Sam.
95. *mutaaga* 'end' < Sam. *muta'aga*. Observe that we also find *mutaga* in Tokelauan.
96. *paē* 'be thin' < Sam. *pa'e'e*.
97. *paepae* 'be white' < Sam. *pa'epa'e*.
98. *paia* 'holiness, holy' < Sam. *pa'ia*.
99. *panihina* 'chalk', cf. Sam. *panisina*, according to TD a borrowing from Samoan.
100. *poa* 'male animal, boar' < Sam. *po'a*.
101. *pou* 'sore, scabies' < Sam. *po'u*.
102. *puā* 'pig' < Sam. *pua'a*. Besides *puā* we also find Tokelauan *puaka* which is frequently used as a term of abuse.
103. *puai*, pl. *pūai* 'vomit' (v.) < Sam. *pua'i*, pl. *pūa'i* (v.), cf. also Tok. *fakahuati* id., and *puaiga* 'vomit' (n.) < Sam. *pua'iga* (n.).

104. *pulelā* 'pulpit' < Sam. *pulela'a*.
105. *pulenū* 'mayor' < Sam. *pulenu'u*. Today the restored Tokelauan form *pulenuku* has replaced *pulenū*.
106. *puleaga* 'sphere of one's control' < Sam. *pule'aga*.
107. *hāofai* pl. *hāofafai* 'sit' < Sam. *saofa'i*.
108. *hāuai* 'ogre' cf. Sam. *sau'ai*.
109. *hēvae* 'shoes' < Sam. *se'evae*.
110. *hilafaga* 'sight', cf. Sam. *sīlafaga*, *hilafia* 'be known', cf. Sam. *sīlafia*, and *hilahila* 'see, look', cf. Sam. *silasila*. TD assumes borrowing from Samoan in these three etymologically related words.
111. *hō* 'frequently' < Sam. *so'o*.
112. *hō* 'anything' < Sam. *so'o*.
113. *hō* 'disciple' < Sam *so'o*. In Tokelauan, we also find *hoko* id.
114. *holofanua* 'horse' < Sam. *solofanua*, cf. *fāfanua* above.
115. *huāū* 'oil' < Sam. *suāu'u*.
116. *hui* 'sew' < Sam. *su'i*.
117. *huhūga* 'sir', cf. Sam. *susuga*. The stem (= Sam. *susū*) of this word is not attested in Tokelauan.
118. *tāinamu* 'mosquito-net' < Sam. *ta'inamu*.
119. *taulealea/taulelea* pl. *tāulelea/taulelea* 'married, mature man' < Sam. *taule'ale'a*, pl. *taulele'a* 'young, untitled man'.
120. *tamāitai* 'lady' < Sam. *tama'ita'i*.
121. *tāmilo*, pl. *tāmimilo* 'go around' < Sam. *ta'amilo*.
122. *tāmū* 'edible herb' < Sam. *ta'amū*.
123. *tātia*, pl. *tātitia* 'lying around' < Sam. *ta'atia*, pl. *ta'atitia* 'lie'.
124. *tāvale* 'car' < Sam. *ta'avale*.
125. *tīgāina* 'be very sick' < Sam. *tīgāina*. The very common Samoan suffix *-ina* is not used in Tokelauan.
126. *tōai* 'persuaded, forced to' < Sam. *tōa'i*.
127. *toeaina* 'old man' < Sam. *toea'ina*, pl. *toea'i'ina*. The original Tokelauan term was *kolomatua* (= Sam. *'olomatua/lo'omatua* 'old woman(!)').
128. *toeitiiti* 'be nearly' < Sam. *toeitiiti*. Cf. *lauiti* above.
129. *tōnai* 'traditional formal meal' < Sam. *to'ona'i*, and *aho tōnai* 'Saturday' < Sam. *aso to'ona'i*.
130. *tūgamau* 'grave' < Sam. *tu'ugamau*.
131. *tumuai* 'top of head' < Sam. *tumua'i*.
132. *vāapiapi* 'be narrow (of road)' < Sam. *vāapiapi*. TD assumes borrowing from Samoan.
133. *vāiti* 'be narrow' < Sam. *vāiti*. Cf. *lauiti* above.
134. *valakau*, pl. *vālakau* and *valakaulia*, pl. *vālakaulia* 'invite' < Sam. *vala'au* and *vala'aulia*. TD assumes borrowings from Samoan, but they must then be restored Tokelauan forms.

135. *vāloaga* 'prophecy' < Sam. *vālo'aga*.
136. *vāloia* 'be predicted' < Sam. *vālo'ia*.
137. *veveni* 'be plump' < Sam. *veveni*. TD assumes borrowing from Samoan.

Notes

1. I would like to thank Elisabeth Lanza, Hanne Gram Simonsen, and Arnfinn M. Vonen for comments and criticism on an earlier version of this paper.
2. The material for this study is based on personal field work in Tokelau and Samoa, field notes from my colleagues Ingjerd Hoëm and Arnfinn M. Vonen (cf. also Hovdhaugen et al. 1989), as well as standard works like Milner (1966) and *Tokelau Dictionary* (1986).
3. Observe that ' = [ʔ] (glottal stop) in Samoan orthography and that [ŋ] is written *g* both in Samoan and Tokelauan.
4. Observe that this is Hale's orthography.
5. 'The confusion in the pronunciation of *k* and *t* is not uncommon, even in those languages in which both the sounds are met with as distinct elements. In Fakaafo [sic!] *aliti* was heard for *aliki*..' (Hale 1846: 233).
6. Atafu was resettled about 1800 and it may quickly have developed its own phonetic idiosyncrasies to mark local identity. Today, the stigmatized differences in language between the three Tokelau atolls are mainly found in intonation and subphonematic phonetic variations plus a few lexical items.
7. Normally in inherited words we find PPN **k* = Sam. ' = Tok. *k*.
8. Normally in inherited words we find PPN **V$_i$ k V$_i$* = Sam. V$_i$ ' V$_i$ = Tok. V$_i$ *k* V$_i$.
9. Example 63 is quite peculiar because it is the Samoan form of a prefix which is used, the root of the word being different in the two languages.
10. Pastors and teachers speak only *tautala lelei*, at least in their official functions.
11. But *auala* 'road' < Sam. *'auala*.
12. Such lexical parallelism is also well attested in the phonologically identifiable borrowings like, e. g., 17, 80, and 101.
13. Observe that 100 years of Catholic mass has only resulted in a very few Latin loanwords (e. g., *pātele* 'father, priest' < Lat. *pater*) in the Tokelauan dialect on Nukunonu.
14. According to the Tokelauan alphabet: *a, e, i, o, u, f, g, k, l, m, n, p, h, t, v*.
15. When nothing else is given, the Samoan words have the same meaning as the corresponding Tokelauan words.
16. There were no dogs in Tokelau at the time of contact with Europeans, but archeological excavations have shown that there were dogs living there formerly.

References

Biggs, Bruce
    1980   "The position of East 'Uvean' and Anuta in the Polynesian language family", *Te Reo* 23: 115 – 134.

Clark, Ross
    1980   "East Polynesian borrowings in Pukapukan", *Journal of the Polynesian Society* 89: 259 – 265.

Elbert, Samuel H.
    1982   "Lexical diffusion in Polynesia and the Marquesan-Hawaiian relationship", *Journal of the Polynesian Society* 91: 499 – 517.

Hale, Horatio
    1846   *United States exploring expedition. 1838 – 42: ethnography and philology* (Philadelphia: Lea and Blanchard).

Hovdhaugen, Even – Ingjerd Hoëm – Consulata Mahina Iosefo – Arnfinn M. Vonen
    1989   *A handbook of the Tokelau language* (Oslo: Norwegian University Press).

Milner, George
    1966   *Samoan dictionary* (London: Oxford University Press).

Ranby, Peter
    1982   "The dual reflexes of Proto-Polynesian *$*s$* in Anuta", *Te Reo* 25: 3 – 11.

Tokelau Dictionary [= TD]
    1986   (Apia: Office of Tokelau Affairs).

"You can never tell where a word comes from": language contact in a diffuse setting

Robert B. Le Page

0. Introduction

This paper is divided into three parts: in Part 1, I discuss some of the problems which orthodox linguistic theories present to variationists and creolists like myself, and I sketch the conceptual framework which our Caribbean data forced upon me.

In Part 2, I outline the case-histories of Belize, in Central America, and of the island of St Lucia in the Windward Antilles, relating each to the various cultural pressures operating on their linguistic evolution. Andrée Tabouret-Keller and I have dealt with these two cases in detail in our book *Acts of identity* (1985). There we illustrate the processes of diffusion and incipient re-focusing from our fieldwork data of 1970 and 1978. We also list and illustrate the four headings under which the psychological and social constraints which operate on the individual's creation of linguistic systems can be grouped.

In Part 3, I return to and explore the use of metaphors for the multidimensional "galactic" framework, indebted to quantum theory and to images drawn from astrophysics, within which one can envisage the kinds of "languages" for which we have stereotypical concepts actually coming into existence and then disappearing again in our multilingual universe. I try to project the universe of "languages in contact" as nearly forty years of work on creole and contact varieties have brought me to see it.

As a preliminary however I give some brief excerpts from our fieldwork data from Cayo District, Belize, to illustrate how our informants themselves saw their society and its languages. The conversations were recorded in 1978.

0.1. Recollections of the past

First, an old man, JW of Bullet Tree Falls. He said he had been born in
1898 in nearby San Ignacio. Thus he was eighty years old. He said that
his "grandfather" was English and his "grandmother" an Indian woman
from Guatemala — but did not say which grandfather and grandmother:

> *My mother used to talk in Spanish to we and my father talk in English. My
> father never talk a half a half one word .. in Spanish .. mia mada yes my
> mother used to talk pure* [= only] *May .. the Spanish and Maya. The
> majority of me children-dem talk Maya .. Carib .. They go amongst them
> an' they learn the language you see.*

He claimed to have ninety grandchildren in the District.

It was clear from JW's memories of his childhood that he felt there
had been quite clearly distinguished "races" in what was then the colony
of British Honduras, and that each had had its language. His own
"English" to me had quite a number of Creole and some Spanish features,
evidenced above — for example, the Creole pluralising suffix *-dem* (after
an already-plural *children*), and the use of *mia mada* (*mi madre*) then
corrected to *my mother*. As we shall see, it is really not possible to ascribe
all linguistic features to any particular named system.

0.2. The present — 1978

Secondly, a young woman MB, sixty years younger than JW, told us that
she used "Spanish, English and English Creole" but that the essence of
being "Belizean" — that is, a citizen of the newly independent state —
was to be "mixed", and that went for the language too:

> *Even from Belize* [City] *to San Ignacio we have a difference in the language,
> right? Because here it's .. be more Spanish. Still it's Creole, right? but just a
> bit more Spanish words an' in Corozal they speak Spanish with a lot of
> Creole words i' ... Ours is English, Spanish, Carib, everything .. Everything
> mixed up .. you can never tell where a word comes from.*

Two more short excerpts from young (early twenties) informants. EA
said:

> *The languages of this country is something mixed specially the Creole .. and
> with Spanish also 'cause sometimes we find weselves talking Spanish and
> notice now and again you put in a bit of Creole or a bit of English.*

and AT said:

Well there is change because the older people used to speak broad Creole as
we call it, but the younger ones coming up now they don't speak it like that
any more you know? .. Some of the Maya Indians even they speak the English,
they don't speak the Creole.

Part 1. A general framework for contact situations

1.1. Theoretical problems

Suzanne Romaine starts her recent book, *Bilingualism* (1989), by saying
that it would be odd to read a book with the title *Monolingualism*, and
yet monolingualism is the underlying construct on which most linguistic
theory and description is based. She ends the book (1989: 287) by quoting
from the late Peter Strevens ("The localized forms of English" in Kachru
1982: 23) as follows:

> .. a central problem of linguistic study is how to reconcile a convenient and
> necessary fiction with a great mass of inconvenient facts. The fiction is the
> notion of a 'language' — English, Chinese, Navajo, Kashmiri. The facts
> reside in the mass of diversity exhibited in the actual performance of
> individuals *when they use a given language*. [my emphasis — Le P]

She then concludes: "This serves to remind us that linguistic theory is
still a long way from being able to deal analytically with performance
and what people do *when they use 'language', rather than a 'given'*
language." [my emphasis — Le P]

In between this beginning and this ending Romaine herself uses such
terms as "English" and "Punjabi" and other language names (as I shall
have to) as a convenient way of referring to abstractions from the behavior
of communities, and to stereotypes[1] about that behavior, while remaining
aware that the referent in each case is very far from being the autonomous
entity which both linguists and laymen tend to have in mind when they
talk about "languages", and when linguists use terms such as "code-
switching" or "code-mixing" or "borrowing" or "interference". A recent
article (1989) by Georges Lüdi on behalf of the European Science Foundation's Code-switching and Language Contact Network illustrates my
point; he writes as if contact-phenomena were the outcome of "contact"
between "pairs" of discrete languages: "The phenomenon of code-switching, to be properly understood, requires the analysis of *many pairs of*
languages in contact...." [my emphasis — Le P] (Lüdi 1989: 8).

Another fairly recent book I wish to refer to is Brian V. Street's *Literacy in theory and practice* (1984). Street is an anthropologist who did extensive fieldwork in the 1970s on literacy in rural villages in Iran. He makes a broad distinction between those theorists who write about literacy as if it were an autonomous and universally-valid aspect of human language, the transference of "the system" from spoken to written symbolism; that same bridge which all communities need to cross in similar manner (implied quite strongly I think in the French term for becoming or making literate, *alphabétisation*) in order to achieve "development" and "objective science" and so on; and those theorists who, like Street himself, believe that we need rather to recognize the ideological nature of "becoming literate", and that it has different meanings and implications from one culture to another.

Both Romaine and Street are making the point, among others, that the way most linguists think about language is strongly conditioned by Western European and American ideologies, theories and practices relating to the functions of spoken and written languages, to the relationship between these, and to the nature of linguistic structure which itself is based mainly upon centuries of study of written texts. They, and I, and many of my colleagues who have worked with the often diffuse vernaculars of contact situations, wish and need to revise that conventional thinking. A somewhat similar challenge to it has been expressed in some recent papers by George W. Grace of the University of Hawaii (see, e. g., Grace 1989).

1.2. "Projection, focusing, and diffusion" as a contribution to a theoretical framework for contact situations, and hence for all linguists

It is fitting that in discussing languages in contact Andrée Tabouret-Keller should take a "highly focused" situation (cf. Tabouret-Keller's paper in this volume) and I a "diffuse" one. Professor Tabouret-Keller is from a country in which the concept of a language called "French", its autonomy, its reification, totemization, and institutionalization are firmly fixed in the public and political ideology, whereas I come from a country whose main language has in turn spawned the many regional varieties known rather inelegantly as "The New Englishes" (or, in Loreto Todd's title, *Modern Englishes*). A project by the organisation AUPELF (Association des universités partiellement ou entièrement de langue française) to prepare a dictionary or dictionaries of African French has run into opposition on the grounds that nobody should be making dictionaries of bad French and if it is good French the dictionaries are already being made in Paris (Marcel Diki-Kidiri 1988). At the level of educated varieties therefore "French" is a very highly-focused concept, "English" more diffuse since we readily talk and write nowadays about American English, Canadian English, Jamaican English, Australian English, Indian English, Singaporean English, and so on, and about dialects within these supposed Englishes; both dictionaries and grammars are available or in preparation for these. The standardizing grammar of Quirk et al. (1972) attempts to define a "common core" of usage, with marked variants.

Even within the English-speaking world however the debate about the proper variety to prescribe for education is by no means over; within the Francophone world the walls of the Académie Française are only just beginning to show hairline cracks. In Mauritius the education system treats "French" as being in effect the local vernacular and denies this status to Mauritian Creole, even though all Mauritians speak Mauritian Creole, on the grounds that it is merely "bad French" (Philip Baker, in *Abstracts 1988*: 40−41). Mauritian Creole has the status of a "non-langue" on the basis of a specious categorization which establishes French as a "langue".

The categories "focused" and "diffuse" are key ingredients in an attempt to establish a theoretical framework for linguistics which is genuinely universal (see *Acts of Identity* p. 202), by reexamining the ontology of the concept "a language". Uriel Weinreich, in *Languages in contact* (1953), makes the point that contact only occurs in the mind of the individual. The one undoubted universal in language is the individual user of language. It is often taken for granted that the concept of a communal language is also universal and can in some way be defined so that, for example, we all know the difference between "a language" and "a dialect", or that such terms as "first language" and "second language" can be used scientifically.

But apart from the concept of "the individual", which is itself, of course, far from monolithic although a necessary prerequisite of language, all of these other beliefs are stereotypes which derive from our particular cultures. Within our culture "Ciceronian Latin" is an autonomous system precisely because it is an abstraction from the finite written texts of a single individual. "The English language", on the other hand, has always been an abstraction from the way the English people have used language from time to time, either a term of art with unspecifiable parameters, or a highly idealised stereotype, behavior reified, totemized, and institutionalized.

1.3. Outwards from the individual to groups

If one takes this view about the centrality of the individual to any scientific study of language then one has to build outwards from that to accommodate the indisputable fact that cultures tend to throw up various stereotypes about the autonomy of their languages; and that these (for example, the concept of "God-givenness", or doctrines of "correctness") sometimes exert a powerful influence on the community so that people defend their implications, talk about "language purity", or about "owning a language", and so on. (A British journalist reported recently that an Italian politician told him "The English have nothing to give to Europe except their language, and we've already stolen that.")

The Chomskyan mode of bridge-building, as everybody knows, was to create a hypothetical idealized speaker-listener with complete knowledge of the linguistic system of a homogeneous language community. Although our experience tells us that this concept is much at odds with some basic and observable properties of language-using individuals such as their built-in innovative and creative faculties, nevertheless similar assumptions underlie many of the ways in which people talk about language learning. There are, it is felt, discrete systems. Every human being has the capacity to "internalize" at least one of them, possibly more. Sometimes when they learn two or more systems they mix them in use, either intentionally, or in a covert but rule-governed way, or from a lack of proper control of the systems. We have such terms as "code-switching", "code-mixing", and "using a mixed code" which presuppose that we can ascribe linguistic features to one external code or another. Then, of course, we run into all sorts of problems of ascription and of writing rules for the constraints on switching and mixing which derive at least in part from our starting point, the idea of discrete external codes being internalized. Many of these problems are discussed in a recent book on Alsatian French by Professor Tabouret-Keller's former student, Penelope Gardner-Chloros. They are touched upon also in Valdman (1989) with reference to the situation today in Haiti. As an English-speaker who has worked for many years in post-colonial countries, I came into contact with varieties of supposed Mandarin or Malay or Hindi or Urdu or

Marathi or Yoruba within which so much "English" had been naturalised as to enable me frequently to pick up the gist of what was being said; and my colleague at York, Mahendra Verma, has recorded much of this macaronic usage from his Indian friends, within which it is impossible to assign clear degrees of indigenization of borrowed features or to write rules to do so.

But suppose we start, not from reified discrete systems like "English" and "French" but from observable human beings using language, is it possible to create and preserve a theoretical framework for talking about language, about "bilingualism" or "diglossia" or "languages in contact" which, while not denying the force of these cultural stereotypes, nevertheless preserves intact the fact that the individual is the sole existential locus of language, and that the only universal source of differentiation, of discreteness in linguistic systems, lies between one individual and another? Charles Ferguson's original (1959) definition and exemplification of "diglossia" stipulated that High and Low codes were in each case varieties of "the same language", and Haiti was one of the four cases cited; but the cultural bias among Creolists since then has shifted towards regarding "Haitian Creole" as one or more languages distinct from French. Andrée Tabouret-Keller has referred (in *Abstracts 1988*) to the fact that officially at least in Alsace "bilingual" means "using both French and German", rather than "French and Alsatian", since Alsatian is not officially a language. In relation to Mauritius. Philip Baker writes (*Abstracts 1988*, p. 40):

> One bias or misconception which outsiders tend to bring to the Mauritian situation is an assumption that each of its five major languages is a self-contained entity. Mauritians are aware, to the extent that they are familiar with two or more of them, that much of the vocabulary of English derives from French, that local French draws heavily on English, that most of M[auritian] C[reole]'s lexicon is shared with local French, that M[auritian] B[hojpuri]'s basic vocabulary is all but identical with Hindustani even though it draws massively on MC for other terms, etc. These relationships have obvious implications for the design of orthographies of MC and MB.

Clearly, what I am asking is difficult to carry through with consistency; to some extent at least it involves keeping the metalanguage which we use for the scientific study of linguistic phenomena distinct from everyday language or customary linguists' usage; it involves constantly putting one set of terms or the other into quotation marks. If however we can at least bear the need always in mind, it may be easier to avoid imposing the stereotypes about discrete languages and the nature of linguistic systems from our own cultures on to other cultures where they do not necessarily apply or apply even less. We can also avoid wasting our argumentation on difficulties caused by our own disparate frameworks for analysis. The International Group for the Study of Language Standardization and the Vernacularization of Literacy (IGLSVL) at its first Workshop in 1986 (see *Abstracts 1986*) spent a good deal of time discussing the way in which linguists, as well as laymen, have exported to multilingual countries in the postcolonial period the stereotypes of their own cultures about the nature of languages. In reference for example to the case of Papua-New Guinea, Peter Mühlhäusler questioned whether it was helpful at all to think about the communal communicative modes of that country in terms of "languages".

1.4. Acts of identification

The bridge between the individual and communal systems is provided in our work (Le Page and Tabouret-Keller) by the concepts of projection and focusing, a cinematic metaphor. Each individual is envisaged using the linguistic systems they themselves have created in order to project on to others the universe as they envisage it, including their own place in it. They each have to establish their own identity, and do this by relating themselves, positively or negatively, to the people or groups of people they discern around them, endowing these with linguistic characteristics. The attraction and repulsion are projected through language use. It is true that we are moving towards the day when genetic science will be capable of uniquely specifying each individual in terms of a very, very long DNA number, but we identify ourselves by creating an idiosyncratic mode of linguistic (and other) behavior, at the same using it to relate to others. We then get feedback from others about the extent to which they in turn accept our universe, find it compatible or incompatible with their own. We may then adjust our behavior accordingly, the others likewise. In this way linguistic groups form in the real world which resemble those in the minds of the participants. People may become more like others in their behavior. This is the process we call "focusing". And since the language of each individual reflects their perception of the language of the group, somebody who succeeds in becoming a member of a focused group becomes similarly focused in their individual behavior. Conversely, where individuals distance themselves from each other that community as a whole is diffuse. It is possible — and is frequently the case in some kinds of multilingual society — to be a member of one highly-focused group among a number of other also highly-focused groups which are nevertheless discrete from, and distanced from, each other, as in a ghetto society, where there is only limited contact, possibly in specific domains such as marketing, between the members of different groups. Lesley Milroy's social and linguistic networks (1980) have proved a useful analytical tool in conditions such as those of Ulster where speakers of "the same language" are nevertheless grouped within religious and geographical boundaries and dialect usage.

If I am a member of a very tightly-knit homogeneous group with only limited access to other groups, my view of "languages" may be that of "my own language" vis-a-vis "all other language". This is a not uncommon chauvinist situation. If on the other hand I live in a community such as that of Cayo District in the 1970's, or Alsace, many groups, and many languages, may be accessible parts of my daily world, the boundaries between them much less clear, and "language" generally a more diffuse phenomenon.

Part 2. The sociolinguistic survey of multilingual communities

2.1. Cayo District, Belize: the social background

In our studies of the people of Cayo District, Belize, in Central America, we deliberately started with a community which as a whole was in a state of post-colonial flux, passing through a period of social and linguistic diffusion in the 1970s.

The 1950s

My first visit there had been nearly twenty years previously, in the early 1950s. It was then still part of the colony known as British Honduras. Internal communications in the colony were quite difficult. The Belize River provided the main route from the coast into the District, and I have recorded the reminiscences of a lady who had been to school near the river; when the regular steamer came up with supplies and sounded its hooter everybody in the little town of San Ignacio came down to the landing stage, and school was suspended. To get to one settlement, the logging camp at Gallon Jug, I started out by road, switched to a boat and finished the journey on a light logging railway to record the story-telling of the foreman, a Creole. Timber cut in the forests was still the main export, although the supply of trees was dwindling rapidly. Another major occupation in Cayo District and across the frontier into Guatemala was tapping the chicle trees for chicle, the gum which was the basis of chewing gum. Another, practised primarily by "Spanish", "Mestizos", and "Indians", was subsistence farming on little milpas. There were a few larger cattle ranches. The total population of the District was very small — about 10,000 people.

There were still rural villages of indigenous Amerindians — Maya and Kekchi — speaking their own well-focused "languages" or "dialects", and, as a second language if they had one, some variety of the Central American Spanish of Guatemala or Mexico. The small towns close to the Guatemalan frontier, of which Benque Viejo was the Cayo District example, were settlements of Spanish-speaking "Spanish" or "Mestizo" people whose grandparents had come in as refugees from Guatemala or Mexico, many of them still having relations across the frontier in Petén Province or Yucatan. The capital of the District, San Ignacio del Cayo, stood on the cayo or island formed by the two rivers which joined there to form the Belize River. It contained some Lebanese/Syrian businessmen who imported goods — flour, tinned food, dry goods, kerosene, and so on — up the river from the port of Belize to supply the loggers and the chicle tappers when they went off into the forest, and arranged for the export of chicle and timber products down the river. It also contained the administrative headquarters of the District — a District Commis-sioner/Magistrate who was British, and a small civil service consisting very largely of Creoles from the coastal District, people who had had an English-medium education and used English for administrative purposes but Creole in their homes. The schools in the District were run by various missions and used whatever medium they could through which to teach English; thus at Mount Carmel School in Benque Viejo there were German nuns teaching Maya children for English-language examinations and using Spanish as the medium of instruction.

Two further ingredients in this ethnic, cultural and linguistic complex were the Miskito Indians, always referred to patronisingly as "Waika", who came up from the coast to work in the forests, and the Garifuna or

Black Caribs, always referred to simply as Caribs, many of whom were teachers or policemen.

Most of the groups I have so far referred to used language which was itself the product of comparatively recent contact situations. The story of the Black Caribs has been told by Douglas Taylor (1951) and by C. J. M. R. Gullick (1976). They were the descendants of West African slaves who had been shipwrecked on, or had escaped to, the island of St Vincent and had taken wives from among the indigenous Island Caribs. After the French Revolution, during which they fought with the French against the British, they were deported en masse to the Miskito Coast and Bay Islands of Central America. The Island Caribs whose women they had taken had themselves earlier invaded and occupied Arawak-inhabited islands in the Antilles and taken Arawak wives. The complex history of the Miskito Indians has been unravelled by John Holm in his sociolinguistic history of the Miskito Shore (1978). They had had close contact with both the Hispanic and the English and Creole English Caribbean settlers since the seventeenth century.

The Creole English of the port of Belize in the early 1950s was still that of a fairly focused community of Creoles living in a small town on a river delta and having in some respects closer trading contacts by sea with Jamaica, through which a good deal of their mahogany was exported and whose ships came in regularly, than they did with the interior of their own country. The reluctance of coastal, urban Creoles to move inland resulted among other things in about half of the teachers in the rural areas being Black Caribs (Douglas Taylor 1951). Their Creole language of course had its origins in the slave trade, and in contact over a period of three centuries between speakers of African languages, speakers of various dialects of English, speakers of Creole, and of Spanish, and the standard English of education, and of the churches.

It was not until a metalled road was built into Cayo District in the 1950s and 1960s (it was still in parts a pot-holed hazard in the 1970s) that Creoles began to take up land for farming in the District, encountering as they did so the "Spanish speakers" moving in from the other end of the road.

2.2. Multidimensional networks or galaxies

The picture I am drawing of linguistic diffusion and focusing in Cayo District requires a view of so-called "languages" as abstractions from more-or-less temporarily focused nodes in a multidimensional network, or galaxy, of relationships and identities. None of the nodes in this network is wholly stable. The basic process in the formation of a node is that of groups of individuals identifying with each other for common purposes. At the end of the last century Hugo Schuchardt, in relation to pidgins and Creoles but also with more general reference, wrote that languages come into being for common purposes and disappear when those purposes disappear. In the early 1950s British Honduras was one of the few British colonies in which the concepts of the Creoles as a readily-identifiable and closely-knit group, and of Creole as a language, were accepted, so that people would for example tell me stories in [ˈkriːa] as well as in Spanish and talk to me in "English" — as one eighty-year-old said:

> *yu fu taak it in Spanish bot ai di trai brok ang iina kriia, nong?*
> 'You should say it in Spanish but I am trying to translate it into Creole, aren't I?'

In Jamaica and other islands, by contrast, the way people commonly spoke among themselves was not regarded as a language but simply as "broken talk" or "bad English", although very similar to Belize Creole. The Creoles of Belize said similar derogatory things about their language within the context of education, but nevertheless called it Creole and identified themselves, with pride and feelings of superiority, as Creoles. One of the reasons for this was their need to distinguish themselves politically and culturally from the Spanish in particular, and also from Caribs and Indians. They were "Bay-born", the culture of the Bay was theirs. They inherited three centuries of hostility between "Creoles" and "Spanish". This hostility was reflected still in both pre-independence and post-independence politics, in the formation of one predominantly Creole political party and one which tried to sublimate racial and ethnic antagonism in claims to a common "national" identity. We had a number of informants like JW who claimed a Creole father who did not speak Spanish to a "Spanish" mother. We had other, "Spanish" informants who could not conceal their distaste and regret at "Creole" replacing Spanish as the lingua franca of their District.

2.3. The discrete communities of the past in Cayo District

The past history of this separateness and antagonism is reflected in JW's account of some of the events of his childhood:

JW: *You see when we come in this part of the worl' there only was Maya*
       .. an' my children gone amongst the Maya people-them, they never
       used to talk Spanish, nor even a word in English, pure [= only] *Maya*
       .. they [my children] *coming with that Maya ..*
LeP: *But they don't talk it today?*
JW: *Yeh, they talk, talk it, yes ... in Bullet* [Tree Falls] *.. the ol' set of*
       Indian you see.
LeP: *Yeh, but not these young people here?*
JW: *No! No! No! − not this young people.*
LeP: *Why did they stop talking Maya?*
JW: *Because ... they got school and they brought the Spanish and the*
       English and they forget that [Maya] *...*
       When we come here the people .. they nearly was naked .. the Indians-
       them, yah. We have big revolution here with the Indians-them you
       know? .. That was 'bout − oh, nineteen-eight [1908]. *.. I will let you*
       know it plain .. the country use to be develop by the .. Guatemantican
       and the Mexican-them you know, because nineteen-ten [1910] *Mexico*
       got a revolution and by the thousand they used to come into the colony
       .. I was a big boy already .. they used to go to the States and buy arms
       to continue fighting. They used to steal money. We have a next
       revolution here that .. they cramp, they cramp the colony .. They tief
       out [= steal) *the chicle-them, they tief out your mule-dem and kill you*
       behind that ..

Cayo District in the 1950s contained relatively isolated and relatively focused settlements in its rural parts, and in some of the small townships also. Benque Viejo then was "Spanish". The next villages along the river, Succotz and Bullet Tree Falls, were mostly "Maya". I was asked by the new District Commissioner to go with him in his launch up and down the river on a tour of inspection; we went from landing-stage to landing-stage often to be greeted by a Creole or Carib policeman in an otherwise wholly Indian village. The prestige language in these frontier villages was still Spanish. In one we were offered entertainment ashore, which the District Commissioner interpreted to me as "some native girls singing". I looked forward to hearing Maya songs; but instead we sat for nearly an hour listening to the Christmas liturgy sung in Latin and Spanish, the girls' nasal "entuning" (very reminiscent of Chaucer's Prioresse) accompanied on a huge marimba.

The "Spanish" of Benque Viejo (laid out in the Spanish fashion with its own Alcalde or Mayor) maintained close contacts with friends and relations across the frontier in Petén Province. The frontier bisected the football pitch of one mission school, and some Guatemantican children came over each day to school. The townspeople were proud of their Spanishness and hostile to any thought of intermarriage with Creoles or Caribs. Some of them claimed "pure Spanish" descent and felt they had cultural links with Spain itself. In practice it was difficult to make any very clear ethnic distinction between Spanish, Mestizo and Indian.

The Lebanese or Syrian traders, known in the colony as *Los Turcos* 'The Turks' — their forebears having emigrated from what had been a Turkish province before the First World War — in the 1950s still tended to look back to the Levant for their wives, although it was acceptable also for them to marry light-skinned "Spanish" women. Some still claimed a command of Arabic, and in 1978 one of their descendants, one of our informants, still claimed that the family was 'Arab':

EE: *[my father] he's a half Arab. My mother is a Spanish but his father is .. was a full Arab you know, and his mother was a Mex .. em Guatemantican. So he was a half Arab. Then my .. my grandfather by my mother's side used to be an Arab too, you know? an' our mother used to be a Spanish.*

LeP: *But if somebody said to you, what do you reckon your family is, what would you say?*

EE: *I would say Arab.*

LeP: *Arab?*

EE: *Mmhm — Anybody ask me I would say an Arab.*

2.4. The changed picture in the 1970s: Mixing

Our sociolinguistic survey of Cayo District started in 1970. By then, considerable changes were in progress, some of the effects of which can be illustrated by continuing the above excerpt from EE's discussion in 1978. Although she lived in Benque Viejo she claimed that at home they mostly spoke "English" except to her father, who didn't understand it. When I commented that the children around us were speaking Spanish among themselves she agreed that they usually did that "among themselves". She had been to school in Belize for a time:

EE: *up there it's more Creole people talk an' that's why we got to talk the English over there. Bika'* [the Creole form of 'because' — LeP] *here most of the time lone* [Creole, = 'only'] *Spanish we used to talk at home. Only when we go* [Creole, = 'went'] *to school we used to talk English.*

LeP: *What sorts of people are living around you here?*

EE: *Pure* [Creole, = 'only'] *Spanish people.*

LeP: *So what language do they talk?*
EE: *The most of the people here talk English .. Unless some of them would talk Spanish .. Some of them can't talk English .. Most of the time they talk the two of them, Spanish an' English.*
LeP: *Do they mix them up at all?*
EE: *Yeh, sometime when they speaking they would talk Spanish and a little bit of English.*
LeP: *When you say English do you mean pure English? or ..*
EE: *No — Creole.*

The informant RQ, a young man in 1978, represented the transitional, post-independence generation among whom the "Spanish" were throwing in their lot with the Creoles. He distinguished "Creole" from "English":

AT-K: *When did you pick up your Creole? Because when you were a small child you spoke Spanish.*
RQ: *.. in school .. here.*
LeP: *The children round here spoke Creole at school, did they?*
RQ: *Yes — Creole and Spanish.*
LeP: *Which most?*
RQ: *The two of them we speak.*
LeP: *Mixed up?*
RQ: *Yeh — .. Our teacher was a Carib ... he used to speak English, you know because he's a teacher he had to. An' Creole... Spanish he .. didn't speak. We speak Spanish with our friends. With our parents. With other grown-ups. [The teacher] he used to talk in English. But we .. understand the English but we usually .. speak Creole. Most useful .. the Creole.*

RQ's father's parents, he said, were "Spanish", his mother's, "Spanish" and "Creole". His father would have described their family as of "mixed" race, and he would describe himself as "mixed". Where RQ worked they usually spoke Creole, although there were a lot of Spanish people there and also Maya Indians from San Antonio.

In 1970 our informant GM, whom I had first recorded telling Anansi stories in 1966, (see Le Page 1968) told us this about her parents, their language use and that of her peer group, with a vivid analysis of the role of the latter:

GM: *[My mother] a Mexican .. my father is a ... Creole .. Belizean ..*
LeP: *When you say "Belizean" what does that mean?*
GM: *His mother was a Belizean from here an' his father is an Irishman but he grew up in Belize so .. they call him a Bay-born .. he was born in Belize anyhow.*

LeP: *So he spoke Creole and your mother spoke Spanish?*

GM: *Well she spoke both.*

LeP: *But with you she spoke Creole?*

GM: *No well she don't .. she doesn't exactly speak Creole to us you know but we .. by going to school an' hear other children well we pick it up .. No she tried to talk to us the proper way but .. you know children .. we want to go our own way .. we pick up Creole...*

LeP: *But she learnt English at school, did she?*

GM: *Mhm.*

LeP: *So she wanted you to speak proper English?*

GM: *.. Now whenever we'd say something out of the way like .. something funny like* [bi'ka·z] *and we don't say* [bi'kɔ:z] *she'd put* [bi'kɔ:z] *and we'd say* [bɪ'ka·] *because we heard that in school you know,* [bɪ'ka·] *that's the way it is, .. we never finish a word .. we always .. cut it short or put more to it.*

LeP: *That school you went to in Santa Elena .. did most of the children there speak Creole?*

GM: *Mhm. And Spanish .. but this .. broken-up Spanish you know .. we call it Creole Spanish too because that's not grammatical Spanish.*

LeP: *But most of the families round there speak Spanish at home, don't they?*

GM: *Mhm.*

LeP: *So what did they talk in the playground, the children?*

GM: *Some Spanish and some* ['kria].

LeP: *Which most?*

GM: *That's* [fʊ] *tell .. I guess it's both. Balance half of each!*

LeP: *Did they ever mix the two up?*

GM: *Mhm ... Have a language spoken like .. for instance you would want to say like .. "catch the ball" .. they wouldn't say "aralami la bola" or something like that they would say "catchia la bola" you know an' ... that's "catch" ..* [laughs].

LeP: *Did your mother ever do that kind of thing when she talked to you?*

GM: *HNG!* [i. e., No!] *.. She spoke good Spanish, yes, because she learned good Spanish from her father .. her father is a pure-bred Mexican.*

LeP: *And when you spoke Creole Spanish did she correct that?*

GM: *Always .. Daddy the same way, because daddy never spoke to us in .. broad Creole* [i.e., Creole English] *.. although he .. right from Belize .. he always .. try to correc' us an' ... get us speak correctly but we never .. we never give up to them ...* [laughs] *as we get to bear children .. there it is!*

2.5. Social reasons for change

There seemed to be three main reasons for the changes noted. The colony was by 1970 well on its way to full independence. Secondly, Guatemala, which claimed Belize as part of its own territory which should have been inherited from Spain had it not been illegally occupied by the British, threatened to annex the whole country as soon as it became independent; as a consequence, a small British defence force remained on the frontier not far from San Ignacio. Thirdly, the road-building programme I have mentioned was by now well under way. The north-south road to Stann Creek on the coast had already been completed, and the east-west road from the port of Belize to the frontier beyond Benque Viejo had been resurfaced and partly macadamised.

These three changes provided fresh opportunities and fresh motivation for the younger generation to regroup themselves. The adoption of the name Belize for the whole country instead of just the port − now called Belize City; the threat of annexation; the roads which greatly increased the mobility of the population and drew people in to settle and farm in what had previously been fairly empty country; a primitive bus service from Benque Viejo to Belize City; more Creole civil servants and policemen moving into the District − all these and more social factors shaped the direction of the search for new identities among the younger generation, and the linguistic attributes with which to project those new identities. These social factors can all be examined under one or other of the four sets of constraints on the main theoretical statement about individual acts of identity (see *Acts of Identity*, pp. 182−186): they identified (with the help of a great deal of supportive propaganda) a fresh overarching group, Belizeans; provided a powerful motive for people to draw closer together for their own defence and in antagonism to "Spanish" Guatemala; and provided for much greater access by young people to "English" in the classroom and "Creole" in the playground in villages where children of different ethnic groups were now mixed up. Education remained for some a step towards higher education in Guatemala, where generous scholarships were available for Spanish-speakers; but for far more now it had become a step towards higher education in Belize, in Jamaica, or in Britain or the United States, or a step towards a better job. One of our Spanish-speaking informants from Benque Viejo went on to higher education in Belize but resolutely refused to be creolised, keeping his eye on a scholarship to study medicine in Guatemala City; but far more were like EE above (2.4.).

2.6. The 1970 evidence

In our 1970 survey we studied the language used by two hundred and eighty children — one in four of the required age-group on the Cayo District school rolls — when spoken to in English, in five modes of an extended recorded interview with each: early rather formal conversation about school subjects; telling both traditional and school-reader stories; later more relaxed informal conversation about, e. g., cooking, and ghosts; and reading. The children were between the ages of ten and sixteen. We were thus able to map the variation between their more formal and less formal linguistic behavior against the variables of their geographical provenance, ethnic provenance, age, sex, and educational level; in addition we talked at length with their families, and matched the children's claims about language use in their homes against what older members of the household claimed. Andrée Tabouret-Keller (1980) made a detailed study of the differences between the claims — the perceptions of the language situation — of the children and of the older generations.

2.7. The 1978 evidence

In 1978 we made a follow-up study of forty members of our original sample, now mostly in their early twenties. We concerned ourselves to record the attitudes they expressed towards language and towards any identities they felt they and their neighbours and families and the community as a whole now had. We were thus able to compare what they now said, and how they said it, with what they and their families had said in 1970, and make a real-time longitudinal study of their attitudes. Pressure at this time from Guatemala had intensified, and not long before the Guatemalan army had caused a panic flight from farms and villages near the frontier by moving up to the frontier in a menacing way. The results of this study have been published in *Acts of Identity*. I do not want to refer to them in detail here, but rather to illustrate them from the 1978 data.

Many of our 1978 conversations illustrated now not only the effects of the school playground described by GM, but the effects of the workplace. Labour had become much more mobile. Government inducements had led to new enterprises in citrus farming, sugar cane growing, garment factories, tourist hotels, and so on. Two devasting hurricanes had led to some population shifts; the first of these, Hattie, had led to the building of the village of Hattieville on the Cayo-Belize road, but the second led to the building of a new capital for the country at Belmopan, near the junction of the north-south and east-west roads. Belmopan was drawing in labour, entrepeneurs, civil servants, medical staff, and politicians from other parts of the country (although many of the civil servants were reluctant to make the move out of Belize).

2.8. Some illustrative cases

"Spanish"/"Creole"

Informant EO was now working at the Government agricultural station, Central Farm. He had been brought up by his grandmother who only spoke Spanish. Both of his parents spoke Spanish to the grandmother, but his mother now working in Belize and his father now working "somewhere around those Jamaicans" on the Pine Ridge road, both had to use Creole at work.

LeP: *At Central Farm, what languages do people use?*
EO: *Creole.*
LeP: *All the time?*
EO: *Yes, mostly.*
LeP: *No Spanish?*
EO: *Well, you got a few fellows .. about ten person ..*
LeP: *They talk Spanish?*
EO: *Spanish.*

Informant DR's father was the fire look-out at St Augustine, in the Mountain Pine Ridge. His parents, DR said, were both Spanish. He himself had done quite well at school in San Ignacio, and had tried to earn a living as a pupil-teacher in Cayo but found he could earn twice as much in a cigarette factory in Belize City. But:

DR: *The city was a bit bright, noisy ... So I finally decide to come back here* [St Augustine] *an' have a job. The only available job at this time now is hard labour .. That's throwing a machete and an axe ..*
LeP: *What sort of language do you need for that? What do they use?*
DR: *Well .. at the moment the language here at home and with the workers, we just use a slang, which is known as Creole, you know? Derived from the English, you know? So, that's our language, you know, we have .. a few Spanish .. that speak Spanish there, so, you know, when we would get together .. I would speak Spanish with them.*

"Maya"/"Spanish"/"Creole"

Informant MM was a young woman of Maya descent from Bullet Tree Falls whose family illustrated well the double shift in three generations from Maya to Spanish to "Creole"; she had a Spanish-sounding name and at first described her parents as "Spanish"; she was doing domestic work in Belize:

MM: *Since I finished school I began to work here in Cayo, I stop working here .. and went back to Bullet Tree then I went to Belize working there.* (laughs).

LeP: *... with what family, Spanish or English?*

MM: *Yes — Spanish ... Till right now I am working with her.*

LeP: *What language did they use in the house in Belize?*

MM: *Mixed. Well — Spanish, sometime they talk in English, too.*

LeP: *Can you speak Creole?*

MM: *Well, that is the language I speak* (laughs).

LeP: *But in your home in Bullet Tree Falls ...?*

MM: *Spanish — pure [= only] Spanish we talk there.*

LeP: *Where did you learn to speak Creole?*

MM: *Well .. in school so an' when I come out from there I learn more here in Cayo and in Belize .. so.*

LeP: *Did your parents know any Indian language?*

MM: *Well, my mother knows Maya so ... Sometimes she talk it. But with us she did not teach us.*

LeP: *Was your father Maya?*

MM: *Yes ... both of them talk the language .. they speak the both languages .. Sometimes they talk in Maya sometimes in Spanish.*

LeP: *And to you children ...?*

MM: *Spanish...*

AT-K: *.. in Bullet Tree Falls, when the children are taught Creole in the school* [as MM had said] *.. from whom do they pick it up?*

MM: *Well, from the teacher ...*

LeP: *Creole rather than English? They use Creole to teach the children?*

MM: *Yes. Well sometimes* /wan a dem fiks dea kriia gud nong/ — *make it sound better.*

Clearly in her perception the boundaries between "Creole" and "English" were rather fuzzy; you could "fix your Creole good, no?"

"Maya"/"Spanish"/"Creole"

Informant SH told us that she felt herself to be a Creole; her mother too she said was "pure Creole" in spite of having had a grandmother who was "a full-blooded Maya Indian .. she spoke only Spanish and Maya ..

my mother was raised with her .." in the Maya village of Baking Pot. Her father was from the Bay Islands of Honduras:

> SH: *A Creole is .. anyone .. that is mixed with Negro and any other .. if the race is white, Spanish, Indian, whatever, as long as .. you had a mixture of Negro then you're a Creole... If you go to a foreign country .. you'd say you're a Belizean .. they use the term "a Creole" right here in the country.*

For her, being a Creole had nothing to do with the language you spoke.

"Carib"/"Creole"/"Mixed"/"English"

Informant DL was of mixed Carib/Spanish descent and married now to a Carib policeman. She was a teacher, and claimed to speak English and Creole and a little Spanish. Ethnically she called herself "mixed", "a Belizean":

> LeP: *.. Do you ever use Spanish?*
> DL: *To outside .. But in school I don't use Spanish, only English.*
> LeP: *Do any of the children come from Spanish homes?*
> DL: *Oh, a lot.*
> LeP: *Can you tell me any of the difficulties they have when you are teaching them?*
> DL: *Well .. we put them along with the children that know English, you know. After a while they can talk it.*
> LeP: *Do they learn to talk English or Creole?*
> DL: *Yes, English. There's mostly Spanish as long as they pick it up. Then the Creole would come right in.*
> LeP: *.. Why is that?*
> DL: *Well, because most people talk Creole.*

"Creole"/"Creole"

Informant AH had left school soon after we had originally recorded her at Black Man Eddy, and had gone to work in a canning factory at Pomona, a twelve-hour day (at the age of thirteen) which she did for eighteen months. The factory was near Stann Creek, a largely Carib area of the coast on the southern part of the north-south highway. When it closed she moved to a garment factory in the new capital, Belmopan, where she now was:

LeP: *What language did they use in the canning factory?*

AH: *Just Creole.*

LeP: *...the people working there, were they all Creoles?*

AH: *No, some were but most were Caribs ... and they could talk Carib but I can't.*

LeP: *Did they talk it among themselves?*

AH: *Yes, but then I don't understand what they said.*

LeP: *So you got your instructions in Creole, did you?*

AH: *Yes, sir.*

LeP: *And what about the garment factory?..*

AH: *Oh .. they talk Creole there.*

LeP: *Are they all Creole people working there?*

AH: *Yes. All .. all Creole... Maybe we have about a few Guatemanticans that speak Spanish but they can talk Creole too.*

"Spanish"/"Creole"/"English"

Finally, informant SH, from a purely Spanish-speaking family in Benque Viejo, was now working in a wine shop in Santa Elena. Previously she had been with her grandmother cooking for the older males of the family who were working in forestry in the Mountain Pine Ridge. Up there, she said, they spoke Spanish and English; in the wine shop, some of the customers spoke Spanish, some Creole, some English and she would answer accordingly. She was living with her aunt nearby, who spoke Spanish because she could not speak English, but all her young cousins in the house (aged nineteen, seventeen and fourteen) used Creole among themselves; as for Spanish, "them can't speak it so good". When I asked her to tell me the difference between "Indian" people and "Spanish" people, she replied "I'd say they were the same thing".

2.9. St Lucia: background

The French-speaking and formerly-French-speaking islands of the Antilles and the mainland territories of Louisiana in the southern United States and Guyane (to be carefully distinguished from Creole-English-speaking Guyana almost next door) on the northeast coast of South America present us with a fascinating series of comparable case-histories of sociolinguistic processes in a multilinguistic, multidimensional framework.

We can mention only briefly in passing Louisiana, Haiti, Guadeloupe, Dominica, Martinique, St Lucia, St Vincent, Grenada, Trinidad, and Guyane (setting aside a number of smaller islands). In no case is it possible to assess the linguistic outcome to date in terms of "pairs of languages in contact". To begin with, the patterns of the slave trade and of plantation slavery were quite complex and changing in terms of the numbers and provenance of both slaves and French emigrants. The Creole French which resulted was the language of communities in continuing contact with speakers of various dialects of French, of English, of Portuguese, of Spanish, of Dutch and of African and Amerindian languages. The period of contact, the demographic and political and economic circumstances, varied from territory to territory. The linguistic outcome is unique in each case although, as in the Anglophone Caribbean, there are sufficient similarities to justify us speaking of "Caribbean Creole French".

There is today an intellectual movement, "Mokwéyol", which has among its aims the establishment of a standardized written variety of Creole French (here called "Antillean"), which could be used in literacy campaigns and in education throughout the formerly-French Antilles and the still-French provinces of Guadeloupe and Martinique. One of the leaders of Mokwéyol is a member of IGLSVL, Lawrence Carrington. His report of December 1988, *Creole discourse and social development*, sets out his program for research and training. If successful, focusing would take place around "Antillean" norms. Some scepticism has been voiced at IGLSVL Workshops about the influence of Mokwéyol and the lack of awareness among the general population of any need for or movement towards literacy in Creole. Parents want their children to become literate in the language that has most economic advantage. Carrington (1988: 46 – 47) himself comments:

> Antillean has had a folk-history and notwithstanding the progress made in Haiti and in particular in the Haitian diaspora, [e. g., among refugees in Florida etc. – LeP] it has not been the language of administrative, political, economic or technological change. In all four of these sectors, the direction of change and movement has been determined by speakers of English and French or by pressures from societies in which Antillean is not present.... For all their similarities the Antillean-speaking countries of the region have had sufficiently different experience of government, administration and technology that they have responded in the lexical domain in different ways.... The readiness of items from one dialect to another lies in the similarity of phonetics, stress patterns, syllable structure, and morphology of all the dialects of the language.

"The language" here is the abstraction being made, "Antillean". Carrington makes a strong case for its instrumentalization while recognizing the antagonism his proposals often raise.

Valdman's 1989 paper on Haiti, referred to above in 1.3., explores the question of a standard form for Creole French in that country, where the metropolitan French of the urban élite exercises a constant pressure on the lexicon of both urban and rural Creole as used in education, but more so on the urban varieties. Valdman finds it necessary to speak of the multidimensional language space in which Haitian speakers move.

2.10. The Survey

When we carried out our sociolinguistic study in St Lucia in the 1970s the population of that island was far more homogeneous than that of Belize. The former British Windward Islands were British colonies from the beginning of the nineteenth century but each of them had had some period of French domination in the eighteenth century. In St Vincent this was very short-lived, and when I did some exploratory fieldwork there in the 1950s I found only one old lady, who was, it was claimed, an Island Carib speaker, who in fact produced a few words of Creole French to support that claim. In contrast, at that time Creole French was the most common vernacular in Dominica (see Christie 1969) and St Lucia, common among the older generation in Grenada, and still known among the older generation in some parts of Trinidad. Recently P. G. Christie (personal communication) gained the impression that young people in Dominica responded to her as much in English as in Creole French, and certainly in Grenada the Creole French has all but disappeared. In St Lucia we were concerned to discover what kinds of English or Creole English would be used by the schoolchildren when they were spoken to in English, and to correlate as in Belize their social and economic circumstances, age, sex, level of education with certain linguistic variables. The details are in *Acts of Identity*.

Our survey showed that the English used by the schoolchildren, supposedly the English they had been taught at school, reflected in a number of morphological features (the level of analysis on which we concentrated) differing patterns of influence from both indigenous and external contacts, today and in the past. In contrast to Grenada, this equally mountainous island had a history of poor internal communications, so that the Creole French of the small villages in the interior was well-focused until recently through lack of external contacts.

Among the external influences however were: the geographical proximity of Martinique to the north, a Department of France still using Creole French and French; of St Vincent to the south, using Creole English and English; and of Barbados to the east, using what can best be labelled "Bajan" and English. The links with Barbados had been particularly important in and around the capital, Castries, in the past for reasons of the colonial administration and of trade. There has been in the past considerable movement of labour in the Eastern Caribbean, including building labour sent from Barbados to St Lucia. In addition the British administration established schools which used English as the medium of instruction, forbidding the use of Creole French, and these were staffed to some extent by expatriate Englishmen or Barbadians.

Although when I was first doing fieldwork in St Lucia in the 1950s the draconian ban on Creole French, or "patois", in schools had been relaxed a little, the older teachers still pretended to have no knowledge or understanding of it; nevertheless, even then what was supposed at official level to go on in the classrooms and what actually did go on were two very different things, and by the time we did our survey the distinctions formerly drawn so firmly between "English" and "patois" were not only being blurred, but blurred differentially among different sections of the population. St Lucia is probably on the same road towards the use of some variety of Creolized Eastern Caribbean English as Grenada and Dominica.

2.11. The Caribbean as a cultural network

Each one of the islands in what is called "the Commonwealth Caribbean", in fact, is a potential node in the networks of cultural relationship which link them — to each other, to North America, to Britain, to France, to Central America and Venezuela, to various parts of Africa, to India from which large numbers of indentured labourers came in the second half of the nineteenth century, to the Cantonese and the Syrian background of shopkeepers and so on. And within each island, groups and individuals are caught up in the post-colonial search for their identity, and are refocusing their linguistic behavior accordingly. Today the tourist industry has an enormous potential influence.

Part 3. Conclusion

3.1. Multiple inputs and the diffuseness and subsequent focusing of multiple outputs in multilingual contact situations

The kind of picture I am drawing of evolutionary linguistic processes in contact situations is anathema to some creolists, who dismiss it pejoratively with the term "the cafeteria principle". That is because they wish to invoke only concepts associated with "contact" between "pairs of languages", coupled with "universals" of grammar.

A cafeteria example

From our St Lucian data it is clear that there are three ways of expressing habitual usage in the verb, in addition to Standard. These are illustrated, as being each one characteristic of the vernacular usage of one of the other islands, from the following replies from informants in Jamaica, St Vincent, and Grenada asked to turn the English sentence 'Good children go to heaven' into their own dialect:

Ø	Jamaica	*gud pikni ga-a hebm*
does	St Vincent	*gud pikni doz gu a hevn*
-ing	Grenada	*gud childrin go-in tu hevn*

(*Acts of Identity* 86)

In the following piece of narrative (from a ghost story) told by a St Lucian child all three occur together:

'They *say* he taking your hair and go with it... they [spirits] *goes go with you*... they *say* they *does take you* and kill you... they *giving theyself to the devil* and they *does give them money.*' (*Acts of Identity* 136)

The use of *does*, *-ing* and Ø as verb markers for habitual aspect was among the criteria we used to group the children. All three forms were available to them. If we take the Eastern Caribbean as a whole we find that the *does* constructions are most closely associated with Barbadian (Bajan) usage, the *-ing* forms with communities affected by contact with Creole French. In St Lucia the *does* constructions occurred most among children in or close to Castries, the *-ing* forms most frequently among the most rural children. Since urban speech has some prestige, if we then view the community as a whole we find an incipient system emerging from this multidimensional and at present diffuse use of "English" in the island within which the tokens available to signal "habitual aspect" are socially marked; and if St Lucia follows Dominica and Grenada in becoming more and more "English-using", focusing of group usage will take place around more frequent, more prestigious and less frequent, less prestigious selection of one of these forms. Similar considerations apply to the incipient social marking and consequent frequency of selection of many phonological, morphological, syntactic, and lexical items. In this way what may initially be regarded as loans from external sources all become absorbed into one indigenous system with stylistic and social variants and possibly also variations of semantic nuance.

3.2. Are Creole situations aberrant?

I see no reason why a sharp distinction should be made between the language of Creole communities and of any other language community. The differences are matters of degree. It is significant that attempts have been made to claim Middle English as a "Creole language", and as often refuted either on typological grounds or on the basis of social history: in the first case, for example, that no pidginizing situation preceded the re-emergence of English writing in its "Middle English" form, and in the second case, that the Norman-French-speaking elite, far from enslaving the English-speaking population, ended the Saxon institution of slavery. But to take the typological case first: a Creole language is simply the language of a Creole — i.e., a locally born as opposed to expatriate — community; it does not appear overnight out of a contact situation, but develops initially with the first few generations of locally born children. Many similarities between Creoles in phonology, in syntactic structure, and in the lexicon have been pointed to as if they were defining characteristics of "Creole languages", but many of these can be shown to be properties of a common substrate or superstrate input or universal characteristics of contact languages such as a reduction of the redundancy or of the stylistic choice available in one of the source languages (see Le Page 1977, 1990). And in the second case, the master — slave relationship was for a great many African slaves only one part, perhaps a small part (because contact between field slaves and their masters on large plantations was extremely limited) of the overall language input for Creole children. (For a recent study bearing out the validity of a gradualist theory of creolization, see Arends 1989.) In all cases of intimate contact between different communities there is likely to be multiple linguistic input to the children's language systematization, and the children will produce for their peer groups initially at least a diffuse and varying output. What happens next is a transactional focusing among peer groups, agreement on the social marking of tokens being exchanged, the emergence within each generation of sets of linguistic attributes assigned to different groups within the community, the use of these differentially by individuals to mark their own identity within the community.

Such an approach seems to me to provide a way of reconciling a great many apparently very different kinds of contact situation with what Thomason — Kaufman (1988) refer to as cases of "normal genetic transmission" — to provide, that is, a valid common general framework for the study of the evolution and change of all "languages". Those of us who come from very stable and highly focused societies may find it difficult to distinguish stereotypes about "normal transmission" from the real facts about language use, variation, and change in use, since we are so accustomed to think in terms of idealized, reified, discrete systems; but it is essential to see all language questions in terms of activity between individuals as they form social groups, even in the most static and highly focused communities.

If we do use such a framework for talking about "languages" we can easily recognise that "codes", "code-switching", "code-mixing" and "mixed codes" are terms of convenience which can, and need, never be defined in absolute terms. We can talk about probabilities within clusters of concomitant circumstances; of the possibilities that individuals have available to them, of the significance of their choices. Code-switching between the customary usage of two highly focused communities — for example, of English and French academics — will have one kind of probable significance; between "Spanish" and "Creole" in Belize switching will be very much harder to define and may pass unnoticed, just another stage in the evolution of "Belizean".[2]

Notes

1. On "stereotypes" see, e. g., Walter Lippman (1922) and much sociological literature since. See also Le Page (1989).
2. Since writing this paper I have received the preliminary draft of Norman Denison's paper for the forthcoming European Science Foundation meeting in Basel (January 1990) "An alternative to the '(single, homogeneous) code'-

view of language in use". Examination over thirty years of the repertoire of the inhabitants of the village of Sauris in northeast Italy has brought him to express views very similar to my own.

References

Abstracts
1986   *Abstracts and transcripts of the York 1986 Workshop of the International Group for the study of language standardization and the vernacularization of literacy*, edited by R. B. Le Page.
Abstracts
1988   Idem, *1988 Workshop*, edited by R. B. Le Page. University of York, Department of Language and Linguistic Science, Heslington, York, GB.
Arends, J. T. G.
1989   *Syntactic developments in Sranan: creolization as a gradual process* (Doctoral diss., University of Nijmegen, Holland).
Baker, Philip
1988   "The major languages of Mauritius and their domains", *Abstracts 1988*: 40 – 41.
Carrington, Lawrence D.
1988   *Creole discourse and social development* (Ottawa, Canada: International Development Research Centre MS Report 212 e).
Chomsky, Noam
1965   *Aspects of the theory of syntax* (Cambridge, Mass: MIT Press).
Christie, Pauline G.
1969   *A sociolinguistic study of some Dominican Creole-speakers* (Doctoral diss., University of York).
Denison, Norman
1988   "Language contact and language norm", *Folia Linguistica* 22: 11 – 35.
Diki-Kidiri, Marcel
1988   Discussant in *Abstracts 1988:* 110.
Ferguson, Charles A.
1959   "Diglossia", *Word* 15: 325 – 340.
Gardner-Chloros, Penelope
1990   *Language selection and switching in Strasbourg* (Oxford: Oxford University Press).
Grace, George W.
1989   "The notion of "natural language", *Ethnolinguistic Notes* (University of Hawaii) 3, 38: 567 – 581.

Gullick, C. M. J. R.
1976   *Exiled from St Vincent: the development of Black Carib culture in Central America up to 1945* (Malta: Progress Press).

Holm, John
1978   *The Creole English of Nicaragua's Miskito Coast: its sociolinguistic history and a coparative study of its lexicon and syntax* (Doctoral diss. University College, London. Ann Arbor: University Microfilms).

Kachru, Braj (ed.)
1982   *The other tongue: English across cultures* (Oxford: Oxford University Press).

Le Page, Robert B.
1968   "Problems of description in multilingual communities". *Transactions of the Philological Society* 1968: 189 – 212. (Oxford: Blackwell).
1977   "Processes of pidginization and creolization", in: Albert Valdman (ed.), *Pidgin and creole linguistics* (Bloomington: Indiana University Press), 222 – 258.
1989   "What is a language?", *York Papers in Linguistics* 13: 9 – 24. (University of York, Department of Language and Linguistic Science).
1990   "What can we learn from the case of Pitcairnese?", in: Rosemarie Tracy (ed.), *Festschrift for David Reibel* (to appear).

Le Page, Robert B. – Andrée Tabouret-Keller
1985   *Acts of identity* (Cambridge: Cambridge University Press).

Lippman, Walter
1922   *Public Opinion* (New York: Harcourt, Brace).

Lüdi, Georges
1989   "Code-switching and language contact", *Communications* (Strasbourg: European Science Foundation) 21: 8 – 9.

Milroy, Lesley
1980   *Language and social networks* (Oxford: Blackwell) (second edition 1987).

Quirk, Randolph, et al.
1972   *A grammar of contemporary English* (London: Longman).

Romaine, Suzanne
1988   *Pidgin and creole languages* (London: Longman).
1989   *Bilingualism* (Oxford: Blackwell).

Schuchardt, Hugo
1882 – 1889 *Kreolische Studien* (Wien, various publishers) edited and translated in part by Glenn G. Gilbert, *Pidgin and creole languages* (Cambridge: Cambridge University Press, 1980).

Stewart, William A.
1965   "Urban Negro speech: sociolinguistic factors affecting English teaching", in: Roger W. Shuy et al.(eds.), *Social dialects and language learning* (Champaign, Illinois: National Council of Teachers of English), 10 – 19.
Street, Brian V.
1984   *Literacy in theory and practice* (Cambridge: Cambridge University Press).
Tabouret-Keller, Andrée
1980   "They don't fool around with the Creole much, as with the Spanish: a family case in San Ignacio, Cayo District, (Belize)", *York Papers in Linguistics* 9: 241 – 259. (University of York, Department of Language and Linguistic Science).
Taylor, Douglas
1951   *The Black Carib of British Honduras* (New York: Wenner-Gren Foundation).
Thomason, Sarah G. – Terrence Kaufman
1988   *Language contact, creolization and genetic linguistics* (Berkeley: California University Press).
Todd, Loreto
1984   *Modern Englishes: Pidgins and Creoles* (Oxford: Blackwell).
Valdman, Albert
1989   "The elaboration of pedagogical norms for second language learners in a conflictual diglossia situation", in: S. Gass – C. Madden – D. Preston – L. Selinker (eds.), *Variation in second language acquisition* (Clevedon, Avon: Multilingual Matters), 15 – 23.
Weinreich, Uriel
1953   *Languages in contact* (Publications of the Linguistic Circle of New York No. 1) (New York).
Young, Colville
1973   *Belize Creole..in its cultural and social setting* (Doctoral diss., University of York).

The substratum in grammar and discourse

Marianne Mithun

Substratum effects can vary substantially in their salience: those involving smaller domains of language, such as vocabulary and clause-level grammar, can be conspicuous to anyone outside of the immediate speech community, while those involving multiple clauses or larger stretches of discourse can be subtle. Substratum effects conditioned by larger contexts can be easily overlooked, yet they can be pervasive, shaping the way information is presented and adding special stylistic dimensions to the language of which listeners outside of the community may be unaware.

Some subtle substratum effects can be observed in several communities in Northern California. Central Pomo is a California Indian language, indigenous to a region one hundred miles north of San Francisco. It is one of seven distinct languages of the Pomoan family. Several other unrelated languages are also indigenous to the area, including Yuki to the north, Patwin to the east, and Wappo and several Miwok languages to the south. All of the languages contain lexical evidence of contact dating from aboriginal times. There was apparently extensive intermarriage among members of these very small communities, and the pattern has continued into the present. People seem to have had a pragmatic attitude toward language, learning new languages readily but expressing little emotion toward any special beauties of one language over another.

The first major wave of European contact to affect Central Pomo was Spanish. The end of the eighteenth century and the first half of the nineteenth brought Spanish missionaries and Mexican settlers into California. A large number of Spanish nouns remain in modern Central Pomo for items introduced during the early nineteenth century: tools, clothing, food, etc.

In the mid-nineteenth century, California was transferred from Mexico to the United States. The Central Pomo lost most of their land and began working for white ranchers. English-speaking missionaries began to arrive, and by the early twentieth century children were attending school in English. One Central Pomo man recalls that when he left the Hopland

Rancheria in 1925 for boarding school, Central Pomo was still spoken in most households. When he returned in 1935, the language of most of these same households, apart from those of a few older people, was English. Speakers alive today cannot remember anyone who was completely monolingual in Central Pomo.

At present there are three Central Pomo communities: Point Arena/Manchester on the coast, and the Hopland and Yokaya Rancherias about forty miles inland, seven miles apart. There is still a handful of Central Pomo speakers in each community, most over the age of seventy five, but the language is not normally used in everyday conversation. The effects of English on Central Pomo are as might be expected. English words of all categories are sometimes borrowed for concepts that have no Central Pomo labels. More often, speakers simply switch to English when discussing non-traditional topics. (For a detailed description of the effects of Spanish and English contact on Central Pomo see Mithun 1990.)

At the same time, some of the English now spoken in these communities shows influences of the Central Pomo substratum. Community residents have remarked that they can identify individuals who have grown up on a Central Pomo rancheria on the basis of their English alone. Some intonational and lexical traces of Central Pomo appear, but grammatical and discourse effects are more pervasive.[1]

1. The lexicon

Words for specifically Central Pomo cultural items appear on rare occasions in English discussions of traditional objects and customs.

(1)   *Put ʔám leaf on there?*   *(ʔám* 'soapweed')
(2)   *Maybe they put p'dú out there.* *(p'dú* 'acorn')

A more subtle lexical effect of the Central Pomo substratum is the relatively high frequencies of certain expressions. A phrase 'and again too' for example appears often, as in the beginning of the sentence in (3), part of a discussion about netting quail in a tree.

(3)   And again too,
       how they gonna čʰáakaw with that ... *(čʰáakaw* 'catch')
       here's that qʰalé.   *(qʰalé* 'tree')

This English phrase is a loan-translation of a Central Polmo expression typically used to present another side of a discussion or an additional point. The high frequency of the Central Pomo model has affected the frequency of its counterpart in English.

(4)   *Méen ʔihlakay...*[2]
         méen   ʔi = hla = kay
         so   be = AGAIN = ALSO
         'And then again...'

(In the examples cited here all words on a line are part of a single intonation unit in the sense of Chafe: "a sequence of words combined under a single, coherent intonation contour, usually preceded by a pause" [1987: 22]. In the Central Pomo examples, the first line represents the material as spoken, the second a morphological segmentation, the third a literal gloss, and the fourth a free translation.)

2. Grammar

Grammatical structures whose domain is a single clause tend to be obvious to speakers and analysts alike, while those conditioned by contexts covering larger segments of speech tend to be less so. As in many language-contact situations, substratum effects on morphology and syntax are variable. Within a single conversation, an individual speaker will typically show a mixture of alternants in identical contexts.

2.1. Clause-level domains

Among the clause-level phenomena that can show Central Pomo substratum influence are verb inflection, nominal number inflection, indefinite marking on nominals, and lexical gap questions.

2.1.1. Verb inflection

Central Pomo verb morphology can be complex, including distinctions of number and aspect. First, second, or third person, and past or present tense, are not usually distinguished, however.

(5)   *pʰdéeʔwan*
      pʰ-dé-·ʔw-an
      BY.SWINGING—move-AROUND-IMPRF
      'swim around/swam around'

Similar distinctions are often omitted in English.

(6)   *If a,*
      what about if rabbit,
      big one come,
      that break the string?

(7)   *And I haven't done it because she say wait.*

2.1.2. Number

Number marking on nouns is not obligatory in Central Pomo. Some nouns and all pronouns referring to human beings have both singular and plural forms, but number is not normally specified for non-humans. In (8) for example, the Central Pomo noun for 'berry' contains no number marker, although it refers to many berries.

(8)   *Hóskʰonṭo ʔel ʔmaya*
      hóskʰonṭo   ʔel   ʔ=ma-ya
      berry   the   COP=2-PL
      'Don't waste

      yóoʔts'eeč'kʰe   *tʰin.*
      yóoʔ-ts'e-·č'=kʰe   tʰí-n
      waste-GOING.TO-IMPRF.PL=INFV   not-IMPRF
      the berries.'

Similarly, in these communities, English nouns referring to multiple non-humans often appear without plural markers.

(9)   *They're very fond of fish...*
      and berry.

Those referring to human beings are generally inflected for number.

2.1.3. Indefinite articles

Central Pomo contains a definite article, the enclitic *ʔel*, but there is no indefinite article. (10) is the opening of a legend in which two characters are introduced.

(10) *šéemi*   *ʔdoma*
      šéemi   *ʔ = doma*
      long.ago COP = QUOT
      'Long ago, they say,

      p'šé   *báyaakay*
      p'šé   *báya· = kay*
      deer   man = ALSO
      (a) man deer

      p'šé   *máaṭakay,*
      p'šé   *máaṭa = kay*
      deer   woman = ALSO
      and *(a)* woman deer.'

When the same speaker retold the story in English, the first noun phrases contained no indefinite article, although the second one did.

(11) *Long time ago,*
      was ...
      man deer,
      and a woman deer.

This variability is typical. (12) was part of a conversation.

(12) A: *So she ..*
         she sings a song.
         That's why she ..

      B: *She sing Indian song?*

      A: *Yeah. Indian song.*

Definite articles are generally not omitted in English.

2.1.4. Lexical-gap question

Central Pomo lexical-gap questions involve no subject-verb inversion comparable to English. Interrogation is shown by an enclitic on the first word.

(13) *Q'ówa*   *muul yhéen?*
      q'ó = wa   *muul yhé-·n*
      what = Q   3   do-IMPRF

'What does he do?'

English question-word questions in these communities often follow a similar pattern, showinng no inversion. Without inversion, *do*-support is unnecessary.

(14)   *And how they make that to slip then?*

(15)   *What they call that?*

2.2. Multi-clause domains

Grammatical structures involving contexts larger than a single clause show more subtle substratum effects. Some of the most characteristic are the use of pronouns and clause linking.

2.2.1. The use of pronouns

In Central Pomo, once a central person or entity has been introduced, this participant need not be overtly respecified in every clause unless there is some discontinuity in the discussion. For this reason, many clauses contain no nouns or pronouns referring to arguments that would be subjects in English. In (16), for example, some people are referred to pronominally in the first clause, but there is no overt mention of them in subsequent clauses.

(16)   *Múuṭuyaakʰe   muul lóq'   ʔe   ʔmúuṭuyaakʰe*
   múuṭuya· = kʰe   muul lóq'   ʔe   ʔ = múuṭuya· = kʰe
   3.PL = OBL that thing COP COP = 3.PL = OBL
   'They had things

   maʔá   qaawáačʼkawʔkʰe;
   maʔá   qa·-wá-·čʼ-ka-w = ʔkʰe
   food BITING-go-IMPRF.PL-CAUS-PRF = INF
   for them to eat.

   tʼabó   qʰadiṭṭaymawʔkʰe,
   tʼabó   qʰadí-č-ṭa-č-ma-w = ʔkʰe
   hay buy-SML-ME-SML-MA-PRF = INFV
   Because *(Ø)* had

péesu   čʰów   méen   ʔín,
péesu   čʰó-w   méen   ʔi = n
money   not-PRF   so   be = AS
no money to buy hay,

kʰé   meenémaʔya,
kʰé   ma·-né-m-ač'-ya
dance   STEPPING-set-DOWN-IMPRF.PL – DFOC
(∅) put on a dance

maʔákay   báʔelšiṭaq'.
maʔá = kay bá = ʔelši-ṭ-q-ʔ
food = also INDF = sell-ME-PL.AC-PRF
(∅) sold food to people.'

The same pattern of pronoun use appears in English in these communities. Continuing subjects are often not respecified in every clause or even every sentence.

(17)   *In the morning early,*
        they get up,
        before sunup,
        (∅) don't eat,
        (∅) don't drink water,
        (∅) going ...
        (∅) going out to hunt.

2.2.2. Clause linking

Central Pomo contains a set of morphemes for overtly linking related clauses. They appear suffixed to the last word of each non-final clause in a series. Note the position of the marker *-ba* 'and then' in (18).

(18)   sélka   ʔel   sʔémmaba
        sélka   ʔel   sʔé-m-ma-ba
        fence   the   build-DOWN-MA-AND
        '(They) built the fence and

        yhéṭač'ba
        yhé-ṭa-č'-ba
        do-ME-IMPRF.PL-AND
        did that and then

> múuṭuya ʔe   mul lóqʼ ʔel qóol   mčámmaw.
> múuṭuya ʔe   mul lóqʼ ʔel qó=·l   mčá-m-ma-w
> 3.PL   COP that thing the out=TO
>   throw.PL-DOWN-MA-PRF
> they threw the things away.'

Because the marker is suffixed to the first clause of a linked pair, it is part of the preceding intonation unit. The same intonation pattern often characterizes English conjoined clauses.

(19)   *See the women would .. sell sandwiches and,*
        you know things like that and,

(20)   *The people that was taking care of it was getting old and ..*
        They can't ... climb the .. hills ..

(21)   *They driving on that road*
        way over that way,
        where the cattles are and
        steal the little cows.
        Little calfs.

3. Discourse

Substratum effects are all the more subtle when they involve larger stretches of discourse. Although both speakers and hearers are typically not conscious of these effects, they may be pervasive.

3.1. Recalibration of pragmatic markedness

Many syntactic options in Central Pomo, as in other languages, indicate the importance of particular elements of information within the discourse as a whole. Especially significant information may be set off by certain syntactic devices such as word order, clefting, etc. The markedness of a particular construction may differ from one language to another. Such differences can result in discourse-conditioned substratum effects.

3.1.1. Word order

Central Pomo is characterized by flexible verb-final constituent order. Note that all nominals precede the verb in (22).

(22) *Mil̓kʰe*   *péesu*   *ʔmiili*
  mí-l = ʔkʰe *péesu*   *ʔ = mí· = li*
  that-at = FROM money COP = that-AT = WITH
  čáač̓   *yawál yačól,*
  čáač̓   *yawál = yačol*
  person   all-OBL
  'The money from the sale of that (mountain land)

  qat̓éeʔyaw.
  qat̓é-·č̓-ya-w
  give.PL-IMPRF.PL-DFOC-PRF
  was distributed to everyone.'

The same order appears in many English sentences in these communities, as in (23).

(23) *Nice fence they had to build*
  to keep the cattle in.
  That's why we got fence over there.

Left dislocation is of course perfectly grammatical in standard English, although it is highly marked pragmatically. The unmarked status of the equivalent word order in Central Pomo has apparently resulted in a recalibration of the markedness of English left dislocation in these communities, where it can appear frequently.

3.1.2. Cleft constructions

Central Pomo contains a cleft construction that is pervasive in the speech of some. Significant elements are set off by the copula *ʔe*.

(24) *ʔúdaaw baasét̓ ʔe* *mun.*
  ʔúdaaw baasét̓ ʔe *mun*
  awful bad COP 3
  'She's really a bad woman.'

It is not a highly marked construction in Central Pomo. Similar structures appear often in English.

(25)   *Just bad one she is.*

As with word order, the existence of the Central Pomo model, not a highly marked construction pragmatically, has prompted a slight recalibration of pragmatic markedness in the English counterpart.

3.2. Arrangement of information

Discourse in Central Pomo, as in a number of North American languages, often displays a particular arrangement of information: a simple clause is followed by elaborations, each filling in information. The sequence in (26) is quite typical.

(26)   *Máa ʔel ʔélšiiyawʔkʰe.*
        máa ʔel ʔélši-·ya-w=ʔkʰe
        land the sell-DFOC-PRF=INFV
        'The land would be sold.

       Danómaa   ʔel ʔdoo   ʔélšiiyawʔkʰe.
       danó=máa   ʔel ʔ=doo   ʔélši-·ya-w=ʔkʰe
       mountain=land the COP=QUOT sell-DFOC-PRF=INFV
       They said the mountain land would be sold.'

The same pattern appears in English in these communities.

(27)   *they gave them cattle.*
        The government gave them cattle.
        Nice .. breed of cattle.

The effect is subtle but pervasive.

3.3. Couplet constructions

Like some other languages indigenous to the New World, Central Pomo is often characterized by couplet constructions. Pairs of intonationally and semantically parallel lines are used to make special points of importance to the discourse as a whole. Note the parallelism between the second and third lines in (28).

(28)   *ṭáwhal yhéṭač'   ʔel dáaʔč'iw*
        ṭáwhal yhé-ṭa-č'   ʔel dá-·č'-č'i-w
        work do-ME-IMPRF.PL the want-RFL-IMPRF.PL-PRF

čʰów
čʰó-w
not-PRF
'They don't want to work

péesu   čʰów   ʔin;
péesu   čʰó-w   ʔi=n
money   not-PRF   be=AS
because there is no money;

manáṭayṭammawʔkʰe   ṭʰin
maná-ṭa-č-ṭa-m-a-w=ʔkʰe   ṭʰi-n
pay-ME-SML-ME-MA-DFOC-PRF=INFV   not-IMPRF

ʔin.
ʔi=n
be=AS
because they are not going to be paid.'

The same couplet structure appears frequently in English.

(29)   *When the payoff came,*
        he got some of it too.
        They paid him too.

Again, the substratum influence is subtle but pervasive.

4. Conclusion

Substratum effects can vary substantially with the size of the context they involve. Lexical effects may be highly salient but scarce when the culture of the speakers of the original language has undergone drastic change. Grammatical devices that express distinctions definable within the clause, such as tense, person, number, definiteness, and interrogation, may also be quite salient.

Those conditioned by larger stretches of speech, such as the use of zero anaphora for continuing topics, the linking of clauses, left dislocation and clefting of significant information, as well as the arrangement of information over series of clauses, may be very subtle. While substratum effects in these larger domains may result in standard grammatical constructions, they can provide speakers with stylistic options that not only structure discourse, but also add a special community flavor.

How long such substratum effects may remain in a language is still to be investigated. The features described here are clearly present in the English of some rancheria residents whose dominant language is not Central Pomo. They are fading, however, due to external circumstances. The Central Pomo communities are very small. The Hopland rancheria, for example, contained only eighteen houses until a few years ago when ten more were built. Most young people move away early and find spouses elsewhere. Few children have two parents from the same community. The children constitute a tiny minority in school and they are of course constantly exposed to standard English mass media. Now that tape recorders have made it possible to examine spontaneous connected speech in detail, it will be interesting to see the extent to which subtle substratum effects on grammar and discourse may live on within a large speech community after the original language has disappeared.

Notes

1. I am grateful to the following Central Pomo people who have generously shared their time and expertise: Mr. Jesse Frank, Mrs. Winifred Leal, and Mrs. Eileen Oropeza of Point Arena, Mrs. Salome Alcantra, Mrs. Florence Paoli, and the late Mrs. Clara Williams of the Yokaya Rancheria, the late Mrs. Alice Elliot and the late Mr. Mitchell Jack of the Hopland Rancheria, and especially Mrs. Frances Jack of the Hopland Rancheria, who assembled all of these people and who has worked with me energetically and patiently for over six years in documenting her language. All of the examples cited here are drawn from spontaneous connected speech, both narrative and conversational. Work on Central Pomo has been funded by the Survey of California and other Indian languages, the Academic Senate of the University of California, and Grant BNS-8801784 from the National Science Foundation.

2. The following abbreviations are used for glosses:

CAUS	causative	1	first person
COP	copula	2	second person
DFOC	defocus	3	third person
INDF	indefinite human indirect object		
INFV	infinitive		
IMPRF	imperfective		
MA	multiple agency		
ME	multiple event		
OBL	oblique		

PL   plural
PL.AC   plural activity
PRF   perfective
QUOT   hearsay evidential
SML   semelfactive

Sequences of dots represent pauses: two dots (..) indicate a very short pause, three (...) a somewhat longer pause.

References

Chafe, Wallace
    1987   "Cognitive constraints on information flow", in: Russell Tomlin (ed.), *Coherence and grounding in discourse* (Amsterdam: John Benjamins), 21 – 51.

Mithun, Marianne
    1990   "Language obsolescence and grammatical description", *International Journal of American Linguistics* 56: 1 – 26.

Dialect socialization in Longyearbyen, Svalbard (Spitsbergen): a fruitful chaos

Brit Mæhlum

> ... tensions, contradictions, and ambivalences within and between theories are not always bad. Coherent theories in an obviously incoherent world are either silly and uninteresting or oppressive and problematic, depending upon the degree of hegemony they manage to achieve. Coherent theories in an *apparently* coherent world are even more dangerous, for the world is always more complex than such unfortunately hegemonous theories can grasp.
>
> Sandra Harding (1986: 164).

1. Introduction

For the following paper on dialect socialization in Longyearbyen,[1] I have chosen for a subtitle the term "a fruitful chaos". The term is cited from a recent interview with the French novelist Marie Cardinal in the Norwegian newspaper *Dagbladet*, an interview in which Cardinal discusses western views on chaos and the chaotic. Here Cardinal makes the following claim:

> Disorder is more natural than order. Disorder is creative, positive if we accept that it is natural, if not, it is disastrous. What is terrible is that the West worships order and fears disorder. (S. Skjønsberg 1989)

Cardinal goes on to describe how electronic microscopes enable us to study the structure of various types of cells, her point being that what one can observe is not the form and regularity we are prone to expect — in other words, no symmetry, no regulated and well-adjusted movements. What we observe, on the contrary, is chaos — not a negative one, but a chaos which functions exceptionally well, Cardinal argues. In fact, what the novelist here draws attention to is the epistemological propensity to try to make reality comply with certain harmonious patterns and structures, and work according to a definite systematic order. This tendency is reflected in science in general as a quest for well-formed, symmetrical theories and models which can be applied to such a well-regulated world. In this connection, the French philosopher of science Émile Meyerson points out that there exists "an incurable realistic tendency in a simple theory ... Whether we like it or not, we feel that a simple, harmonious theory reflects an ontological order, expressing our conception of reality" (É. Meyerson, cited by Føllesdal 1973: 261).

2. Longyearbyen — a chaotic speech community?

Without necessarily wanting to claim that Longyearbyen, as a speech community, represents total chaos, it is nevertheless obvious that it is difficult to find a uniform and unifying linguistic model or theory which can be applied directly to the language situation of this community. The available methodological and theoretical apparatus is unable to capture the existing complex plurality both in terms of language and social context. It is necessary, first, to look at a brief sketch of what is the starting-point of this potentially chaotic situation. I have undertaken a study of children and adolescents who have been raised in a community characterized by a pronounced linguistic heterogeneity. People from all over mainland Norway have settled on this group of arctic islands which is strategically situated between the Scandinavian continent and the North Pole and for centuries had the status of *No man's land*. An important additional feature is the lack of an indigenous and genuine basic dialect; only since the beginning of the twentieth century has Svalbard had a permanent Norwegian settlement. The children and adolescents I have observed represent a fairly limited, but at the same time relatively constant, nucleus of the inhabitants in an otherwise very unstable and turbulent population. Normally, people settle in Svalbard for a few years only, the average being slightly more than ten years for families, and they practice, moreover, a form of migratory cycle because they usually spend the summer months at their original domicile on the mainland. My principal concern, therefore, has been to investigate what variant or variants of Norwegian the more permanently settled children adopt in this unstable community. What are the particular strategic choices they make within an amorphous social and linguistic situation which involves a conglomerate of different Norwegian dialects?

While the language situation in Longyearbyen may appear to be chaotic and insignificantly structured, the reason for this is basically that a socially unifying and distinct dialectal norm has never existed, nor has it been allowed to crystallize. The continual turnover in the population has created social conditions which have been insufficiently stable for a uniform linguistic structure and a collective basis of language norms to develop. This, then, raises the question of what social unit or units have the greatest normative impact on children raised in such a community, where under no circumstances will there be a complete correlation between the language varieties of the various social groups. These are questions, therefore, which draw attention to more fundamental problems in relation to the theme of language socialization. Within this particular field of the sociology of language, there are in principle two main theories. The preferred view of sociolinguistics in that under conditions where there is no correlation between the dialect of the parents and the dominant spoken language in the community, children will as a rule adopt the language of their peer group (see, e. g., Trudgill 1983: 31; Weinreich — Labov — Herzog 1968: 145). The opposite view, which is found within the field of general theories of language socialization, argues on the contrary that the parents are given the role of the children's primary model of identification (see, e. g., Halle 1962). It is a problem, however, that so far very few specific scientific data have been presented in support of either theory. Both individual observations and an unstructured, and partially anecdotal, empiricism clearly indicate that the question of the relative normative effect of parents versus friends finds no immediate and unequivocal answer — not even in relatively homogeneous language communities with a locally-conditioned majority language is this a possible task (see, e. g., Kazazis 1970; Mæhlum 1985). As a kind of third alternative to these conflicting theories, it may be relevant to refer to what possibly can be seen as a kind of compromise solution; in a study of children's acquisition of dialectally-determined phonological distinctions, Tse — Ingram (1987: 281) state that "the results are interpreted as supporting the claim that children use all available input in acquiring language rather than limiting themselves to a primary language model".

In Longyearbyen it seems as if this — possibly chaotic — model is able to provide the best and most adequate picture of the dialectal strategies of the "native" Svalbard children. I would therefore like to construct a framework or a model which, at least initially, is a harmonious one, and which may contribute to illustrating the relevant social conditions for the language socialization of children in this community. Initially, the two primary social units, parents and friends, represent opposite positions along a continuous scale. If one should choose to expand the social parameters somewhat, these opposite poles may be referred to as, respectively, the family-internal and the family-external poles. It would then be possible to situate each of the relevant language users on this axis, in greater or lesser proximity to one of the two poles. In many specific cases, it would moreover be necessary to divide the family-internal part of the scale into two so as to enable us to differentiate between the different dialects of the father and the mother. In addition to this, however, it becomes absolutely necessary to distinguish carefully — or perhaps rather to complicate — this preliminary binary opposition by expanding the model by introducing two normative "ceilings" (see figure 1). These "ceilings" characterize two varieties of language which, by being based on specific social and cultural conditions, have obtained a privileged position as units of social impact. Primarily, this concerns what in this context I will refer to as "spoken North-Norwegian". Although it is true to say that a number of different North-Norwegian dialects are represented in Longyearbyen, together they form a group with specific, common linguistic features which makes it justifiable to say that "North-Norwegian" is the majority language of the community. Somewhat more than half of the total number of adult inhabitants in Longyearbyen come from Northern Norway.

The second point of normative delimitation is, on the other hand, established on the basis of quite different social conditions; here we find standardized East-Norwegian, a spoken variety which, within the Norwegian language community in general, must be said to have obtained the status of a supra-regional prestige variety (I will return to this point below). This separating of North-Norwegian and standardized East-Norwegian does not, however, imply that these varieties may not also be represented by one, possibly by both, of the extremes on the axis of socialization. Practically speaking, the family-external areas within an individual's social network will — without exception — contain a certain proportion of North-Norwegian components. When expanding the proposed linear model with these two normative points, we get figure 1 — a figure which represents the social and normative space of the individual (the asterisks represent individual speakers located along the normative axes).

What, then, characterizes the situation of the relevant group of children and adolescents in Longyearbyen is the fact that every individual language user will find a place within this social framework — in a certain proximity

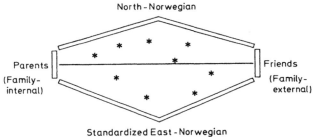

North-Norwegian

Parents
(Family-
internal)

Friends
(Family-
external)

Standardized East-Norwegian

Figure 1.

to, or at a certain distance from, the different normative units. And as I intend to show in what follows, in a considerable number of cases it has proved absolutely necessary to situate the individual language user in a position where all the factors to some extent have had a normative effect. In reality, this means that the use of pronounced mixed dialects is a common strategy in native Svalbard children, a result I wish to return to in greater detail shortly.

The resulting picture must by necessity be complex and also far from harmonious, if by harmony one refers to well-regulated and orderly being (where the language users would, for instance, have been classified in relation to specific social parameters, thus forming a definite pattern and a specified quantitatively-based structure of distribution). If I were to suggest something which approached an overriding pattern or a tendency in the Longyearbyen material according to this proposed model, it must be that the dialects of the parents here seem to influence the spoken language of the children to a greater extent than is usually the case in mainland Norway. In other words, parental impact is greater here than among other individuals where we also find a discrepancy between the family-internal and the family-external dialect conditions. This tendency, then, may to a great extent be seen as the product of a community where social and dialectal conditions are so unstable that the parents are precisely the ones who normally represent the most, or even the only, really stable social unit over some period of time. For this reason, too, it is reasonable to expect that the mother and the father possess a particularly significant normative potential in relation to the spoken language of their children.

The only real pattern emerging within this language landscape is, however, an idiosyncratic one. More particularly, this means that the individual language user constitutes the socially and analytically most relevant unit. This phenomenon also emerges in cases where significant areas of the social and linguistic conditions are practically identical, as in the case of siblings, so that Longyearbyen gives us instances of significant, often radical, individual differences in dialectal practice. When related to the perspective implied in the proposed model, such pronounced individual features show how the various language users occupy different strategic positions within their respective social and linguistic frameworks. This implies, in other words, that there are great differences in the degree of susceptibility, or sensitivity, to the varying stimuli of the different social units. The sociolinguist Richard Hudson (1980: 14 – 15) has characterized communities where language individuality is dominant as the fundamental opposite of a linguistically uniform community. "The amount of variation actually found within any given community," he argues, "will depend on the relative strengths of these two forces, so that conformity will predominate in some communities and individualism in others." In Longyearbyen, individualism is undoubtedly more prominent and significant than conformity. The terms "diffused" and "focussed", which were introduced by Robert Le Page, have gradually become the accepted terms for this polarity (see, e. g., Le Page 1980, Le Page – Tabouret-Keller 1985). "Focused" or "focusing" denotes a situation where a relatively uniform, homogeneous, and socially unifying language norm is at work, whereas "diffuse" is the accepted term for a situation which is more variable, heterogeneous, and unclear.

3. "Strategies of neutrality"

In the preceding discussion, it is precisely the dominant diffuse situation found in Longyearbyen that has been emphasized. It is a language community where a number of different dialectal norms are represented, even within the social framework of the individual, and where all the social units to varying degrees prove potentially able to exert a real normative influence on each language user. A basically diffuse situation of this kind may then in turn be documented on different social levels and considered in relation to various verbal strategies. But rather than analysing the language situation in Longyearbyen directly within this perspective, I wish at the same time to add another analytical dimension which may help us to understand more fully the children's dialectal choices within this community. This dimension may therefore contribute to explaining why the children here speak the way they do; it may also be used as the point of departure for a description of the way they speak, that is, which verbal strategies they choose. An implicit and absolutely fundamental perspective when approaching the problem from this angle entails considering all language activity as expressions of specific "acts of identity" (Le Page – Tabouret-Keller 1985) – or in the words of Carol Scotton, "code selection is seen as a personally-motivated statement of social identity" (1980 a: 328). Within fairly well-established relationships of social roles, such a perspective will entail different linguistic choices to be seen either as marked or unmarked, a polarity which is essential in this context. Here, however, we arrive at one of the crucial points in this line of reasoning: "When speakers must choose a language under conditions of uncertainty, strategies of neutrality dominate. People seek a linguistic variety which avoids commitment to the socially meaningful attributes which may be salient" (Scotton 1976: 919). Naturally, this strategy of neutrality will have to be related both to the relevant social identity of the language user and to the actual linguistic code chosen. The "neutral" dimension, then, will be realized through various linguistic means of expression signaling no specific socio-cultural affiliation, i. e., a verbal code that is unmarked. All this can be seen in relation to what Suzanne Romaine (1989: 203) says about marking in general: "there is also an associated theory of markedness, which dictates that in the absence of evidence to the contrary, the child will select the unmarked options."

In connection with this theory of affiliation and identity, we may now directly relate the notion of neutral strategies to the thoroughly diffuse language situation in Longyearbyen. The fact that regular linguistic focussing has occurred neither on the level of social groups nor on the level of the individual will to a great extent be explained in terms of the lack of a dialect identity, or – at least – of the unclear dialect identity of many Svalbard children. Most of the children who have grown up in these islands in fact exhibit an extremely ambivalent, and even double, geographical and social affiliation. Normally, they feel connected to one or more places on the mainland, while in another respect they belong to Svalbard, where they live most of the year. This unstable and conflicting sense of belonging provides no basis for a salient dialectal identity, and this diffuse state of affairs has caused many to be especially susceptible to many different and changing linguistic impulses. As Carol Scotton (1976) has pointed out, it is in a situation characterized by uncertainty that the so-called neutral strategies may represent particularly pragmatic social and linguistic choices.

What, then, are the neutral communicative strategies represented in the spoken language of native Svalbard children? To answer this question, I wish to concentrate in principle on three different ways in which neutrality in language practice may come about in this community. We should note, however, that in the spoken language of the individual language user these different principles may appear together, thus taking part in various forms of individually conditioned syntheses.

3.1. Choosing a specific "neutral" variety

Probably the simplest strategy within social contexts containing disparate elements of uncertainty consists of selecting one particular established linguistic variety which signals the value [+ neutral]. In Longyearbyen, as indeed in the rest of the Norwegian language community, a standardized spoken East-Norwegian variety comes close to fulfilling this function. Because of its correlation with the written language *bokmål* and because it has traditionally been the dominant spoken language in the State broadcasting media, this variety has obtained a position as a supra-regional and therefore geographically-unmarked dialect. The strong normative effect of standardized East-Norwegian in Longyearbyen must, however, be related not only to its value as a dialectally unmarked variety, but also to its function as a spoken variety implying social status and prestige. I would nevertheless like to argue that this aspect of status is to some extent secondary to the neutral quality for the Svalbard children. If the signaling of status, and hence an implicit relationship to Oslo and the culture of the capital, had been primary, this would have represented an especially salient social marker, and the quality of neutrality would have become a totally irrelevant and negligible factor. However, the status dimension, and also the specific geographical connection, will nevertheless almost involuntarily be a part of what I have termed standardized East-Norwegian. This may partly explain why the variety as it is practiced by most of the Svalbard children is so inconsistent. On the other hand, the fact that sequences and variants of standardized East-Norwegian enter into synthesis with other varieties can in turn provide further means for negotiating dialect neutrality. The first of these two more complex strategies of neutrality is code switching.

3.2. Code switching

"Code switching" may here be defined as a systematic linguistic alternation conditioned by changes in the communicative context. This kind of switching will in general appear in a number of fundamentally different ways and serve different social functions (see, e. g., Appel — Muysken 1987: 118 ff.). However, when related to the overriding principle involving selection of a linguistic code as an expression of particular acts of identity, code switching represents a pragmatic strategy for relating to a variable social context. In Longyearbyen this occurs primarily in the form of various distinct alternations between different dialect structures. On a synchronic level, such switching by the individual may, somewhat sketchily, be said to occur both between different social situations (family-internal versus family-external contexts here appearing to be a particularly relevant parameter) and within a single situation, that is, when communicating with the same person. In cases of situational switching, the neutrality consists of the selection of the language code which in the relevant context is felt to be the most unmarked and thus neutral. This usually involves an adjustment to the spoken variant of the conversational partner. Through such socially-conditioned patterns of switching, several of the Svalbard children have developed what can be referred to as bi-dialectalism — and possibly also multi-dialectalism. On the other hand, when the code switching takes place within a single situation, the neutrality is realized precisely through the fact that no definite, socially-marked variety is chosen. Instead, several complementing varieties coexist in a kind of alternation, and thus form an unmarked synthesis of dialects. Both of these principles of code switching can thus be related fairly directly, first, to what I have said about the absence of — or possibly double or ambivalent — dialect identity of many of the Svalbard children; and secondly, to what Carol Scotton characterizes as "the multiple identities maxim" (1980 b: 363 ff.). Within the framework of this maxim, code switching becomes a particularly strategic choice under certain complex social and cultural circumstances where the individual wishes "[to] negotiate for himself something of the favourable statuses and role relationships with which each code is associated as an unmarked choice. In an additive fashion, then, he negotiates a multiple identity" (1980 b: 363).

The third and last strategy of neutrality found among the Svalbard children is code mixing.

3.3. Code mixing

It is true that code mixing as a principle in many cases can be virtually indistinguishable from code switching, in particular where switching takes place on an intra-situational level. It would be beyond the scope of this paper, however, to try to establish exact criteria for drawing the boundary between these two forms. Besides, both principles — code switching and mixing — may often be present at the same time in the individual strategies found among the children in Svalbard.

I have already mentioned the different types of mixed dialects which are frequent in Longyearbyen, and code mixing on different linguistic levels must be said to be a constitutive, and perhaps the most salient, principle in the pronounced idiosyncratic language varieties we find in the community. In this context, I wish to draw attention to two phenomena, drawn from two different linguistic levels, which can both be important components in these interdialectal varieties (for the concept "interdialect", see Trudgill 1986: 62 ff.).

(A) Interdialectal variants on a phonological level. I would here first and foremost characterize a special distribution of certain *l*-variants as being the result of a form of code mixing, probably with a dialect-neutralizing function. Firstly, the phenomenon appears in informants with a North-Norwegian family background. Within the North-Norwegian dialect area, we normally find palatalization of originally long dentals, like *l*, according to rules which are too detailed to explain in this context. Several of these Svalbard children, however, employ a retroflex lateral articulation in such positions (corresponding to [ɭ] in the IPA). This is shown, for instance, in words like *alle, ball, aldri, holde*. By choosing a retroflex articulation, these language users distance themselves from the palatalized variant, which is certainly felt to be a salient North-Norwegian dialect marker; but they do not adopt an alveo-laminal pronunciation of *l*, which possibly would have signaled a specific East-Norwegian connection to too great an extent. The result can be interpreted as a kind of compromise or hybrid variant, a variant the language users themselves — either consciously or more probably unconsciously — feel to be dialectally unmarked and neutral. This retroflex *l* is, however, also present in the spoken language of several of the children who do not have a North-Norwegian family background, and who have not adopted other North-Norwegian features into their language to any great extent. Among the other things, I have observed this phenomenon in several informants who use a predominantly standardized East-Norwegian variety.

I here add — as a curiosity — that these East-Norwegian speaking children, through this feature, develop a spoken variety corresponding to that in Østfold, the only area in Østlandet, as far as I know, where retroflex *l* is used in these particular positions, and where it also possesses an especially pronounced signaling function as a dialect marker. This should, however, be considered a concurrence of linguistic coincidences which could not possibly have exerted any real motivational effect on the verbal strategies of the Svalbard children — one obvious reason being that this typical Østfold feature traditionally has been strongly stigmatized within the Norwegian language community.

The occurrence of retroflex *l* in these other groups should therefore be interpreted as a strategy of neutrality, as was the case with the North-Norwegian children. And here there are two possible interpretations: (1) either this phonetic quality may have arisen directly as a hybrid in the spoken variety of these East-Norwegian language users, who via their parents receive the primary language input without palatalized dentals; or as an alternative, (2) these individuals have adopted the retroflex variant of *l* directly from the group who has already modified, or neutralized, their palatilized variants to retroflex ones, i.e., from the quantitatively dominant group in Longyearbyen, those who come from Northern Norway.

(B) The second interdialectal and neutral strategy involves the conspicuous word and sentence intonation which is practiced by many of the native children in Svalbard. This must undoubtedly be considered as an integration or synthesis of elements deriving from different dialect structures, that is, a special form of code mixing. At these prosodic levels, many of the native Svalbard youngsters follow often completely individual patterns of intonation, thus often differing quite considerably from the conventional prosodic structures found within the dialect areas on the Norwegian mainland. The probably most salient feature is that several of these individual varieties consist of mixtures of high-tonal and low-tonal contours, in other words they are mixed intonation systems. (Conventially we consider the intonation systems of spoken varieties in Norway to be of basically two distinct types; either high-tonal dialects or low-tonal dialects — cf. Fretheim—Nilsen 1989.) Precisely because the word and sentence melody constitutes one of the most basic and salient indicators of a dialect, these individual varieties emerge as geographically unidentifiable. It is difficult to place the greater part of them within any particular region on the mainland. Because of this, the spoken variety of these children is often considered extremely peculiar and special, which is a reaction the children often encounter in both Longyearbyen and on the mainland. The children themselves often use expressions such as "nothing" or "everything" to characterize their own language. And on several occasions I have also heard people characterize these children as *dialektløse*, i. e., 'without any dialect.' What is striking, then, and also seems something of a paradox in this context, is the fact that these idiosyncratic intonation structures actually can be said to function as more or less unmarked dialect strategies. At the same time, however, these individual varieties are often felt to be extremely deviant and strange, and thus in a special way socially marked, precisely because they do not conform to, or resemble, any of the established, regional structures of intonation. Moreover, the fact that a person's spoken language tends to become dialectally unmarked at the level of prosody is obviously a marked feature in itself.

By attempting in this manner to relate and interpret the language codes within a specified social and psychological framework, we are afforded greater scope for understanding the more or less unconscious language strategies of the individual language user. Thus we may also arrive at a better and more thorough recognition of circumstances concerning dialectal socialization and language contact in general. Not least because Longyearbyen in this respect appears to be an excellent research laboratory, I wish to characterize the situation of this community as an extremely fruitful one — though possibly chaotic, to return by way of conclusion to the concepts of Marie Cardinal.

Note

1. The paper is based on parts of my doctoral dissertation (Mæhlum 1990).

References

Appel, René — Pieter Muysken
    1987   *Language contact and bilingualism* (London: Edward Arnold).
Fretheim, Torstein — Randi Alice Nilsen
    1989   "Romsdal intonation: Where East and West Norwegian pitch
                contours meet", in: *Papers from The 11th Scandinavian Conference
                of Linguistics* (University of Joensuu), 442 – 459.

Føllesdal, Dagfinn
1973   "Vitenskap og virkelighetsforståelse", *Kirke og kultur* 78:
            258 – 272.
Giles, Howard – W. Peter Robinson – Philip M. Smith (eds.)
1980   *Language. Social phychological perspectives* (Oxford: Pergamon
            Press).
Halle, Morris
1962   "Phonology in generative grammar", *Word* 18: 54 – 72.
Harding, Sandra
1986   *The science question in feminism* (Ithaca – London: Cornell Uni-
            versity Press).
Hudson, Richard Anthony
1980   *Sociolinguistics* (Cambridge: Cambridge University Press).
Kazazis, Kostas
1970   "The relative importance of parents and peers in first language
            acquisition: the case of some Constantinopolitan families in Ath-
            ens", *General Linguistics* 10: 111 – 120.
Le Page, Robert B.
1980   " 'Projection, focussing, diffusion' or, steps towards a sociolin-
            guistic theory of language, illustrated from the sociolinguistic
            survey of multilingual communities ...", *York Papers in Linguistics*
            9: 9 – 31.
Le Page, Robert B. – Andrée Tabouret-Keller
1985   *Acts of identity* (Cambridge: Cambridge University Press).
Mæhlum, Brit
1985   "Modifisering – et aspekt ved språklig variasjon og forandring",
            in: Tove Bull – Anton Fjeldstad (eds.), *Heidersskrift til Kåre Elstad*
            (Tromsø: Institutt for språk og litteratur), 117 – 131.
1990   *Dialektal sosialisering. En studie av barn og ungdoms språklige
            strategier i Longyearbyen på Svalbard* (Tromsø: School of Lan-
            guages and Literature).
Romaine, Suzanne
1989   *Bilingualism* (= Language in Society 13) (Oxford: Basil Black-
            well).
Scotton, Carol Myers
1976   "Strategies of neutrality", *Language* 52: 919 – 941.
1980 a   "Bilingualism, multilingualism, code-switching. Introduction", in:
            Giles et al. (eds.), 327 – 328.
1980 b   "Explaining linguistic choices as identity negotiations", in: Giles
            et al. (eds.), 359 – 366.
Skjønsberg, Simen
1989   "Det fruktbare kaos", *Dagbladet* (April 13th, 1989).
Trudgill, Peter
1986   *Dialects in contact* (= Language in Society 10) (Oxford: Basil
            Blackwell).

Tse, Sou-Mee — David Ingram
    1987   "The influence of dialectal variation on phonological acquisition:
                    a case study on the acquisition of Cantonese", *Journal of Child
                    Language* 14: 281 — 294.
Weinreich, Uriel — William Labov — Marvin I. Herzog
    1968   "Empirical foundations for a theory of language change", in:
                    Winfred P. Lehmann — Yakov Malkiel (eds.), *Directions in histor-
                    ical linguistics* (Austin — London: University of Texas Press),
                    95 — 195.

Ethnolinguistic minorities within the European community: migrants as ethnolinguistic minorities

Peter H. Nelde

1. Contact linguistics and migrants

Research on the language behavior of migrants is above all an area of enquiry for contact linguistics and the related disciplines of psycho- and sociolinguistics. This is due to the phenomenon of multilingualism, to which migrants are often more exposed than are populations indigenous to a given area. Language contact in the case of migrants can refer to the individual speaker or to the language community. Although all types of migrants can serve to illustrate contact-linguistic phenomena in general, language-contact research in Europe from its beginning (Weinreich 1953) until the 1980s concentrated on the influence of the economically conditioned south-north migration, i. e., on the so-called "guest workers". A model of linguistic contact of migrants, not unlike that of other multilingual contacts (e. g., between indigenous ethnic groups), could be drawn as seen in Figure 1.

Numerous European contact-linguistic studies on language shift in multilingual groups have shown that contact without conflict is very rare and that lack of conflict often results in linguistic and cultural assimilation.

2. Indigenous and non-indigenous minorities

Migrants are usually linguistic minorities. In the following, migrants will be classed as minority groups. In the past, contact linguists and sociolinguists have concentrated too little on investigating the similarities between European migrant groups, similarities based on a more-or-less comparable starting point, legislation, and public interest. The effort to compare ethnic groups and minorities (guest workers, immigrants, marginal

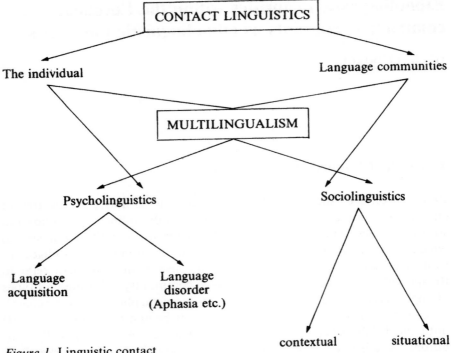

Figure 1. Linguistic contact

groups, linguistic and cultural minorities) could be of direct use to the migrants themselves, especially in the areas of pedagogy and didactics.

Given that, according to UNESCO figures, more than half of the world's population is multilingual, the European dimension is part of the international problem of refugees, racial and minority oppression, and disadvantage found on other continents. Listing common factors of minorities and migrants however must not ignore the unique nature of specific group characteristics, since this would lead to inappropriate descriptions of ethnic or linguistic groups. To develop an "appropriate" step-by-step approach to minorities from various backgrounds, the similarities between native ethnic minorities and migrants should be emphasized, and then the difficulties of defining minorities discussed. The self-assessment of these groups will also play a role.

2.1. Similarities

At first glance indigenous ethnic minority groups (e. g., French in Switzerland, Italy, and Belgium; Catalan in Italy/Sardinia and France; Basque in France and Spain) seem to have little in common with migrant groups. With few exceptions most migrant groups in Europe consist of "guest workers", political refugees, immigrants, economic refugees, or executives and businessmen from "affluent" countries. Nomadic peoples in Europe such as the Samis and Gypsies are often included as migrants. The Romance language area is home to a great number of native minorities as a result of the numerous migrant groups who have settled there, beginning with the great migrations of the Germanic peoples into Italy and France; some of these groups are in fact older than the Frankish settlements in western and southwestern France. The ethnolinguistic multiplicity of the Romance language area, however, is surpassed by the multiethnic landscape of the Slavic countries. Both indigenous and non-indigenous minorities in Europe are stigmatized to a greater or lesser degree, and the term "minority" often has a negative connotation and is applied to both groups in a discriminatory fashion.

Both groups, then, bear the double burden of bi- or multilingualism which makes rapid integration into the school system of the majority or of the host country difficult and helps restrict professional possibilities. However, it does not appear possible at present to replace the negative term "minority" — even the new terminology of the European Community with its *langues moins répandues* or *moins enseignées, lesser-used languages* or *lesser-taught languages* helps very little.

In addition, the usual term "minority" is imprecise, since it does not express the actual size relationship. There are, for example, school classes in Stockholm, Brussels, and Berlin in which Finnish, Arabic, or Turkish minorities are in the majority; the so-called Flemish minority, the Dutch-speaking population of Belgium, is in fact the majority; in the Irish context the term "minority" is at the very least problematic.

In most cases both native and foreign groups use their native language as a "group language", differentiating them clearly from their surroundings. This is true both of migrant groups, including those which speak non-European languages, and groups settled in border areas in mostly rural language communities. The social use of the native language is clearly restricted in both groups: it is used in family domains and in some cases in semipublic ones (in clubs, bars, and restaurants), and rarely in public ones. For both groups the native language lacks prestige, a fact

which promotes assimilation and rejection of the native language. Retention of the family language is not always explicable in terms of respect
for this variety or a strong sense of tradition; rather, it sometimes lies in
the inability to learn a second language at an appropriately high level
while desiring to communicate well in at least one language. So-called
semilingualism, linguistic mixing, and language avoidance in both groups
attest to unsuccessful attempts to acquire the prestige variety.

For both groups, new arguments in support of bi- and multilingualism
are constantly being brought into the discussion. Surprisingly, these
arguments seem to be applied only to the minority groups, not to the
majority, once again unevenly allocating burdens. Linguistic minorities
with languages of international importance (e. g., French and Arabic)
find that their language does not help them advance in their region (e. g.,
in Val d'Aosta in Italy) and thus does not serve as so-called "natural
bilingualism" so strongly promoted by language pedagogues. It is for this
reason that Swedish children in Sweden rarely learn the migrant language
Finnish (artificial bilingualism), while Finnish children (in Finland, as
well as in Sweden) often learn Swedish (natural bilingualism). In Alsace-
Lorraine, English has begun replacing German as the first "foreign"
language in secondary schools (thus shifting from natural to artificial
bilingualism).

2.2. Differences

Along with lack of uniformity in terminology and lists of common
linguistic/social/cultural stigmas, there are also problems in defining and
characterizing minorities. The point of departure in contact linguistics is
an insufficient data base. Census-like surveys, as carried out in the United
States and the Soviet Union, are of little value in areas of linguistic
heterogeneity with native or foreign linguistic minorities. The lack of
terminological congruity alone in such surveys leads to doubt and lack
of comparability, as shown by Canadian, American, and Soviet examples.
There is, indeed, cause for doubts about the synonymy of the terms
*Erstsprache, Muttersprache, mother tongue, langage du foyer, home lan-
guage*, etc. In addition, countries with language statistics have changed
or adapted their survey methods repeatedly, making direct comparison
impossible. During the short history of Belgian linguistic censuses
(1846—1947), the survey criteria and the questions were changed ad
absurdum; the last government-conducted linguistic census in Belgium
was carried out four decades ago.

Accordingly, official census figures in a multilingual setting are unconvincing. The statement "320,000 Finnish migrants in Sweden speak Finnish" is not very informative, since language behavior associated with domains, especially language shift, can be determined only through contact-linguistic research, not through census-taking.

Language shift, the yardstick of integration efforts, is the result of contact-linguistic factors which cannot be determined quantitatively, factors such as social pressure on a minority, the prestige of given language varieties, the strength of identity consciousness, language loyalty based on extralinguistic factors, prejudices, stereotypes, and attitudes of an ethnic group (Nelde 1984: 32). There are a number of other factors which cannot be determined quantitatively and which to a great extent preclude comparability:

— Bilingual groups without monolingual speakers are in a transitory stage (language shift) to monolingualism. Group-specific extralinguistic factors may result in unique exceptions, such as the Sorbians in the former German Democratic Republic or the Berbers in Brussels.
— Monolingual speakers with positive attitudes toward bilingualism or diglossia. The latest development in Provence, for example, indicates a sympathetic attitude on the part of young people towards Occitan, despite the fact that it is precisely the young people who scarcely have an active command of *langue d'oc*. French-speaking Canadians in Belgium ("affluent migrants") sympathize with the Belgian form of multilingualism, empathizing with Dutch as a minority language in overwhelmingly Francophone Brussels, yet without actually learning Dutch. Quantitative survey methods would certainly give an incorrect picture of this attitude, if they could determine it at all.
— In many cases a form of bilingualism appears (Portuguese and French or Luxembourgish in Luxembourg, English and French in Quebec) which leads automatically to language shift. However in some cases, such as in Quebec, the importance of the native language increases along with the increase of bilingualism. Regular censuses inadequately reflect this kind of development.

2.3. Language planning concepts for indigenous and non-indigenous minorities

For the reasons cited above, current contact-linguistic research does not rely on the results of language censuses for the exact determination of a minority, since such censuses can merely indicate a trend. Rather, contact linguistics includes self-definition of minorities along with contact-linguistic methods.

2.3.1. Defining minorities

While census-type survey methods are used with greater care today, little has changed in the criteria of self-definition of minorities over the past decades. Along with the principle of self-classification of members of the minority, there is, on the part of the majority, above all the question of origin, with newcomers being accepted only in the second or even in the third generation (Haarmann 1983: 22 – 24). A third determining factor is the similarity of cultural and linguistic patterns, which in most cases form the dividing line between the minority and the majority surrounding them. Particular forms of social organization could be seen as a new criterion of membership, as expressed in associations and ideologically, politically, and religiously conditioned patterns of behavior. Here, however, no unambiguous studies have been conducted which could determine the validity and appropriateness of this sort of criterion. By using descriptive and interpretative profiles ("socioprofiles"), contact linguistics is expected to provide reliable results in assessing minorities, examining the socially-conditioned communication structure of multilingual communities, especially minorities whose linguistic behavior is undeterminable using normal survey methods such as language statistics, in such a way that an explanation for thus far insufficiently-explained language-shift factors can be found. This includes consideration of extralinguistic factors which in the past were more familiar to sociologists, political scientists, economists and advertising specialists than to linguists.

2.3.2. Territoriality versus individuality

In the area of language planning, the Belgian state — like the Province of Quebec — has striven to apply the concept of territoriality (as opposed to the concept of individuality) which requires that the inhabitants of a given region use the language of that region. In the case of Belgium it is left to the autonomy and generosity of its three regions (Dutch, French, German) to what extent linguistic minorities have the right to maintain their native language — not a very pleasant position for stigmatized minorities such as migrants and small native ethnolinguistic groups. In contrast, the individuality principle, as has been implemented at least partially in Belgium's capital, appears to be a more liberal concept: speakers of either of the two authorized languages may choose freely between the two, since both recognized languages enjoy the same rights, each has its own cultural network, and each has its own language- and culture-specific infrastructure, thus discriminating no more against the monolingual than against the multilingual speaker.

However, neither the concept of individuality nor that of territoriality, given their areas of application in officially-prescribed domains, has given stigmatized linguistic groups — minorities and/or migrants — more equal opportunity than other models of coexistence in a population with various languages. In order to achieve this, the socio-economic causes of linguistic discrimination would have to be uncovered. Studies of immigrant workers from the Mediterranean and minorities in fairly open economic/industrial border areas have shown that native-language maintenance in many cases can be explained in terms of the socio-economic backwardness of these minorities.

3.   Migrants as a non-indigenous minority

3.1.   Internal migrants

In contrast to German-speaking countries, which for decades have experienced a socio-economically conditioned rural exodus to urban centers, the Romance countries have witnessed significant internal migration, usually south to north, also for economic reasons. Two examples are given here:

a) Since the Second World War, thousands of Sicilians and southern Italians have moved every year to the industrialized north *(Triangolo industriale)*, where the gross regional product is often twice as high as in the south. As a result, changes have occurred in speech patterns, dialects, and urban speech varieties which are to some extent comparable to the language-shift situations of Italian workers abroad (Berruto 1982). In Turin, for example, a regional lingua franca has developed alongside the dialects (40% of the inhabitants of Turin speak southern Italian, Piedmontese, or rural "low varieties" in the Fergusonian sense) which is slowly developing in the direction of a standard language.

b) In Brussels, with a French-speaking majority, the gross regional product is approximately 30% higher than in the agricultural areas of West Flanders, the coastal province. For this reason, there has been a constant internal migration of West Flemish families seeking higher status. These economic migrants, interested in rapid professional advancement, try to adopt the highly-prestigious Brussels standard French as quickly as possible, sending their children to French schools, beginning conversations with strangers in French — ending with a shift in language and culture and thus a shift in identity. In this way, they have hindered the efforts of the Brussels Flemings to achieve linguistic and cultural equality (which on paper they have achieved) and to stop, or reverse, the historical frenchification of Brussels (since the end of the 1970s, however, this trend towards frenchification has in fact slowed and partly stopped). A random sampling of Flemish immigrants to Brussels has shown that the majority use French in Brussels, despite the possibility of using their native language. The sampling also shows that along with a willingness to undergo language shift, social pressure factors (language use with a physician or with neighbors) also promote French.

Figures 2 and 3 show the language use of Dutch-speaking immigrants in Brussels as percentages for French, French-plus-Dutch, Dutch. Figure 2 shows what percentage of internal migrants use which language in language-contact situations with neighbors, policemen, physicians, and salespeople (contact with the outside world). Figure 3 shows what percentage of these same subjects use which language in language-contact situations with their spouses, children, relatives, and in-laws.

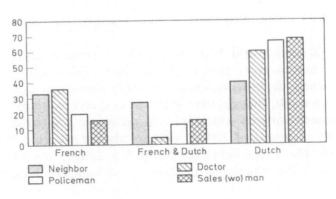

Figure 2. Contact linguistic situations I

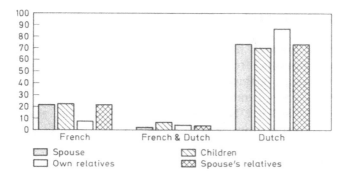

Figure 3. Contact linguistic situations II

3.2. Immigrants

The phenomenon of non-indigenous minorities who leave their countries of origin for economic, political, climatic, or social reasons is as old as mankind. The relative ease of travel across great distances and borders has increased the numbers of migrants worldwide to such an extent that there are already countries (e. g., the Comoro Islands) with more immigrants than indigenous inhabitants, that is more non-indigenous than indigenous language communities. This modern mass migration has increased the already prevalent language contacts in a multilingual world, bringing about new forms of language conflict on a greater scale than ever before.

3.2.1. Political and economic emigrants and refugees

Although there have always been political and economic refugees, people seeking asylum, people driven from their homelands, these categories of migrants have reached such proportions that they have become not only a general political problem for many states, but also a problem for language policies and language planning. In Europe the wave of asylum-seekers in the 1980s has been even greater and more conflict-laden than were the groups of refugees (from Eastern Europe and North Africa) in the 1950s and 1960s and the "guest workers" of the late 1960s and 1970s.

3.2.2. "Affluent minorities"

Up to now little research has been carried out on the wave of highly-qualified "guest workers" from the so-called affluent countries of Europe and North America ("affluent foreign minorities"). The internationalization of the economy (multinational firms) and of politics (European Community, UNESCO, UN, OECD) has also created new minority populations, the proportions of which often equal those of a small city (some thirty thousand Germans and eight thousand French in Brussels). The European capitals, especially Paris, Geneva, London, and Brussels, are home to many such groups. These migrants typically differ from migrants from poor countries in the following ways: higher socio-economic status, higher-than-average income, high degree of education, relatively good command of foreign languages, and usually shorter periods of residence in the host country. A contact-linguistic concept must still be developed in this area. Cohen (1977) and de Vries (1979) use the sociological notion of "expatriate communities", which is based on North American conditions and is not universally applicable without modification. Cohen characterizes these migrants as follows:

a) Representatives of state or international institutions develop expensive lifestyles and are seldom willing to adopt the values and behavior of the host society.
b) They create their own ecological subsystems, thus increasing the distance between themselves and the host society.
c) They set up their own institutions for the sole purpose of meeting the personal, social, and cultural needs of their group.
d) Affluent migrants form socially-closed communities.
e) They have great difficulties in adapting to the prevailing circumstances.
f) Interaction occurs between representatives of the (language) community and is restricted to contact with the local upper-class.
g) Affluent migrants have little motivation to adapt to the host society and to have close contacts with members of that society (Cohen 1977: 76–79).

3.2.3. Migrants from poor countries

The phenomenon of (e)migrant workers exists throughout the world (seasonal workers, guest workers, etc.), but was especially in the forefront of the political and linguistic/cultural discussion until the beginning of the 1980s. Some twenty two million migrants moved either permanently or temporarily to the industrialized countries of Europe, most of them coming from Mediterranean countries. Along with migrants from the traditional emigrant countries of Greece, Turkey, Yugoslavia, Poland, Italy, Spain, and Portugal, there were also many immigrants from North African countries, especially in France and Belgium. Much of the linguistic literature of the past few years has dealt with the problem of integration and assimilation of these immigrants. This discussion has often centered around applied, practical, even ideological, points rather than on theoretical and methodological questions. Apart from social class membership and limited chances for economic improvement in their countries of origin, the situations in the various host countries are so different that generalizations are hardly possible — one need think only of the immigrants from the former colonies in France, Great Britain, and Portugal who immigrate as citizens of the host country rather than as "foreign workers".[1]

4. Integration problems

It is difficult to identify heterogeneous minorities such as the migrant workers in Europe. In general they can be seen as belonging to a sub-system of the national social system. Often they differ from the host population in language and culture. The problems connected with this difference, which have been at the center of discussion on migrants for years, have lost some of their importance, as shown by the example of Brussels, though this is not necessarily representative for all minorities. In answering the question of what Brussels' residents thought were the greatest problems in Brussels, fewer than 10% of the respondents in a survey replied "immigrant workers". Unemployment, high taxes, language problems, environmental pollution, and high cost of living are apparently more burning issues (see figure 4).

The series of urban problems (in percentages) mentioned by a representative population sample in a European city (Brussels) which has witnessed the greatest influx of immigrants since the Second World War appears to show that the problem of migrants is currently considered relatively unimportant.

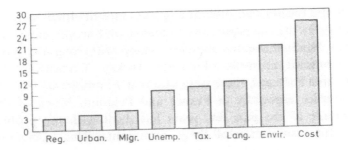

Reg.	= Regionalisation
Urban.	= Urbanisation
Migr.	= Migrants
Unemp.	= Unemployment
Tax.	= Taxation
Lang.	= Language
Envir.	= Environmental pollution
Cost	= Cost of living

Figure 4. Present-day problems in Brussels.

4.1. School language and cultural integration

There are differences of opinion in the literature on school language and cultural integration of migrant children of Mediterranean origin. To what extent should the pre-schooler know his own language and culture before he learns the host language and culture? Vansteelandt-Debauche (1983: 216) starts particularly early, suggesting that host-language teaching should begin at day school (at one and a half years old), with the goal that the migrant child reaches a comparable level with the native child by the time schooling begins. This requires thorough teacher training (Giesinger 1983: 250) and a structural comparison between host language and migrant language (Schlemmer 1983: 294), class size of under twenty pupils (Detiège 1981: 145—147), not too great a cultural distance between the two cultures in question (Stölting 1980: 431—431), and maintenance of the first language through special programs (Fritsche 1980: 509—514). Sociocultural uprooting should be prevented, so that confrontation of the value systems of the two cultures does not lead to conflict but rather to integration on the road to biculturalism (Forgione 1980: 170).

4.2. Linguistic transfer

Immigrant workers and especially their children behave diglossically in the Fergusonian sense, i. e., their native language becomes the low variety and the host language the high variety, so that the influence of the host language on the migrant language is greater than the reverse. Spanish migrant children in France and Belgium, for example, show much interference in their Spanish on the lexical level, and to some extent even on the morphological level, while the phonetic level remains basically untouched. Little Spanish interference in French can be seen (Lafontaine 1981: 172—173). In a study done in Germany, di Luzio (1981: 105) comes to a similar conclusion. Di Luzio speaks of code switching because of embarrassment and one-way language transfers, the enrichment of the other variety being only a "by-product". Of greater importance is the great reduction in the scope of structure and use of the Italian varieties because of their small relevance for socialization and minimal use in school, mass media, family, and peer groups.

4.3. Multilingualism models as a solution?

The case of the immigrant worker rarely involves the coexistence of two monolingual varieties of equal status (cf. the British subway workers in Brussels who maintain their language without exchange, transfers, or influence from the conflict-laden host languages Dutch and French, remaining separate and negating the linguistic environment); even rarer is symmetrical, equal-status bilingualism, which offers migrants the possibility of integration without assimilation. In Europe, school-language policy is generally not concerned with the languages of European neighbors and gives little support to European languages other than English, thus rarely, if ever, giving migrant children the advantage of "natural bilingualism" (i. e., migrant language as school language). Because their languages of origin are not recognized, migrant children are exposed in school to artificial bilingualism (i. e., in addition to their native language, they must learn both the host language and a prestigious foreign language such as English).

5. Outlook

Besides the continuing assimilation and integration of immigrants, the fact that unemployed workers are sent back to their countries of origin, as well as a restrictive integration policy, and new forms of forced migration (e. g., Vietnamese Boat People) makes the language problems of immigrant workers appear sociopolitically less important than in the 1970s. This is yet another reason to look at the question of migration not exclusively as a linguistic/cultural problem of "guest workers", but rather within the context of a mobile world population in which new forms of migration continue to appear. The basically monodisciplinary research approaches of the last two decades dealt insufficiently with the variety of changing migration structures.

Note

1. The situation and the linguistic problems of Mediterranean migrant workers in Belgium have been extensively described by Yannopoulos (Greeks in Wallonia), by Forgione (Italians in Belgium), by Garcià-Husquinet (Spaniards in Wallonia), by Lurquin and by Lafontaine (Turks in Belgium), and by Vansteelandt-Debauche (Spaniards, Turks and Arabs in Belgium).
   The linguistic situation of Mediterranean "guest workers" in Germany has been described by di Luzio, Auer (Italians), and Schlemmer (Turks).
   Spaniards, Portuguese, and Algerians and their linguistic situation in France have been described by Dabène, Italians and Spaniards by Lüdi.
   Linguistic problems of Moroccans in the Netherlands have been discussed by Vermeer.

References

Allardt, Erik – Karl Johan Miemois – Christian Starck
   1979   *Multiple and varying criteria for membership in a linguistic minority* (Research Report 21, Research Group for Comparative Sociology, Helsinki).
Auburger, Leopold
   1981   "Deutsch als Ko-Sprache der Gastarbeiterkinder: Das Mannheimer Mehrsprachigkeitsprojekt", in: Peter Nelde et al. (eds.), 69 – 82.

Auer, J. C. P.
1981   "Einige konversationsanalytische Aspekte der Organisation von
            'Code Switching' unter italienischen Immigrantenkindern", *Revue
            de Phonétique Appliquée* 58: 126 – 148.
Berger, John – Jean Mohr
1976   *Arbeitsemigranten* (Reinbeck: Rowohlt).
Berruto, Gaetano
1982   "Langues et dialectes en contact dans les villes industrielles de
            l'Italie du Nord: bilinguisme et migrations italiennes", in: René
            Jeanneret et al. (eds.), 111 – 146.
Cohen, Erik
1977   *Expatriate communities* (London: Sage).
Dabène, Louise
1987   "Caractères spécifiques du bilinguisme et représentations des pra-
            tiques langagières des jeunes de l'immigration en France", in:
            Georges Lüdi (ed.), 77 – 97.
Detiège, Léon
1981   "La scolarisation des enfants de travailleurs migrants. La situation
            dans la circonscription de Mons", in: Peter Nelde et al. (eds.),
            145 – 156.
Fleis, W.
1981   "Les enfants de migrants placés dans les centres de rééducation",
            Revue de Phonétique Appliquée 58: 149 – 152.
Forgione, A.
1981   "Contribution à l'étude de la migration: difficultés psycho-péda-
            gogiques vécues par les enfants de migrants", *Revue de Phonétique
            Appliquée* 58: 168 – 180.
Fritsche, Michael
1980   "Der Verlust schriftsprachlicher Fähigkeiten in der Muttersprache
            und Maßnahmen der Therapie", *ZDL* 32: 509 – 514.
Gazerro, Vittorio
1983   "Multilinguistische Kontexte und Interferenzprobleme bei Emi-
            grantenkindern in der Schweiz", in: Peter Nelde (ed.), 231 – 240.
Giesinger, R.
1983   "Zum praktischen Nutzen von Sprachvergleichen für Lehrer von
            Gastarbeiterkindern", in: Peter Nelde (ed.), *Vergleichbarkeit von
            Sprachkontakten* (Bonn: Dümmler), 241 – 252.
Haarmann, Harald
1983   "Kriterien ethnischer Zuordnung", *Language planning and lan-
            guage problems* 1: 21 – 41.
Husquinet-Garcia, Presentación
1981   "Importance des régionalismes dans l'espagnol des enfants im-
            migrés de la région liégeoise", in: Nelde et al. (eds.), 181 – 189.

Jeanneret, René – Georges Lüdi – Bernard Py (eds.)
1982   *Actes du colloque sur le bilinguisme* (TRANEL 4) (Neuchâtel: Institut de Linguistique).

Keim, Inken
1974   "Sozial- und Bildungsprobleme der Gastarbeiter in der Bundesrepublik", in: Heinz Kloss (ed.), *Deutsch in der Begegnung mit anderen Sprachen* (Tübingen: Narr), 139 – 201.
1978   *Gastarbeiterdeutsch* (Tübingen: Narr).

Lafontaine, Dominique
1981   "Bilinguisme et scolarité: le cas des enfants espagnoles de première année primaire dans la région liégoise", in: Peter Nelde et al. (eds.), 167 – 174.

Liebkind, Karmela
1984   *Minority identity and identification processes: a social psychological study* (Helsinki: Societas Scientiarum Fennica).

Lüdi, Georges
1985   "Zur Methodologie der Interpretation der Rede von Zweisprachigen über ihre Sprachenwahl", in: Peter Nelde (ed.), 105 – 118.
1987   *Devenir bilingue – parler bilingue* (Tübingen: Niemeyer).

Lüdi, Georges – Bernard Py
1983   "Propositions pour un modèle heuristique du bilinguisme d'un ensemble de communautés migrantes. Comment peut-on être Italien, Espagnol ou Suisse Alémanique à Neuchâtel?", in: Peter Nelde (ed.), 145 – 162.

Lurquin, Georges
1981   "L'enfant immigré turc", *Revue de Phonétique Appliquée* 58: 181 – 187.

Luzio, Aldo di
1982   "Für eine Untersuchung der Muttersprache italienischer Gastarbeiterkinder in Kontakt mit Deutsch", in: René Jeanneret et al. (eds.), 23 – 110.

Mimois, Karl Johan
1980   *The minority client's view of public administration in a bilingual society* (Research Report 26, Research Group for Comparative Sociology, Helsinki).

Nelde, Peter
1982 a   "Conflit ethnoculturel et changement de langue à Bruxelles", in: Jean Caudmont (ed.), *Sprachen in Kontakt – langues en contact* (Tübingen: Narr), 37 – 57.
1982 b   "Migration interne et changement de langue à Bruxelles", in: René Jeanneret et al. (eds.), 147 – 166.
1982 c   "Sprachsoziologische und soziolinguistische Überlegungen zur deutschen Minderheit in Belgien", in: Hans Moser (ed.), *Zur*

	Situation des Deutschen in Südtirol (Innsbruck: Institut für Germanistik), 35—49.
1983 a	*Tendances actuelles de la linguistique de contact* (Plurilingua I) (Bonn: Dümmler).
1983 b	*Théorie, méthodes et modèles de la linguistique de contact* (Plurilingua II) (Bonn: Dümmler).
1983 c	*La comparabilité des langues en contact* (Plurilingua III) (Bonn: Dümmler).
1984	"Sprachkontakt als Kulturkonflikt", in: Wolfgang Kühlwein (ed.), *Kultur und Gesellschaft* (Tübingen: Narr), 31—40.
1985	*Methoden der Kontaktlinguistik — Methods in contact linguistic research* (Plurilingua V) (Bonn: Dümmler).
1987	"Aspects méthologiques de la détermination de langues minoritaires", in: Georges Lüdi (ed.), 157—169.

Nelde, Peter, et al. (eds.)
| 1981 | *Sprachprobleme bei Gastarbeiterkindern* (Tübingen: Narr). |

Oksaar, Els (ed.)
| 1984 | *Spracherwerb, Sprachkontakt, Sprachkonflikt* (Berlin—New York: Walter de Gruyter). |

Perdue, Clive
| 1982 | "L'acquisition d'une deuxième langue par des adultes immigrés", in: René Jeanneret et al. (eds.), 57—86. |

Phillipson, Robert—Tove Skutnabb-Kangas
| 1985 | "Can increased metacommunicative awareness solve intercultural communication difficulties?", in: Peter Nelde (ed.), 299—308. |

Rebaudières-Paty, Madeleine
| 1987 | "Etude des marques identificatoires dans le langage de familles immigrées de différentes origines dans le Bassin Houiller lorrain", in: Georges Lüdi (ed.), 191—210. |

Schlemmer, Heinrich
| 1983 | "Die sprechaktbezogene sprachliche Repräsentation der Zeit im Türkischen und im Deutschen. Zur didaktischen Funktion der kontrastiven Linguistik", in: Peter Nelde (ed.) 1983 a: 293—304. |
| 1985 | "Zweisprachigkeit, didaktische Methoden und Kontaktlinguistik", in: Peter Nelde (ed.), 309—315. |

Stölting, Wilfried
| 1980 | "Einige methodische Probleme der Beschreibung des Sprachwechsels bei Gastarbeiterkindern", *ZDL* 32: 431—434. |

Vansteelandt-Debauche, A.
| 1983 | "L'enseignement du français parlé à des jeunes migrants. Typologie des procédés et techniques pédagogiques", in: Peter Nelde (ed.) 1983 b: 215—222. |

Verdoodt, Albert
    1982   "L'enseignement en langue maternelle aux enfants des travailleurs migrants: une étude de cas à la lumière d'arguments théoriques", in: René Jeanneret et al. (eds.), 167–196.

Vermeer, Anne Rende
    1981   "Volgorde in de verwerving van het Nederlands door Marokkaanse kinderen op de basisschool", in: Peter Nelde et al. (eds.), 129–144.

Vriendt, Marie Jeanne de
    1981   "Quelques réflexions sur la formation des enseignants prenant charge des enfants de migrants", in: Peter Nelde et al. (eds.), 65–68.

Vries, John de
    1979   "Demographic approaches to the study of language and ethnic relations", in: Howard Giles–Bernard Saint-Jacques (eds.), *Language and ethnic relations* (Oxford: Pergamon).

Yakut, Atilla
    1983   "Ein Analysemodell der deutsch-türkischen Zweisprachigkeit", in: Peter Nelde (ed.) 1983 c: 219–229.

Yannopoulos, Panayotis
    1981   "Les enfants de migrants face au problème d'apprentissage de leur langues maternelles: le cas des Grecs en Belgique", in: Peter Nelde et al. (eds.), 101–110.

Isolation, contact, and lexical variation in a tribal setting *

Jørgen Rischel

1. Introduction

This paper makes some very tentative statements about the linguistic situation of two ethnic groups in Indochina. One of these minority groups (Tin) is made up of subgroups of indigenous hilltribe peasants, the other (Mlabri) of a few families of shy hunter-gatherers. For centuries, it seems, both tribes have been living in more or less the same area, i.e., the easternmost mountainous regions of Northern Thailand and the adjacent part of Laos (i.e., an area that used to belong to Thailand).

A linguistic comparison of the languages of these two ethnic groups provides evidence of both old and recent contacts between them. Likewise, when considered together as one hilltribe stratum, they exhibit evidence

* The work on "α-Mlabri" (and much of the philological study of Bernatzik's "Yumbri") was done in close collaboration with Professor Søren Egerod of the East Asian Department, University of Copenhagen, who first invited me to join the field of Mlabri studies. Up till 1985, we worked together with Professor Theraphan L. Thongkum of Chulalongkorn University, Bangkok. Lately, this work has been supplemented by my own work on various dialects of Mlabri and Tin; in the latest phase of the work on Tin, I have profited much from the generous help of Dr. David Filbeck, Chiengmai, and Mr. Gene Long and his family in Phrae Province.

The Carlsberg Foundation supported our fieldwork, on Mlabri 1982 – 1988, and I also received financial assistance in some phases of the work from the Danish Research Council for the Humanities and from the Swedish-Danish Einar Hansen's Fund (promoting the cooperation between the universities of Lund and Copenhagen). My present research on language contact is financed in part by a DANIDA research grant. — The National Research Council of Thailand and the Tribal Welfare and Development Centre in Nan Province have been of much assistance in providing the settings for our fieldwork.

of old and recent contact with the Thais (taken here to include also Northern Thais and Laotians). *A priori* all of this is what one would expect to happen in a tribal setting within a multi-ethnic community, and thus the Tin-Mlabri scenario may serve as an illustration of this type of contact situation (although it must be conceded that it is rather premature to make definite claims about the Tin-Mlabri issue: much more research is needed to accurately depict the situation, and to substantiate the speculations made in this paper).

The overall situation in this and probably in many other cases is characterized by what happens in the lexicon rather than in any other component of language. What we observe, partly as a corollary of language contact and partly as a consequence of other factors within the ethnic community, is lexical variation, lexical split, and rapid lexical change. In the present case study, the most conspicuous phenomenon is the particular language profile, each language exhibiting two or more quite distinct varieties, which differ considerably in lexicon but which differ significantly less in linguistic structure. This is maybe not so clearly the case with Tin as with Mlabri, although the issue whether the two main varieties of Tin, Mal and Prai, should be termed different languages (as suggested by Filbeck) certainly would not arise from a consideration of phonology alone. In the case of Mlabri there is a dramatic difference in vocabulary between the language norms of different groups, but their phonology is practically the same (as is their morphosyntax). This puts into focus the controversial status of such concepts as "same language" and "same dialect" when applied to a multi-ethnic tribal setting such as the one comprising Mlabri and Tin in all their varieties.

As indicated below, there is a lot of mystery connected with the Mlabri, their origin, and their language, and with some intriguing aspects of the relationship between Tin and Mlabri. Thus, an attempt to sketch this scenario also serves to illustrate the complex problems one may encounter when dealing with little-known tribal languages in a sociolinguistic and comparative linguistic format. It will be apparent from the presentation below that contemporary Mlabri has some features which may possibly invite characterization of it as a "mixed language".

Language mixing is a topic *par excellence* for contact linguistics. However, as I shall argue later in this paper, there is some reason to take issue with the concept of "mixed" as a totally special type of language development if this means that the behavior of such languages is of marginal interest for the study of more "well-behaved" languages and their development in contact situations. Anyway, with tribal languages in a "primitive" setting it is less complicated to give an overview of the socio-cultural parameters which are relevant to linguistic borrowing than in highly complex literate societies. In "primitive" societies, the coexistence of languages in contact seems to be the norm rather than the exception, but it is easier to achieve an understanding of the functions of the languages in such a community than in a highly-developed community. Thus, studies of tribal languages (including "mixed" languages) may significantly contribute to the understanding of which kinds of linguistic material are easily borrowed in simple contact situations, and which kinds are more resistant to change.

In the area dealt with here, i. e., a central region in Indochina, the dominant hilltribes (this term being used here to include peasant minorities who are little integrated into the dominant culture) are the Hmong (Miao, Meo) and the Yao (Mien), who have migrated to this area from the North in relatively recent times; the Hmong are said to have entered Thailand towards the end of the nineteenth century. Both tribes are montagnards living in small villages in the mountain complexes, although some of them were moved from the mountains in the border area between Thailand and Laos and resettled in nearby lowland villages because of the guerilla activity and border fighting which made Nan Province a sensitive area up through the first part of the 1980s. The Hmong and the Yao belong to the same "small" language family, which has affinities with both Tai and Sino-Tibetan, although its genetic placement is a matter of controversy. (Hilltribes of the Sino-Tibetan phylum which are found elsewhere in northern Thailand, such as the Akha and the Lisu, have never settled in the area under consideration here.)

Although the Yao are traditionally characterized by a high culture and relative wealth, the Yao in Thailand have on the whole become rather impoverished in recent years. This is not true to the same extent of the Hmong, although they, too, have a difficult time because rapidly increasing deforestation has caused the government to put severe limitations on their use of the traditional slash-burn approach to agriculture and to make them settle in permanent villages and cultivate dry fields ("rai"). Opium used to be an important source of income for these hilltribes, but its economic importance is receding very much since it is prohibited to cultivate poppy fields for opium production, and illegal fields are destroyed if discovered. Nowadays, sugar cane, corn, and cotton are important products. The Yao and the Hmong also raise pigs and in some cases cattle (and today even goats, the meat of which is precious to urban Muslims).

The Hmong, who have the highest social status among the hilltribes in this part of Indochina, are also the ones that live at the highest altitude, typically more than 3,000 feet above sea level. In connection with the introduction of permanent settlements, some villages have been moved to lower altitudes, although they are still rather high up in the mountains and often quite far from the towns of the Thai lowlanders. Nowadays, all children are obliged to go to school, and each mountain village either has a school teacher (usually a Thai) or is close to another village in which there is a school. School training is difficult to enforce, however, and illiteracy is still widespread.

Most hilltribe villages were, until recently, difficult to get to except on foot. This has changed very much with the construction of dirt roads over the last three decades, but in many areas such roads degenerate into trails a few years after construction so that they can only be frequented by highpowered cars. There are no regular buses in the mountains, but the Yao and Hmong make frequent visits to the lowlands by using trucks loaded with people or motorcycles. Likewise, they are frequently visited by Thai officials, e. g., from the Tribal Welfare and Development Centre, and in many places also by tourists. Several of the Hmong and particularly the Yao in this area have relatives who have migrated to the United States and who, in some cases, keep in touch with their native villages, and occasionally also assist their relatives back home financially.

The Yao and Hmong languages, though related, are very different and certainly not at all mutually intelligible. There is apparently little linguistic differentiation within Yao in spite of its distribution over a large geographical area (extending into China, from where they have come in recent times, like the Hmong). Hmong consists of some very distinct dialects which, however, are reported to be mutually intelligible. In the area of interest here, there are both "White Hmong" and other groups of Hmong (named after a typical color in their garment). In some places, there are Yao and Hmong villages quite close to each other, which may entail intensive contact between the tribes, especially if one village has a shop and the other does not. The Hmong and the Yao then typically converse in Northern Thai rather than using one of the two tribal languages.

The two languages to be dealt with in this paper, viz., Tin and Mlabri, are unrelated to Hmong and Yao, but sociolinguistically it is important to see their speakers in the context of the two socially more powerful tribes, particularly the Hmong.

The language generally referred to as Tin (or T'in) is spoken by hilltribe people. These seem fairly homogeneous in material culture. They are poor peasants, living in rather small villages on the hillsides in mountainous regions, particularly in the northeastern and northern districts of Nan province (i. e., southeast of the "Golden Triangle" and close to Laos). Here, within a rather small geographical area, we find a puzzling multitude of very different dialects of Tin. According to David Filbeck (personal communication), it seems likely that the Tin became a distinct ethnic group with a separate language in the very core area of their present habitat, i. e., the mountain slopes just northeast of the district city of Pua. Because of guerilla activity close to the Laotian border in the last couple of decades, some of the Tin villagers have been moved to new settlements at a much lower altitude, like some Hmong and Yao.

The Tin villagers are altogether less visible to outsiders than the Hmong and Yao; they are culturally very close to the poorest Northern Thai farmers living in the highlands. One source of income for the females is to make materials for thatching, which are sold at a low price.

The other language, and its speakers, dealt with here, are referred to in the current reference books as "Mrabri" (and "Yumbri") or perhaps more frequently as "Phi Tong Luang", which is a pejorative name meaning 'Spirits of the Yellow Leaves' in Thai. The correct term (used by the tribe itself) is Mlabri (the equivalent of Thai: Khon Pa), which means 'forest people'.

These "Spirits of the Yellow Leaves" are a mysterious tribe of hunter-gatherers who live in the eastern part of northern Thailand and in adjacent Laos. They were first mentioned in the scholarly literature in the 1920s, but there was very little factual information since they were so evasive that few people — and up till then no Westerner — had ever seen them. Nothing was known of their language, although the Danish major Seidenfaden (1927: 47) cited a layman's statement, according to which "their own language seems to consist of a collection of strange guttural and staccato-like sounds, in which the letter R does not occur. To the observant ear their language sounds like a piping and unmanly sort of gibberish".

The first detailed description of this strange tribe was given by the Austrian explorer and anthropologist Hugo Bernatzik, who heard of them and met them in the forest on a journey in 1936. He published a book called *The spirits of the yellow leaves* (Bernatzik [1938] 1941) with beautiful photographs, a surprisingly detailed description of their life and habits, and two word lists: a list of kinship terminology and a list of other words. The name of the tribe, according to Bernatzik, was "Yumbri".

There was some scepticism about Bernatzik's story until the learned Thai banker Kraisri Nimmanhaeminda took the initiative to head two expeditions to the habitat of the "spirits" in 1961 and 1962. He met them, and in addition to anthropological and other information gathered by him and his associates, he published a word list (Nimmanhaeminda 1963) to document their language, which he claimed was called "Mrabri".

The people Kraisri met were not of the same group as those encountered by Bernatzik almost a quarter of a century earlier, although they clearly represented the same culture, which has been described as moving from a "bamboo age" into modern time. One researcher characterized the state of their material culture as follows: "1. The Mlabri have not known a stone age (no stone implements, no pottery of any kind). 2. ... the Mlabri do not make their own clothing. ... 3. The Mlabri do not practice agriculture. 4. The Mlabri do not build houses. 5. The Mlabri wear no ornaments." And he continues: "It will be difficult to find groups of human beings in this world that live in similar conditions" (Boeles 1963: 150). At the same time, Boeles characterized some of their accomplishments as impressive, e. g., their linguistic skills ("Many Mrabri speak several languages").

Bernatzik approached the Mlabri through the Hmong, who were the most knowledgeable concerning their whereabouts, and from whom he had to seek permission, as it were. This is in a sense still true. The Mlabri associate with the Hmong and also the Yao, not in order to barter (as was the case in old days, when such articles as fabric and knives were obtained in return for bees' wax and honey) but to labor in the dry fields of the Hmong and the Yao. The Mlabri wander about in very small groups; at intervals they enter a village, approach a Hmong (or Yao) villager whom they know and agree with him to work in the dry field for a while in order to get food and various other goods in return. Then they will move to another place, perhaps keeping to themselves in the deep forest as long as they do not feel they suffer too much from starvation.

The researcher wanting to work with the Mlabri must, in most cases, approach a Hmong (or Yao) who happens to have hired a Mlabri, and it is then necessary to reimburse the peasant for the unavailability of his temporary farm-hand. As for the Mlabri themselves, their highest priority is to receive a pig, the sacrifice of pigs being an important feature in their culture, and the partition and consumption of pig's meat being the highlight of social life. Otherwise, their daily life is led on a very subdued note; they are excessively timid people whose whole appearance reinforces the low esteem that other people have of them. The Mlabri are undoubtedly perfectly adapted to the "wild" forest life (which is strongly regulated by their dependence on the benevolence of spirits), but they are extremely vulnerable in other environments.

It goes without saying that it is an interesting challenge to study the language of such a group, and local anthropologists have emphasized (personal communication) that they look forward to the information about the enigmatic Mlabri tribe which they hope to gain from linguistic studies.

Let us now have a look at the classification and general characteristics of the languages of the Tin and Mlabri tribes.

Tin is a Mon-Khmer (i. e., Austroasiatic) language. It has been classified together with Kammu (Khmu') into a Kammuic (Khmuic) branch of Northern Mon-Khmer. This subdivision of Northern Mon-Khmer to comprise a special Kammuic branch rests largely on lexicostatistic evidence. Words in these two "Kammuic" languages bear no close phonetic resemblance to each other, and so far nobody seems to have established regular phonological correspondences to substantiate this alleged subbranch of Mon-Khmer, although there is by now an authoritative descriptive literature on both Kammu and Tin. In recent language surveys, Mlabri (or "Mrabri", see below) is normally included in this Kammuic branch of Northern Mon-Khmer, though this is a controversial issue (see Rischel 1989 b).

2. Recent research on "Kammuic" languages

Until the last three decades, next to nothing had been done on these languages. The American linguist William A. Smalley published a monograph on Kammu nearly thirty years ago (Smalley 1961). Shortly afterwards, Kraisri Nimmanhaeminda (1963) published some word lists of various dialects of Tin and Kammu along with a specimen of Mlabri after a journey in the Nan district in 1962. His linguistic data were not presented in a rigid phonetic or phonological format and are difficult to use. Quite recently, two Thai linguists, Suwilai Premsrirat (1987, 1988 a, 1988 b) and Choltira Satyawadhna (1987), have published monographs about the Tin and Kammu peoples, with linguistic introductions and with texts. The very appearance of such publications is significant in provoking a wider interest in these ethnic minorities.

Otherwise, the recent linguistic research on the Northern Mon-Khmer languages has been entirely dominated by foreign scholars. The bulk of research on Tin has been done by the American David Filbeck of the Christian Mission to the Orient and the Phayap University in Chingmai (Filbeck 1978). Another American missionary, David Jordan of the New Tribes' Mission, is working on Prai. As for Kammu, the major research has been done by the Swedes Kristina Lindell and Jan-Olof Svantesson (cf., e. g., Lindell 1974, Svantesson 1983) at Lund University in cooperation with a native Kammu, Damrong Tayanin, who is now permanently working on Kammu in Sweden.

As for Tin itself, it has been shown by Filbeck (1978, 1987) that there are two very different dialects, or as he puts it, languages: Mal and Prai. The Thai word "Tin" literally means that they are people speaking a dialect, a patois, and thus is not restricted to this ethnic group. The Tin themselves prefer to be called Lua' (which is also ambiguous) or either Mal or Prai, depending on the subgroup. The two types of Tin, Mal and Prai, are phonologically very closely related. This is true typologically and also genetically: Mal and Prai differ only on some points and are altogether united by straightforward correspondence rules. In this sense, the difference is certainly very modest considering what kinds of dialect differences may be found in languages all over the world. However, Mal and Prai show considerable differences in lexicon, so that they are for communication purposes not nearly as similar as tables of perfect cognates with correspondence rules would suggest. As shown by Filbeck, Mal falls into a phonologically very conservative (sub)dialect "A" (apparently spoken in only one small village surrounded by speakers of other Mal dialects), a somewhat more advanced (sub)dialect "B", and a very advanced (sub)dialect "C" (characterized by simplifications of consonant clusters). Prai, according to Filbeck, falls into at least two (sub)dialects "A" and "B", the latter now being called Pyai (/r/ is shifted to /y/ here). In addition, there is a transitional dialect spoken in one village, Chuul, which Filbeck characterizes as Mal spoken on a heavy Prai substratum. Filbeck has suggested that Tin may have split into Mal and Prai somewhere between two and three hundred years ago (1978: 106, 1987: 136); he assumes the "A" (sub)dialect of Mal to be very close phonologically to Proto-Tin.

I myself have gathered data from altogether four dialects representing the Prai branch, the Mal branch, and a transitional dialect, with the purpose of finding out about the relationship between Mlabri and Tin. It is obvious that there is a close connection between the two languages, which share a substantial part of their lexicon, but it is still unclear to what extent this is due to genetic relatedness and to what extent to extensive borrowing (Rischel 1989 b).

Now to Mlabri. As mentioned already, the earliest specimens of the language were gathered by Bernatzik and Nimmanhaeminda. More recently (1964), Michel Ferlus took down some words from a small Mlabri group he met in Laos. This word list has not been published, but was recently kindly put at the present writer's disposal by Ferlus. The variety of Mlabri that Ferlus observed, and which I here refer to as β-Mlabri (cf. Rischel 1989 a), is on some points clearly closer to Bernatzik's "Yumbri" than to Kraisri's "Mrabri". Over the last couple of years, I have occasionally met speakers of this same β-variety of Mlabri on the Thai side of the border and recorded a substantial amount of data from them. Those speaking this kind of Mlabri seem to amount to less than a dozen people in Thailand.

Søren Egerod and I (both from the University of Copenhagen) gathered data on Mlabri in Thailand over the years 1982 – 88, the first three years together with the Thai linguist, Theraphan L. Thongkum, who is a specialist on Mon-Khmer linguistics, and who has published (in Thai) on some semantic characteristics of Mlabri. The variety of Mlabri we have studied together (Egerod – Rischel 1987) is the same as the one recorded by Nimmanhaeminda (we even had his main informant as our informant almost thirty years later). I shall refer to this as α-Mlabri.

If we look at the linguistic specimens in Bernatzik's and Kraisri's accounts, these do not look very similar, and it has been doubted whether "Yumbri" and "Mlabri" were the same language at all. The American linguist William Smalley (1963) applied a lexicostatistic test to the data (which in my view was rather problematic, considering the nature of the data), and he found "Yumbri" and "Mrabri" to be two different languages, rather on a par with Tin and Kammu. This linguistic statement was not, of course, invalidated by the ethnic similarity between the two groups encountered by Bernatzik and Kraisri, although the two descriptions, with photographs, etc., are indeed strikingly alike.

Egerod and I have tried to show that "Yumbri" and "Mrabri" are in fact one language, which is called Mlabri by the people themselves (Rischel – Egerod 1987). This same name applies to both of the currently existing varieties of the language. The word /mla'briː'/ means 'people of the forest', which is the only designation of their tribe that they themselves accept. Bernatzik's "Yumbri" may be /joːŋ briː'/, i. e., 'men of the forest', or /jɤːm briː'/, i. e., 'to live in the forest' (personally, I rather believe in the latter interpretation). Kraisri just misheard /mla'briː'/ as "Mrabri" because the initial cluster was unfamiliar to him. As for the popular name "Spirits of the Yellow Leaves", this is what the Thai usually call the tribe, although the Mlabri resent the nickname very much. The Thai version of this expression has also entered linguistic reference works as the standard name of the language: "Phi Tong Luang".

As it will appear from the survey above, there is in a way quite an amount of data on the Mlabri language. However, most of it consists of short word lists taken down in quasi-phonetic notation by amateurs; the only professional linguist apart from us is Ferlus, and his material is extremely limited and stems from a brief accidental encounter with a couple of people (apparently close relatives of some β-Mlabri people whom I met twenty-five years later in Thailand). Moreover, it was unpublished and not available to us during our fieldwork on α-Mlabri. We therefore had to start from scratch ourselves, except for a tape recording which the Danish curator Jesper Trier had kindly put at our disposal. Only after working for years on Mlabri have we been able to rationally interpret the data of other researchers as being more or less identical with Mlabri as we know it.

There is an American missionary, Gene Long, who is associated with the Mlabri in the province of Phrae (south of the area we have frequented but having people from the same "α-Mlabri" group as the one we work with). The Long family are the only outsiders with considerable command of the language, but so far they are not directly involved in descriptive linguistic work. It should be mentioned also that Trier has visited the Mlabri people numerous times over the last two decades and has collected valuable material consisting of oral ritual texts. Only a few of these have been published, in a short but interesting paper on the customs and supernatural beliefs of the Mlabri (Trier 1986); his paper does not really overcome the problems of transcribing and translating Mlabri texts, however.

In Thailand itself, very little research has been done on the Mlabri since the early sixties. There was a period in the early eighties when the archeologist, Surin Pookajorn, from Silpakorn University (Bangkok), together with a research team, studied Mlabri society and their material culture. This resulted in a report to the National Research Council of Thailand (Pookajorn et al. 1984), a work which, like most of the literature on Mlabri, is of limited linguistic interest because of gross inadequacies in the rendering of Mlabri word forms (e. g., personal names). The more recent report (Pookajorn 1988, in Thai) has a chapter on the language by Theraphan Thongkum, with important grammatical and comparative information.

In our fieldwork over the years, we have taken down whatever lexical information we got, although we often had serious trouble with Mlabri word semantics. This is an important point, since it means that we should not compare the Mlabri lexicon to that of other languages without being aware all the time that we undoubtedly have a somewhat skewed picture of the vocabulary of Mlabri and even, in some instances, a quite faulty interpretation.

The Mlabri are basically very shy, and it is partly for that reason that we worked on our own on the most recent field trips, without any interpreters or other kinds of assistants. This seemed to ensure a minimum of psychological strain, while at the same time it made our task of elicitation of linguistic material very difficult at times.

From the point of view of lexical borrowing, our general impression of Mlabri is that there are a number of different strata. I shall not deal with the question of very old Austroasiatic components in Mlabri here but rather start with the relationship between Mlabri and Tin.

As stated already, it now looks as if all accounts of "Yumbri", "Mrabri", and Mlabri deal with the same language. It seems that there are only very slight differences in phonology but very great differences in the lexicon between the linguistic varieties of the various groups. It is possible that these linguistic varieties are kinds of clan sociolects. Such different varieties may have developed not only because of lack of contact between different nomadic groups, but also because of a certain polarization between them. The Mlabri themselves distinguish rigidly between one group that uses tattooing and formerly used spears, and another group that lacks these characteristics, and each group warns against the alleged hostility of the other. Some α-Mlabris identify β-Mlabris, whom they have only heard of, as a frightening Laotian tribe which they call /talɛː/, i. e. 'the ugly ones', though they know that that tribe, too, is a kind of Mlabri. The linguistic differentiation between α- and β-Mlabri may reflect this cultural difference. However, we still know too little about the social organization of the Mlabri to decide what kind of ethnic differentiation this is. It may be meaningful to speak of different clans.

3. Mlabri and Tin dialects

As explained above, both Mlabri and Tin exhibit dialects differing much more in the lexicon than in phonology. An essential research task is to compare the dialects of Mlabri and Tin to see how the lexical divergence within Mlabri compares with that of Tin. This paper addresses the question of contact phenomena in certain languages in Indochina, but this issue is tied up with an understanding of the unusual lexical variation which is observed across the dialects of each of these languages. Therefore, the lexical variation in itself will be exemplified first.

Tin, as already mentioned, occurs in at least two clusters of dialects (called different languages by Filbeck) which are very similar in the phonological make-up of the etyma they share but which differ quite a lot in the lexicon. I shall cite here a handful of typical shared original etyma (not loans from Thai), which in these instances are phonologically alike in Mal and Prai:

> 'mouth' (ŋkaːp/,
> 'one's behind' /lɔːl/,
> 'stomach' /mphul/,
> 'rain' /miʌ'/,
> 'foot' /cɤŋ/,
> 'to drink' /'ɔːk/.

On the other hand, there are very many instances of totally different lexical items in Mal as opposed to Prai, e. g., 'pig': Mal /siŋ/, Prai /'i'/.

It is, I take it, these lexical differences, not the very modest phonological differences between Mal and Prai, that are likely to hamper intercommunication and that make it possible to argue that Mal and Prai are in a sense different languages (each with its set of dialects), as Filbeck does. Personally, I have difficulties with this extension of the term "language" to cover spoken norms that are closely related in all relevant respects except for differences in individual lexical items. The Mal and the Prai peoples seem to consider themselves as rather distinct groups, but it is unclear to me how much or how little sense it makes to talk about them as making up "the Tin people" together. As for Mlabri, the two lexical varities α-Mlabri and β-Mlabri differ so little in phonology that the vast majority of shared words are phonologically identical. The following examples of shared words have been picked somewhat at random:

'man, human being' /mlaː'/,
'husband' /glaŋ/,
'child' /'ɛːw/,
'house (a lean-to)' /gɛːŋ/,
'tiger' /rwaːj/,
'snake' /tum'oː'/,
'nose' /mɔh/,
'chin' (wɤːŋ/,
'breast' /boː'/,
'to return' /wʌl/,
'I' /'oh/,
'you' /mɛh/.

At the same time, the α- and β-Mlabri differ drastically in terms of the lexicon, and as in the case of Tin Mal and Prai, this is true of many of the most common everyday terms, e. g.:

'woman' (α) /luŋguh/, (β) /mɯlh/,
'blanket' (α) /pol/, (β) /gɯncɛj/,
'chicken' (α) /sɯrkɛŋ/, (β) /joc/,
'pig' (α) /cəbut/, (β) /siːŋ/,
'mouse, rat' (α) /hnɛl/, (β) /hwɤːk/,
'dog' (α) /braɲ/, (β) /soː'/,
'neck' (α) /ŋlɯ'ŋlɛ'/, (β) /kukɔː'/,
'water, to drink' (α) /wɤːk/, (β) /ɟrʌːk/,
'to sit, to dwell' (α) /hŋuh/, (β) /jɤːm/,
'to speak' (α) /tʌɲ/, (β) /gla'/,
'to be able' (α) /mʌc/, (β) /bɤːn/.

It is often the case that the β-Mlabri word is still known to some old α-Mlabri speakers (and is maybe even found in Bernatzik's old word list, see Bernatzik 1938). This is true of the words for 'dog' and 'pig' above, for example. In some cases, the β-word even exists in current α-Mlabri, though with a different meaning (/joc/ in α-Mlabri means 'wild fowl'). It is less often the other way round, with old β-Mlabri speakers remembering the α-term (this is true, for example, of the word for 'neck'). Thus, one may speculate that α-Mlabri is the more innovative dialect.

The fact that there is lexical differentiation across dialects may be said to be trivial, but it is nevertheless noteworthy that such differentiation is very considerable in this case, even though it is a matter of tiny groups of people whose dialect is virtually the same as regards the segmental phonology of the shared words (i. e., apart from the lexical differences and apart from the prosody). This is suggestive of the speed with which lexical differentiation can develop in the case of separate nomadic groups. One interesting issue is to what extent the differentiation reflects differential cultural contact with other peoples in quite recent time.

The Mlabri people are an anachronism, entirely out of place in the Mekong area, where they live close to the Golden Triangle. One does not expect hunter-gatherers to wander about in the forests there, and as indicated by the quotation from Boeles above, the Mlabri represent an unusually "primitive" type of material culture with virtually no technology of their own, no agriculture of any kind, no animals except the dog, and no real houses. They live in a kind of bivouac which is covered with banana leaves and which is used only for a few days. These delapidated lean-to constructions were the only trace of the shy Mlabri that the Thais used to see — hence their name "Spirits of the Yellow Leaves". Their language is altogether extremely conservative, at least in its phonology.

In this part of the world, we expect languages to be tonal; the vast majority of Southeast Asian languages are tonal either from very old times or due to more recent influence from neighboring tonal languages. Jan-Olof Svantesson (1989) has shown how several Mon-Khmer languages have become tonal by various kinds of tonogenesis, so this process is not a unique phonetic development but rather a general tendency toward typological similarity as an areal feature, tonemicity being fashionable in Southeast Asia, as it were. Both Tin and Mlabri are among those languages that have not become tonal (except for the borrowing of Thai loanwords in tonal form in one Tin dialect) and have not acquired register. Mlabri has even preserved the manners of articulation of obstruents that were found prior to the "consonant mutation" which has affected Southeast Asian languages very widely (causing voiced stops to become voiceless, for example), and it has also preserved old voiceless continuants, like the most conservative dialect of Tin. All of this can be seen, for example, by looking at the sound structure of early loanwords in Northern Mon-Khmer and comparing them with Thai (cf. Rischel 1989 b).

Thus, the general picture of Mlabri is that of a very conservative language spoken by a very small tribe of people who have a habit of hiding in the forest and avoiding much contact with other people. The layman hearing about such a tribe invariably expects its language to be "primitive" in the sense that it has little or no orderly grammar, a very limited lexicon, and a very simple sound pattern, though possibly with strange sounds. Linguists regard such a concept of "primitivity" as quite naive, of course. Nevertheless, it may be appropriate to mention that Mlabri phonology happens to be characterized by a complex consonant and vowel inventory (cf. Egerod — Rischel 1987: 36 — 42), and that Mlabri morphosyntax is rather intriguing. On the one hand, it exhibits very old Austroasiatic features such as prefixation and vestiges of infixation and other expected areal features such as SVO word order and the use of noun classifiers; on the other hand, there are some unexpected features, which may be of considerable antiquity in the language. One such feature is a genitive construction consisting of possessor noun plus possessive particle plus possessed noun (typologically reminiscent of the Germanic *s*-genitive construction). This very un-Mon-Khmer construction occurs in Mlabri side-by-side with the expected attributive construction, i. e., possessed noun + possessor (the difference between the two construction apparently having to do with reference and specificity). The latter construction is what we find in Tin and in numerous other languages in this area, including Thai.

On the whole Mlabri and especially Tin syntax exhibit similarities with Thai which may be due to influence from some dialect of Thai. The same is true even more of phraseology in both Mlabri and Tin. This is what one expects in this part of the world. The Tai languages Siamese (Central Thai), Northern Thai (Khammueang), and Laotian have exerted a very strong influence on several minority languages of the Mon-Khmer family in this part of Indochina. This influence, which is very conspicuous in contemporary languages, applies to the lexicon as well as to phraseology and syntax.

In Mlabri, there are very many expressions which have exact counterparts in Thai, with Mlabri either having a calque of the Thai expression or having borrowed the expression directly with greater or lesser phonetic modification. Of the following four expressions, the first is genuinely Mlabri and expresses an idea about the involvement of the heart which is alien to Thai (and apparently to Tin), whereas the rest are perfect mappings of Thai (the third and fourth examples are specifically β-Mlabri):

/klol ɟuːr/ 'heart sinks', i. e., 'I am happy'
/klol pluŋ/ = Thai /caj rɔ́ːn/ 'heart hot', i. e., 'choleric'
/klol met thɛh/ = Thai /caj mâj diː/ 'heart not good', i. e., 'unkind'
/thɛh klol/ = Thai /dicaj/ (/diː/ 'good' + /caj/ 'heart', i. e., 'glad, happy'

(Tin has an analogous expression literally meaning 'good' +
'heart')
/glɤ' klol/ = Thai /hŭa caj/ 'head (of) heart', i.e., 'heart'.

Similarly, we find serial verb concatenations mapping Thai expressions,
e.g. (from a text in β-Mlabri about making holes in the ears for earrings):
/toc wʌl sɛj/ = Thai /'aw maː saj/ lit. 'take come place', i.e., 'get hold
of it (the earring) and insert it'.

Tin seems very much influenced by Thai phraseology. This is easily
seen if one takes a look at the recent translation of the Gospel of St.
Mark into Tin Mal made by Dr. Filbeck in cooperation with native
consultants (who accepted the final version as "the way we speak",
personal communication). Not only are many features of word order the
same, but we also find that the semantic range of verbal operators, for
example, is the same, though that certainly is not predictable from a
"universal" semantic scheme (such as speakers of Western languages
might envisage universal semantics). One example is the verb/particle
/pɔːn/ in Tin, which matches Thai /dâːi/ in several meanings, i.e., 'to get',
'to be able', and assertively 'to have indeed performed an action' (or, in
combination with a preceding operator 'not': 'did not'). The difference
between the latter two meanings is correlated with the position of the
operator before or after a main verb, both in Tin and in Thai, as can be
seen in the following examples showing a morpheme-per-morpheme
match between Tin and Thai, although the languages do not have a single
etymon in common in these instances: (i) Tin /kan kaih pɔːn/ = Thai /
thâː pen dâːi/ 'if be can', i.e., 'if possible'; (ii) Tin /'əɲ pɔːn ntuah/ =
Thai /chăn dâːi bɔ̀ːk/ 'I did tell', i.e., 'I have said before'; (iii) Tin /man
'er pɔːn təːm 'ɛː to'/ = Thai /khaw mâi dâːi taːm raw maː/ 'he not did
follow us come', i.e., 'he was not in our company'.

β-Mlabri has an etymological equivalent to Tin /pɔːn/, i.e., /bɤːn/,
which, however, does not seem to have the same range of usages as Thai
/dâːi/, but instead seems to have a meaning akin to 'to be able' or 'to
have experienced' (like its etymologically-unrelated α-Mlabri counterpart
/mʌc/). This would suggest that the older meaning of Tin /pɔːn/ may be
of this kind, and that the extended use of this word in accordance with
Thai /dâːi/ may be secondary.

The linguistic relationship between Thai and these languages is complicated by the fact that there are many words in Thai which ultimately
stem from Mon-Khmer, i.e., from Cambodian. Thus the "Thai" words
in modern Mon-Khmer languages are in several cases originally Mon-

Khmer words. Moreover, hilltribe languages borrow to a greater or lesser extent from other hilltribe languages, typically, of course, from languages of higher social prestige. Mlabri and Tin are both languages with a very low prestige compared to other hilltribe languages spoken in the same area, such as Hmong and Yao; still, it is clearly the case that Mlabri has borrowed from Tin, as will be demonstrated in this paper. Along with other words borrowed from Tin, Mlabri may also have borrowed a substantial part of the old Thai words which are abundant in Mlabri.

Now some words about the lexicon of Mlabri in particular. Needless to say, there is much emphasis in the lexicon of this language on terms for natural phenomena and apparantly less emphasis on abstract terms. Today the language seems to be becoming gradually impoverished in its lexicon. The Mlabri spend more and more of their time in non-Mlabri speaking environments. The elders complain that adolescent people do not properly learn the very extensive botanical and zoological vocabulary of traditional Mlabri. This is because the Mlabri have to depend for their survival on temporary dry-field labor for the Hmong (Miao) people. There is no more game left in the forest, and in some places hardly enough edible roots (wild taro) either. There is, in fact, not much forest left at all.

There are many good reasons for studying the linguistic situation of the Mlabri and the Tin. Firstly, if the nature and extent of older and more recent contact between Mlabri and Tin can be determined, one stands a much better chance of determining the genetic placement of Mlabri in relation to the various branches of Mon-Khmer (or more generally, Austroasiatic). It is definitely possible that Mlabri will turn out to be "originally" from a quite different branch (or possibly not a Mon-Khmer language at all). This is one incentive for the study of the Mlabri-Tin relationship. At the same time, of course, these contact phenomena are of both principled and specific interest in their own right. Mlabri being the language of a very "primitive", migrating tribal society, and Tin being the language of a peasant society represented by a low-status hilltribe, this is inherently an interesting field of study from the point of view of contact linguistics. Finally, because of the specific situation of these peoples, a study of contact phenomena in their case may help to throw light on the very complex and in part little-known history of migrations in central Indochina. Such considerations should also enter contemporary issues having to do with the cultural, political, and economic situation of the mountainous border area between Thailand and Laos.

Contemporary research within this area is mainly concerned with the minority groups which are politically and economically most important, namely the Hmong (Miao) and the Yao (Mien). The so-called Northern Mon-Khmer languages, on the other hand, are spoken by comparatively small ethnic groups which belong on the bottom of the social ladder within Thai society. These groups, such as the Kammu (Khmu') and the Tin Mal and Tin Prai, are poor peasants living in the not very fertile mountain regions and having extremely limited sources of income. These peoples are not conspicuous by their cultural features like the Hmong and Yao, who used to be wealthy people (although this is no longer the case), who wear impressive national costumes and have handicraft traditions which appeal to tourists, and who, to some extent, have had a tradition of literacy in their own language (this is certainly true of the Yao). The Tin and Kammu are not distinctive in this sense, although they have become to some extent a political issue because many of them have come from Laos as refugees in the last few decades (this is true of Kammu in particular, but also of Tin). The Tin are liable to be absorbed into Thai society by a transformation into Northern Thai peasants; this process is facilitated by the fact that the term "Tin" just means "patois" in Thai, so that the naming of these people does not clearly set them off from other low-status peasants. As a consequence of this relative cultural invisibility of the Northern Mon-Khmer peoples, and the Tin in partic- ular, there has been very little research on their culture and language.

The Mlabri language is generally classified as belonging to Northern Mon-Khmer and indeed to the same branch as Kammu and Tin. This classification has certainly been made on meagre evidence; recently, the present author (Rischel 1989 b) has shown that there are perfect phono- logical regularities between Mlabri and Tin, so that from this point of view, Mlabri is much closer to Tin than either is to Kammu. Thus, Mlabri might well be a sister-language of Tin Mal and Tin Prai, all of these forming a "Tinic" sub-branch of Kammuic. However, this proximity to Tin applies only to a subsection of the lexicon; much of the lexicon is not shared at all. Thus it is so far an open issue whether the obvious cognates stem from genetic relatedness, in which case the great lexical divergences must be due to the socio-cultural conditions under which the two tribes have been living for centuries, or whether they are all loans (old and recent) from Tin into Mlabri.

After these remarks about the general situation, a few examples will be presented to illustrate the phonological similarity of shared lexical items in Mlabri ("M") and Tin ("T", in this case Tin Prai):

'head' T /k(l)ɯ'/, M /glɤː'/
'house' T /kiaŋ/, M /gɛːŋ/,
'eye' T & M /mat/,
'string' T /thaːr/, M /tar/,
'nose' T /muh/, M /mɔh/,
'bear' T /piʌk/, M /(α) bɛːk, (β) biɯk/,
'chin' T /wʌŋ/, M /wɤːŋ/,
'fish' T /khaː/, M /kaːʼ/,
'hand' T /thiː/, M /tiːʼ/,
'blood' T /miʌm/, M /mɛːm/,
'breast' T /po'/, M /bo'/,
'thunder' T /khɤːr/, M /kɯr/.

Although there are such cognate pairs in large numbers showing a close affinity between the two languages, it should be noted that there is very considerable lexical differentiation between the two languages, maybe more so for some word classes than for others. A comparison of a subset of the verbs we have recorded indicates that maybe only some twenty percent of the verbs in Tin Mal or Prai show direct cognates in either α- or β-Mlabri. This suggests that the close association between these languages was severed quite some time ago, although the observation cannot be translated meaningfully into anything like a time depth.

If indeed Mlabri is a sister-language of Tin, there is the task of explaining the unique cultural situation of the Mlabri, since both the Tin and the Kammu are on a much higher technological level than the Mlabri. Did the Mlabri undergo cultural regression after taking refuge in the deep forest for some reason? There is a myth in Thai history about a Northern Thai king releasing some two hundred slaves in the seventeenth century so that they fled into the deep forest, and some people have associated this story with the Mlabri. This is not out of the question, according to a Thai anthropologist I have talked to; he thinks it might explain why the Mlabri are so notoriously fearful of other people and so extremely good at hiding themselves. However, other anthropologists and physicians who have studied the Mlabri have seriously questioned the probability of the above contention, one argument against it being that the Mlabri are very uniform in physical appearance and blood groups, which is suggestive of their descending from a very small family. Gebhard Flatz in 1963 stated that medicine and anthropology cannot decide whether the Mlabri are an ethnic unit, and he called for linguistics and sociology to solve the issue. As he said: "The clarification of their linguistic affiliation will ... be of great interest for the anthropologist. If it can be proved that their language belongs to the austroasiatic (Mon-Khmer) group their presence in Southeast Asia can be dated back 2000 years" (Flatz 1963: 171).

The Mlabri themselves have told us that, according to their oral tradition, there were Mlabri in Northern Thailand at a time when there were few other people around. So far, the linguistic classification of Mlabri poses a problem, but the linguistic evidence is certainly not in favor of the myth about the released slaves.

There are many strange features in Mlabri that call for an explanation and are suggestive of a separate origin. There may be evidence for a southerly origin of the Mlabri: they seem to resemble some tribes on the Malakka peninsula more than they resemble the surrounding tribes in the area where they now live. Thus, there is an alternative hypothesis, to which I adhere at present, namely that the Mlabri spoke a language that was not particularly affiliated with Tin and Kammu but at some point in time received a strong lexical influence from Tin. This is understandable if there has been extensive contact between the Mlabri and the Tin. We do not know about remote times, except for the inferences one can draw from loanwords, but there is indeed evidence for more recent contact, although there is nowadays no particular association between the Tin and the Mlabri in Thailand.

We must, then, assume that Mlabri has been spoken in the Thailand-Laos border area for centuries, like Tin. Both languages (and Kammu as well) have plenty of old words from some kind of (northern or northeastern?) Thai, which in some cases are preserved in a fossilized form more or less corresponding to Old Thai, e. g.:

'good'	Thai /diː/, Mlabri /ˀdiː/,
'to stand'	Thai /jɯːn/, Mlabri /ˀjɯːn/,
'iron'	Thai /lèk/, Mlabri /hlek/,
'ink'	Thai /mùk/, Mlabri ('tattoo') /hmɯk/

Several such words occur in both Mlabri and Tin. In the most conservative dialect of Tin, these words have preserved old features such as preglottalization and voicelessness (or clustering with /h/) in continuants. Mlabri has even retained preglottalization in stops, which has been lost in all Tin dialects (like in Thai). Mlabri is thus today the most conservative of all. (The manner of articulation features just mentioned are reflected in the Thai spelling but were lost in these consonants hundreds of years ago in spoken Thai). It is a perfectly plausible assumption that several (if not all) words of this category have entered Mlabri via Tin. This would explain how such an overly shy tribe as the Mlabri could absorb so many Thai words in the shape they had several centuries ago.

4. Recent borrowings

In addition to the old strata of words shared with Tin, there is also a handful of recent loans from Tin into Mlabri, such as:

> 'spear' Tin (Prai) /khɔt/, Mlabri /khɔt/,
> 'to stab' Tin /sat/, Mlabri /sat/,
> 'head louse' Tin /se'/, Mlabri /seː'/,
> 'taro' Tin (Mal) /khwaːj/, Mlabri /khwaːj/

Mlabri also has numerous modern loans from Thai. Some of these seem to have come via Hmong since their pronunciation is consistent with the assumption that they have been filtered through Hmong phonology, e. g.:

> 'tape recorder' Thai /thêːp/, Mlabri /theːt/,
> 'Bangkok' Thaik /kruŋ thêːp/, Mlabri /kuŋ theːt/

The word for 'spear' above is particularly interesting. The Mlabri form must have been borrowed from the Prai dialect of Tin since it shares with Prai the development of a final stop instead of a former continuant in this word. Of course we cannot say on this basis that Mlabri has been associated only with the Prai dialect in recent years. Anyway, the Mlabri have recently adopted some Tin loanwords; I think the interesting aspect of these is that they may have been borrowed simply because they were designations for items that the Mlabri got from the Tin. The spear may well have been a cultural borrowing from the Tin. Not all Mlabri groups used the spear, and it is assumed to be a rather recent addition to Mlabri culture (although today it has already fallen out of use again). Bernatzik in 1938 thought that the Mlabri had gotten the spear from the Hmongs, but the linguistic evidence must override that assumption. By and large, the recent Tin words in Mlabri are those that may have entered the language through very rudimentary communication in connection with the trading I mentioned. Maybe some of the words with an initial palatal sibilant are suggestive of more intimate contact, since they refer to head lice, feeling pain, and so on. It is puzzling to me why we find exactly this strange set of words with the initial sibilant.

I have come across an elderly man in the village of Chuul where they speak Prai with a superstratum of the other Tin dialect, i. e., Mal. This man told me that when he was a boy and lived with his family up in the mountains, it sometimes happened that the Mlabri came to the cottage to exchange honey, etc., for other goods, and then his father spoke to them in a language which the boy did not know. It seems most likely that they spoke Northern Thai or possibly Laotian together, since he remembered that the Mlabri had called his father and mother by the Northern-Thai designations /pɔ̂ː/ and /mɛ̂ː/. The terms in Mlabri are /mʌm/ and /mɤː'/, and the Tin say /'aw/, /mɤj/.

As the uppermost lexical stratum in Mlabri, we encounter some quite recent words from Thai. Some of these are obviously borrowed via Hmong, since they have sound substitutions which are motivated by phonotactic limitations in Hmong but not in Mlabri; others may stem from contacts with Thai people. Because Mlabri is not a tone language, the tones in loanwords are lost; it is the case now that Northern and Central Thai do not differ very much in segmental phonology, but they certainly differ in tones and also in the lexicon. Thus it is difficult to decide whether a word that exists in Central Thai has come directly or via Northern Thai, but I presume that the Mlabri have not until now had any contact to speak of with Central Thais, so the lending language probably is Northern Thai (also called Khammueang) in most cases.

Living in Laos, the Mlabri have also been in contact to some extent with Laotian, which is historically the same as the northeastern Thai dialect spoken in Thailand. Thus, with recent Thai words there is the additional difficulty that some may be Laotian. Bernatzik referred to all such words as "Lao", but he was not aware of the difference between Laotian and Northern Thai.

A Hmong peasant who had encountered some Mlabri coming across the Mekong river from Laos some twelve years ago told me that he was surprised that they had quite a good command of Northern Thai; he did not know how they had acquired this competence. I shall later return to this puzzling command of Northern Thai on the part of several adult Mlabri males; at this point I shall just mention that the preponderance of recent Thai loanwords in Mlabri is understandable on this basis. By far the closest contact that the Mlabri have had with any other ethnic group over the last fifty years has been with the Hmong, who live high up in the mountains in regions where the Mlabri also live. As regards the use of the Hmong language in intertribal communication, Pookajorn (1984: 7) claims that "80% of the Phi Tong Luang can speak the Maeo language fluently"; I have no idea about the validity of this figure, which is at variance with my own impression. When Mlabri people communicate with the Hmong, I have mostly heard them using Northern Thai (Kham-muang), which is a lingua franca spoken daily among hilltribes. Hmong and Yao, and similarly Hmong and Tin fellow villagers address each other in this language, although it is unrelated to their own domestic languages.

The symbiosis of Mlabri and Hmong people might be expected to have caused a profound influence from Hmong on Mlabri, but that is not at all what we observe. On the contrary, there is apparently not much of a Hmong stratum in the Mlabri lexicon. As I said before, the Mlabri have some Thai words which have been filtered through Hmong, so it seems that the Mlabri used to speak Northern Thai when conversing with the Hmong. This situation still prevails, at least in some social settings, although several of the Mlabri do speak some Hmong as well.

Let us now make a digression into a particularly interesting subset of the vocabulary, i. e., the numbers. Both in Tin and Mlabri, there is a set of numerals from 'one' to 'four' which are of the old Mon-Khmer type (recurring, e. g., in Khmer and even in Mon):

Tin
'one day'	/me ŋe'/
'two days'	/piʌ ŋe'/
'three days'	/phɛ' ŋe'/
'four days'	/phon ŋe'/

Mlabri
'one'	/mɔːj/
'two'	/bɛːr/
'three'	/pɛː'/
'four'	/poːn/

For the numerals from 'five' to 'ten', Tin has the Thai numerals only, but in Mlabri there are separate non-Thai lexical items for these numerals as well. Now, although all adult Mlabri know of the existence of the whole set of numerals from 'one' to 'ten' and seem to be proud of that knowledge, only the numerals for 'one', 'two', and 'four' are really used in expressing number, and of these the latter two numerals tend to be replaced by the terms used in Thai. The numerals 'five' and 'eight' (like those for 'two' and 'four') survive only in lexicalized expressions with a vague meaning of plurality. Thai numerals are always used in referring to numbers above 'five'. The entire set of Mlabri numerals exists only as a kind of nursery rhyme, and in fact many speakers seem to have difficulties keeping complete track of the higher numbers even when they recite this series while counting on their fingers.

Another interesting detail is that the odd numbers 'three' and 'five' can be expressed in genuine Mlabri but without using the corresponding simple terms. Instead, they use complex expressions meaning something like 'two and an additional one' and 'four and an additional one', e. g., /bɛːr mla' hloːj/ (or /sɔːŋ mla' hloːj/) meaning 'two person(s) and-an-additional-one'; /pon mla' hloːj/ meaning 'four person(s) and-an-additional-one', i. e., 'five persons'. This usage is often combined with the use of classifiers (which is an important areal feature occurring in Chinese and Thai, for example). Thus, the word for 'person' can be used as its own classifier: /mlaː' bɛːr mla' hloːj/ meaning 'person(s) two person(s) and-an-additional-one', i. e., 'three persons'. Both the Mlabri numerals above 'four' and the constructions with /hloːj/ are strange features in a Northern Mon-Khmer context. Tin has nothing of the sort, and neither has Thai, the other important lending language. Here, then, we have a section of the language which has been singularly resistant to linguistic influence from likely sources within the period of several hundred years for which a symbiosis of Mlabri with Tin and (later?) Lao or Northern Thai can be assumed.

Today many Mlabri, expecially adult males, speak Northern Thai very well (Pookajorn 1984: 7 claims that this is true of as much as seventy to eighty percent of the Mlabri), and some have picked up quite a bit of Central Thai as well. This raises the question of whether we have reached a state of diglossia among the Mlabri. It is my impression that command of Thai is generally much poorer for women, which is not surprising, since the traditional role of the women is to keep close to the "house", look after the children and prepare food, except when they make short visits into the forest to look for firewood, banana leaves, and some herbs. Thus they have less opportunity than the men to meet outsiders, and this is also what the male Mlabri prefer. So the husband speaks Mlabri with his wife, and the mother speaks Mlabri with her children, to the extent that they speak at all, which is not always very much.

Nevertheless, the Mlabri do speak Northern Thai, even when they are among themselves, as I have esperienced sometimes when they thought I was asleep, and the men then chatted about funny events that had taken place during the day or some time earlier. If they referred to things happening in neighboring villages, they would often switch to Northern

Thai, whereas they seemed to speak Mlabri instead when talking about their own domestic life. All of this is quite trivial for anybody familiar with diglossia, and maybe I have been tempted to interpret the situation of Mlabri in accordance with my expectations. However, I think it is beyond doubt that Mlabri is rapidly being replaced by (Northern) Thai (along with Hmong) as the effective means of communication. Mlabri is still the domestic patois (at least among the α-Mlabri), but Northern Thai creeps in to a greater or lesser extent, and code shifts occur very frequently, especially of course when there are non-Mlabri persons present. Even in such a genuine setting as the slaughtering of a pig I have heard young men using Northern Thai phrases jokingly or to appear smarter (although others found it more proper to use Mlabri even though I was present). They speak Mlabri fluently, but some seem to find it a little bit funny and out of fashion to speak Mlabri even though they still live much of their time out in the forest in the most primitive manner one can imagine. The Mlabri culture is undoubtedly on the point of extinction, now that this small tribe is getting into much closer contact with the outer world. Thus, one can expect language death in the not very distant future.

As for the Tin, on the other hand, there is no comparable imminent danger of language loss, although these people are bilingual with a rather fluent command of Northern Thai and sometimes even of Central Thai. These linguistic skills are clearly a function of intensive inter-tribal daily communication and are not correlated with a high level of education. Their situation is characterized instead by relatively low motivation to go through the school system and acquire a higher education to improve their own conditions. For quite some time, at least, the Tin may be expected to continue as a people with — in most cases — little or no formal education and with no incentive or no immediate means of changing their social situation within a short time span. From this perspective, one can perhaps say that the Tin language is not immediately endangered.

I wish to conclude by returning to the question of a "mixed language", which was formulated in the beginning of this paper. The concept of "mixed language" implies that multiple linguistic origin is a marginal type of language history (but cf. Thomason—Kaufman 1988 for an insightful discussion). This, then, should contrast with purportedly well-behaved language histories, which are supposed to be characteristic of most languages of the world. Since most of the general thinking about linguistics and sociolinguistics is based on insights about languages belonging in established civilizations, which have a well-established written norm and for which the complex past histories are known in considerable detail, there has been a spectacular success with the notion of family tree or pedigree (Stammbaum) as against its competitor, the wave theory, especially when the notion of Stammbaum is coupled with the notions of substratum and linguistic borrowing to take care of the irrefutable deviations from the expected "pure" Stammbaum development.

It is an inherent risk that one may inadvertently project the insights from such a scenario to other situations which on closer inspection may be radically different. Of course, the Stammbaum model is not limited to Indo-European, Finno-Ugric, and the like. There are many clusters of languages which are, or until recently were, tribal and which nevertheless can be related to more or less well-defined families. This is what one may expect in cases where peoples are known to have split up by migrations to remote areas. But then there are other languages which neither fit neatly into a Stammbaum nor form linguistic isolates. This complex, intermediate status may not be what one expects *a priori* for the language of a tribe which at first glance is assumed to have been living in more or less complete isolation for a very long time. Since we often have little or no knowledge of the socio-political and ethnic situation in the remote past in the case of languages of more "primitive" ethnic groups, it can easily happen that one's thinking is influenced by an implicit prejudice about such languages, i.e., that these do not have a complex cultural history like the "civilized" languages do.

The stereotype, if exaggerated a little, would be that each of the tribal languages we encounter has been handed down from one generation to the next in an essentially invariant culture and almost in a linguistic vacuum, except for possible recent exposure to some dominant language accompanying the approach of civilization. This picture being clearly counterfactual, it is very tricky to approach tribal languages in a socio-historical perspective. On the other hand, a phenomenological description of the hereditary complexity of such languages may often be illuminating for the reason mentioned at the beginning of this paper: in compensation for the lack of historical knowledge, factors influencing the linguistic situation in the present and near-present time are often easier to discern than in highly-developed and highly-complex societies.

At the same time, the study of "primitive" societies gives emphasis to the highly specialized function of linguistic norms in communication: different norms, different dialects, or even totally unrelated languages are used for different communicative purposes. In the habitat of the Tin and the Mlabri, one may hear two, three, or even four different languages used for daily purposes in the same village and sometimes by the same people, depending on whom they address and for what purpose. How many highly-developed countries, with their formal school-training, can compete with this?

Rather than considering allegedly "mixed" languages as marginal phenomena, one should be aware of the global normality of genuine, functional bilingualism (being something sharply different from the acquired semi-bilingualism which occurs in societies with foreign-language training at school), a situation which must probably be projected far back in time. Ultimately, this means that an ever-repeating emergence of new languages as the result of massive language contact (and the "death" of languages as well) may have been the norm rather than the exception in the development of the world's languages in more or less multilingual settings. Seen in this perspective, the study of such cases as Mlabri, which seems highly complex in spite of the legendary isolationism of its speakers, is of some principled interest.

References

Bernatzik, Hugo
  1938   *Die Geister der gelben Blätter* (München 1938; Leipzig 1941).
  1947   *Akha und Meau, Probleme der angewandten Völkerkunde in Hinterindien* (Innsbruck, Kommissionsverlag Wagner'sche Universitätsbuchdruckerei).
Boeles, J. J.
  1963   "Second expedition to the Mrabri ('Khon Pa') of North Thailand", *Journal of the Siam Society* 50, 2: 133 – 160.
Egerod, Søren – Jørgen Rischel
  1987   "A Mlabri-English vocabulary", *Acta Orientalia* 48: 35 – 88.
Ferlus, Michel
  1964   (Word list from a Mlabri dialect taken down in Laos; unpublished).
Filbeck, David L.
  1978   *T'in: A historical study* (Pacific Linguistics Series B-49. Canberra: Australian National University).
  1987   "New ethnic names for the Tin of Nan Province", *Journal of the Siam Society* 75: 129 – 138.
Flatz, Gebhard
  1963   "The Mrabri: anthropometric, genetic, and medical examinations", *Journal of the Siam Society* 50.2: 161 – 177.

Lindell, Kristina
1974   "A vocabulary of the Yuan dialect of the Kammu language", *Acta Orientalia* 36: 191 – 207.

Ngaeng law lueang Phajesu e Malako porn khian ja' (Gospel of St. Mark in Tin (Mal) and Thai, Chiengmai; no date of publication).

Nimmanhaeminda, Kraisri
1963   "The Mrabri language", *Journal of the Siam Society* 50.2: 179 – 184 (with linguistic appendices).

Pookajorn, Surin, and staff
1984   *Preliminary report. The Phi Tong Luang: A hunter-gatherer group in Thailand.* (The Ethno-Archeological Research Project 1982 – 1983) (Faculty of Archeology, Silpakorn University, Vol. 3.1).

1988   *The "Phi Tong Lueang" tribe in Thailand* (in Thai) (Fine Arts Department, National Museum of Thailand).

Premsrirat, Suwilai
1987   *Khmu, a minority language of Thailand* (Papers in South-East Asian Linguistics No. 10) (Pacific Linguistics Series A-75).

1988 a   *Khmu life style in 50 conversational lessons* (in Thai with Kammu texts) (Institute of Language and Culture for Rural Development, Mahidol University).

1988 b   *"Prai" Medical Conversations* (in Thai with Prai texts) (Institute of Language and Culture for Rural Development, Mahidol University).

Rischel, Jørgen
1989 a   "Fifty years of research on the Mlabri language. A re-appraisal of old and recent fieldwork data", *Acta Orientalia* 50: 49 – 78.

1989 b   "Can the Khmuic component in Mlabri ("Phi Tong Luang") be identified as Old Tin?", *Acta Orientalia* 50: 79 – 115.

Rischel, Jørgen – Søren Egerod
1987   "'Yumbri' (Phi Tong Luang) and Mlabri", *Acta Orientalia* 48: 19 – 33.

Satyawadhna, Choltira
1987   *The Lua of Nan Province* (in Thai) (Mahidol University).

Seidenfaden, E.
1927   "The Kha Tong Lu'ang' ", *Journal of the Siam Society* 20: 41 – 48.

Smalley, William A.
1961   *Outline of Khmu' structure* (American Oriental Society Essay No. 2).

Svantesson, Jan-Olof
1983   *Kammu phonology and morphology* (Travaux de l'Institut de Linguistique de Lund XVIII).

Thomason, Sarah Grey — Terrence Kaufman
    1988   *Language contact, creolization, and genetic linguistics* (Berkeley: University of California Press).
Thongkum, Theraphan L.
    1988   "The Mlabri (Phi Tong Lueang) language" (in Thai), in: Pookajorn et al. 1988: 47 — 71.
Trier, Jesper
    1986   "The Mlabri people of Northern Thailand: social organization and supernatural beliefs", *Contributions to Southeast Asian Ethnography* 5: 3 — 41.

Language contact in focused situations

Andrée Tabouret-Keller

Introduction

If one envisages a language as a repertoire of socially marked systems (Le Page — Tabouret-Keller 1985: 116, hereafter quoted as *Acts*), language situations in Europe are as diverse and complex as in any other part of the world. Conversely, if one envisages Europe as a community of states — there will be twelve states within the Single European Act in 1992 — what comes to the fore is a picture of linguistic blocs, each of these states (with the exception of Great Britain) having its official language, or as in Ireland, Belgium, or Switzerland their official languages, and in a few cases autonomous policies for regional languages, e. g., Basque and Catalan in Spain. Each of these languages appears as a self-defined entity, the reality of which is not questioned.

If one envisages society as a multidimensional space for language, we can recognize, in the terms of the optical model of projection by Le Page (*Acts*: 115 ff.), the activity which goes on "as processes of diffusion through initial contact, and then, in the right circumstances, of focusing, or convergence, towards various vernacular norms. Then subsequently, — possibly under the influence of literacy or (today) of broadcasting or television, there is focusing towards more regional norms, and the subsequent institutionalization of some prestige norms as standard languages which may form the basis of prescriptivism within a society. We then find prestige or stigma being transferred from the group whose norm has been so marked, to a construct which comes to be thought of as autonomous — such as "Standard English" or "the Cockney Dialect". People come to believe that a particular way of speaking is intrinsically "good" or "bad", "correct" or "incorrect", and "unchangeable" (*Acts*: 187).

We can recognize among the most generally, if not universally, present agencies which promote focusing: "(a) close daily interaction in the community; (b) an external threat or any other danger which leads to a sense of common cause; (c) a powerful model — a leader, a poet, a prestige group, a set of religious scriptures; (d) the mechanisms of an education system" (*Acts*: 187). To those we certainly can add all kinds of constitutional or legal institutions best shown by the case of France that I will take as an example of one among the most highly focused situations in Europe. Briefly it is a case where the processes by which a language comes to take shape as a powerful normative apparatus derive their importance from the great weight attached to the legal status of the language.

Three events in French history are decisive for the shaping of *le français ou la langue française* as an ideal and as a normative entity: (1) the Edit de Villers-Cotterêts of 1535, through which King François I decided to make *langaige maternel françois et non autrement* obligatory for all legal purposes in the kingdom; (2) the French Revolution, which led to a constitution enshrining French as the national language, and (3) the fact that at the beginning of the Third Republic, in the 1880s both military service and primary education became universal and obligatory. The public primary schools became free, compulsory, and secular, and the system has developed into a highly centralized body throughout which the selfsame language, French, has become operative as the common yardstick and norm through which republican democracy has had to work. At the same time compulsory military service has now for nearly a century brought together successive generations of young men from every part of France, and has operated as a levelling influence linguistically among speakers of different regional languages or, at least, of different regional accents.

Thus for some centuries the existence of French as an entity has been an unquestioned dogma, a major symbol of national unity and one of the main instruments of achieving that unity (Tabouret-Keller 1986: 4).

The first part of my paper deals briefly with the picture of the European language situation as it is shown in the work of the Standing Conference of Local and Regional Authorities of Europe (Resolution 192, March 1988): this picture is that of an overall highly focused situation; in the second part I shall deal with language contact in my home province Alsace, a Germanic dialect area in Northeastern France. As a part of the territory of France, Alsace belongs to the highly focused French language situation, as described above, but as regards its own regional language, it is an area of increasing diffuseness, not only because the spoken dialectal varieties are numerous and of great diversity (from Rhenish-Frankish in the North and Low Alemannic for the largest part of its territory to High Alemannic in the South), but also because there is no single written form for these idioms, nor are any of the available orthographies in widespread use, and lastly also because today a high degree of mixing of French and Alsatian takes place, particularly in towns (Gardner-Chloros 1990: 12 ff.).

1.   A focused picture of the European language situation

1.1. The European Charter on regional or minority languages

In the Resolution on regional or minority languages in Europe (adopted on 16 March 1988, referred to hereafter as *Res.*) four linguistic terms only are used: regional languages, minority languages, dialects, and national languages. "Dialects" is used only once, in reference to a previous report presented to the Parliamentary Assembly; we can leave it aside. "Regional" or "minority" languages are used as entities different from national languages as, for example, in the following quotation from the preamble: "... the defence and promotion of regional or minority languages in different countries and regions of Europe, far from constituting an obstacle to national languages..." (*Res.:* 3). In the General Provisions, however, Article 1, dealing with definitions, makes use of different criteria in order to specify the general category of regional or minority languages. Five sets of features are basic to their definition:

1. Regional or minority languages belong to the European cultural heritage, they are also said to be traditional.
2. They are traditionally spoken within a region of the state territory. The idea of traditional territory is that of "the geographical area in which the said language is the mode of expression of a number of people justifying the adoption of the various protective measures provided for in this convention" (Res.: 3). (It is obvious that the phrase "a number of people justifying the adoption..." leaves entirely open the question of the criteria which will decide on the number that indeed is felt to justify anything).
3. They are different from the language or languages spoken by the rest of the state's population.
4. They are spoken by nationals of the state.
5. They are spoken by a group numerically smaller than the rest of the state's population, hence the use of the term "linguistic minority" and the comparison with "speakers of more widely-used languages" (Res.: 3).

These five sets of features give an accurate image of the foundations of focusing processes as they affect not only the language situations in Europe but also the overall view that most European linguistics has of language itself.

1.2. Space, time and law

Three main factors emerge from this image: space, time and law. The idea of space has its roots in the notion of "language territories", possibly the most powerful basis to support an abstract ideal of language as a unit with strictly limited borders. In linguistics this abstraction is founded on the works of dialectologists; for example in J. K. Chambers and P. Trudgill's *Dialectology* in the figure of the large dialectal areas that map Europe (1980: 7). In my own experience the border between the Romance area and the Germanic area is not just an abstraction: I met it between two villages in the early fifties when as a student I was distributing left-wing leaflets against the Marshall Plan in one of the valleys of the Vosges. In eastern France the language boundary does not follow the mountain crest but follows some of the river valleys as, for example, that of the River Bruche where, in the fifties, at one place, the right bank still had an Alsatian-dialect speaking village, Natzwiller, whereas the left bank had a French-speaking village, Neuville. We had at that time two sets of leaflets, one in German and one in French and had to distribute them according to the side of the language boundary we were visiting. Today this situation has changed and the use of French, particularly of written French, makes a German version no longer necessary. A different and additional factor of focusing is at work here: the written form of language. The fact that French and German each possesses a standardized written form acts as a powerful focusing factor, firstly, by reinforcing the distinction of the two languages in reference to their separate written forms, and secondly, by excluding Alsatian, as a minor idiom with no standardized written form (Tabouret-Keller 1985: 14). When after World War II written French became the dominant language in education, business, and on the labor market, it gradually took over the ground not only of the written media but of the spoken also, and it is at present gaining ground among the younger generation as the most commonly spoken form.

Time appears as a factor superimposed upon space: the longer a territorial identity is perceived as embedded in the use of an idiom —

more often than not subsumed under a unique ethnic term that might designate the territory, the people, and their language — the stronger the representation of a highly focused unit of internal coherence. The strength of such a representation does not depend on the fact of permanent variation and change in language use: on the contrary, it helps to overlook these in favor of a unique identity supported by this unique term. This representation is even more focused when language as a named object, e. g., "French" as an identification label, not as a linguistic behavioral reality, becomes by way of law the expression of power at the same time that it becomes also the main instrument through which this power is expressed and applied. As I showed above, French is not only the name of a territory, of the people who live there, of the language that is supposed to be spoken by them, it is also by constitution the language of the citizen of the state of France.

The cases of the other European official languages are not always as clear-cut as the French case but overall each of the Western European states has an official language, *de facto* or *de jure*. Among the few exceptions one can quote Switzerland with three official languages but four national languages, Belgium with two official languages, or countries like Spain where two regional languages, Catalan and Basque, have status as official languages in the territories of these regions.

As a matter of inherent paradox, though not openly expressed, the formation of states rests on discourse (and eventually on law!) justified by mother-tongue ideology and calls on ethnic territorial identity at the same time that these states in setting their frontiers ignored the language people used and their identity (Tabouret-Keller — Le Page 1986: 252). As a result, frontiers between states more often than not do not coincide with dialectal areas and therefore most, if not all, European states include territories where a language different from the official language of the state is in use. This situation may change in the future if Article 11 of the Charter on "Transfrontier exchanges" is applied (Res.: 11). Its aim is "to maintain and develop specific cross-border relations between regional and minority languages used in two or more member states in identical or similar form".

Present-day surveys of speakers and their actual language behavior are not only scarce but their information is biased by the focused picture of language, particularly language in its written form and language as a juridical object, both contributing to the appearance and the influence of language as a reified entity. The Charter does not give any list of minority or regional languages and it does not pretend and certainly would not have been able to consider, and to go on from, the situations themselves: proper data are not available, by which I mean data such as including at least a sociolinguistic description: what the linguists say about the language; and what people say about it and about their own behavior.

In many cases the language situation is in a state of rapid flux towards a situation where the minority language is hardly any longer the medium of social life. At any rate we should not only know the history of the use of the language, its present-day situation but also the motivations people have and actually demonstrate about using it any longer.

The Charter can only provide a framework in which the legal status and promotion of such languages is possible. For similar reasons, it could not take into account the new situations created by labor migrations. The proportions of immigrant populations in Western Europe vary from about one tenth of the population in Switzerland, between five and ten percent in countries like France, the Federal Republic of Germany, or Belgium, to between one and five percent in southern countries like Spain, Italy, or Portugal. In contrast to the focused picture of official languages, we have to deal here with an overall diffuse picture although it is certain that some immigrant communities, as in certain London suburbs, might have evolved a quite focused language behavior among themselves through close interaction. But in such cases most of the processes that sustain focusing are lacking: shared territory, shared powerful oral and written mass-media, and related reinforcement of each of these by the others.

2. Sociolinguistic and psychological consequences in focused language situations

2.1. A brief remark on terminology

In Europe two main consequences of contact in highly focused situations are, on the one hand: 1) various and complex cases of the modes of contact in a given population — the term "bilingualism" is used as a partially misleading cover term for them all, 2) various and complex behavioral modes in the individual ways of using the languages — the term "bilinguality" (Hamers — Blanc 1986: 15 ff.) again is used as a cover term for them all, 3) various and complex cases of functional distribution in society of the languages, among them that referred to by the term "diglossia"; and on the other hand, the shrinking of the use of minority languages. The case of Alsace, my home province, is a case in point to illustrate them.

First of all we have to consider the terminology itself, "bilingualism", "bilinguality", "diglossia", and other such terms, both as a symptom of the power of focusing agencies and as a focusing factor within the sociolinguistic situation itself.

Over a century, from 1850 to 1950, people in my province had to change their official language and citizenship five times: from French before 1870 to German in 1871, back to French again after the First World War, to German again in 1940 with the Nazi invations, and back to French again at the end of the Second World War. My parents' generation, born at the beginning of the century, have learned to read and to write in German, had their higher education, if any, in French, but became German citizens again for four years from 1941 to 1945. People of my generation born around the 1930s have learned to read and write in French but had to continue for their secondary education level in German and to go on with their education in French after the Second World War. Bilingualism, the term generally in use to label the Alsace situation, clearly refers to those two languages, French and German, that were in turn the languages of literacy and education and the languages of administration and law; the Alsatian language does not come into this picture as it does not fulfill any of these social and political functions. Even today few people in Alsace would speak, for example, of a "trilingual" situation, by including their dialect. They would rather talk about "two languages", French and German, being written, having grammars (that is, rules on how to use them properly), and about Alsatian as a dialect that is not a proper language. Alsatian shows a good deal of geographical and written variation; written Alsatian is not at all widespread, not popular and, more often than not, not taken seriously.

2.2. The case of two related families in Alsace

The result of focusing both by education and administrative agencies and by normative vocabulary can be illustrated by the cases of husband Xavier and his wife Madeleine (G3) in Figure 1.[1] Madeleine, born 1911, acquired literacy and education after 1918 in French, but her husband Xavier, born 1906, acquired it in German. Both were born in Rosheim and have spent all their lives in this small town. Madeleine is still alive

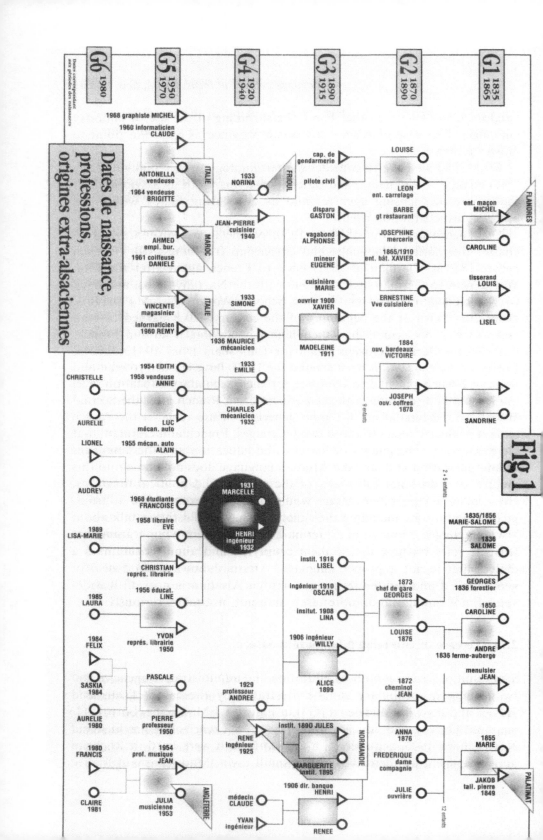

Fig. 1

Dates de naissance, professions, origines extra-alsaciennes

Dates correspondant aux périodes des naissances

| G6 1980 | G5 1950 1970 | G4 1920 1940 | G3 1890 1915 | G2 1870 1890 | G1 1835 1865 |

and a direct informant to me, but I have also known Xavier. Involved in left-wing trade-union politics, Xavier brought standard German literature into the household: between 1918 and 1940 standard German was still the most widely-read language in the working and agricultural classes. That is how Madeleine became a German-language reader. But for Xavier to be knowledgeable in politics he had to read the national news and he therefore learned to read and write in French. To sum up their cases: Madeleine writes only in French, she reads French and German but prefers German because she reads it fluently whereas she reads French with some difficulty; Xavier could read and write both German and French but was more at ease with German. Neither of them would use oral standard German except when forced to during the Nazi occupation. Talking about her identity, Madeleine says that she is from Rosheim, from Alsace, speaking the language of the place where she was born, but she would refuse to say she was bi- or trilingual for in French she only writes and in German she only reads.

The idea and the term diglossia are not known to her, nor generally in Alsace. The idea of a language (French or German) for higher social functions and of another one (Alsatian) for lower ones is not one people would easily accept here where, for example, cooking or viticulture would hardly seem lower occupations than the schoolteacher's reading and writing occupation.

We now take the case of Xavier's and Madeleine's grandchildren (in G5): they are still living in Rosheim, their families living close together. All are using the Alsation dialect for their daily family life, but learned to read and write and had their primary education in French, which they all talk and read fluently as long as it is in daily use but which they do not necessarily write fluently once they have left school for several years. Standard German no longer belongs to their daily experience even if they have learned some at school. They would not talk about bilingualism, the dialect not being a proper language in their view, nor about diglossia, because they have not heard the word.

Another consequence of powerful focusing agencies is, as I said before, the shrinking of the use of many of the regional languages in Europe. The Alsatian dialect is such a case. In the figures we can see six generations of two families related by the marriage in 1954 between Marcelle and Henri (in G4). In a report published elsewhere (Tabouret-Keller 1990) details are given on methods and data. Two points have to be recalled here. Firstly, we use terms like "Alsatian", "French", "Italian", "English" as they are being used by our informants, not knowing what linguistic or sociolinguistic realities they cover on any particular occasion. Secondly, the same terms are being used by our informants and by myself to name language behavior that must have utterly changed over the one hundred and fifty years we are dealing with. In the case of the six Alsatian-speaking generations (Figure 2, G1 to G6, in the family on the left-hand side) who have lived all their lives in the same place, the small town of Rosheim, the local form of Alsatian has kept a number of distinctive features, particularly on the phonetic level, but has changed on the lexical level. In using the names of languages as if for single and permanent entities we are of course both under the influence of the focusing agencies and playing a part in them.

What I want to present is an overview of the data bringing to the fore the fate of the regional language. In the first generation (G1) born between 1835 and 1865 Alsatian was the language used within the families with two exceptions, Michel (at the left top end) coming from Flanders, being said to have spoken "a komisch ditsch" and Jakob (at the right top end) coming from the Palatinate, being said to speak "plat". All their children (G2) grew up learning to speak in the Alsatian language with one exception: that of the children of Louis and Liesel (G1), who had left Alsace for Reims to escape germanization. Their daughter Ernestine who grew up in a French-speaking environment came back to her parents' place Rosheim, and was never heard to speak French by her granddaughter Marcelle who, as a child, lived with her. But something else happened in this generation (G2). In the families on the right-hand side the men got jobs that brought them and their families to live in town. Both Jean and Georges entered the railway company and, as a consequence, had a regular income and sent their children to have more education than they had had themselves. Some of the girls became schoolmistresses, the boys engineers or bank-clerks. In the family on the left-hand side, things went differently: the Fleming Michel had built up a flourishing building company (he had about 30 employees), his son Xavier went on with it but died in an accident at the age of forty five, leaving his widow with five children. There was no social security at that time and poverty ensued. Xavier-junior, the youngest son, was a builder like his father but he got asthma from the dust and he could not afford education for his children who either got artisan jobs, still in the same small town, or left, as Marcelle, through marriage, or as Jean-Pierre who, as a good cook, found a much better-paid place in Switzerland.

In (G4) (that is people born between 1920 and 1940), only Simone and Maurice, and Emilie and Charles have not left Rosheim, their parents

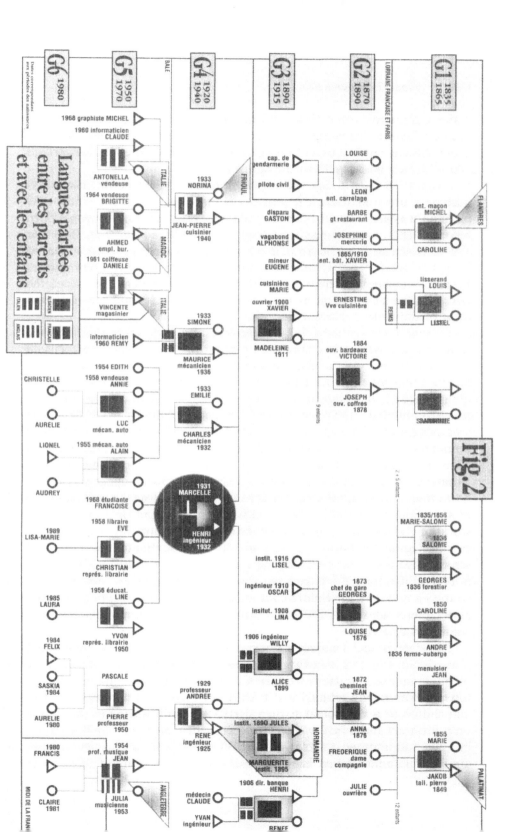

Fig. 2

and grandparents' place; they still keep up the use of the Alsatian language today, whereas all the others have shifted to French although they still live in Alsace with the exception of Jean-Pierre who settled in Switzerland and of Jean who settled in the South of France.

From 1918 until today the social mobility of the middle classes has become more and more dependent on the use of French. Until 1939 German was also required in the public services because, for people born before 1918, it was the sole language they could read or write. But after 1945 this generation began to die out and the younger generation needed French, since not only intellectual jobs but any office job now requires French. Nowadays there are hardly any jobs left where the use of the written form of language is not needed even if it is only the restricted form of the word processor's code.

To sum up: over the last one hundred and fifty years the linguistic situation in Alsace has changed in many respects as have the focusing factors. In the middle of the nineteenth century the term Alsatian had a certain focusing role as a factor of a regional identity linked to the use of a dialect in a geographical area — itself a factor of the focusing process-limited in the west by the language boundary with Romance languages and in the east by the river Rhine which was also a political boundary. The idea of a common dialect referred to an abstract and ideal form of language actually covering a wide range of local and/or social varieties. Nevertheless, as a common vernacular this language was felt to be dominant in the numerical sense: in the villages it was the only language of the majority of the farmers and wine growers and, in towns, of the working classes and together these two social groups were the majority of the regional population. It was also felt to be dominant in the functional sense that it was the only language spoken by this majority. The couples in (G1) illustrate the village situation: the only language between these couples and with their children was Alsatian, with the exception of Louis and Liesel who after 1871 at the beginning of the German occupation emigrated to Reims.

The deep social changes during the nineteenth century culminated towards the end of it in two main consequences from the point of view of the language situation: 1. masses of people left the villages to go to towns where they gradually lost features of their local variety of dialect and shifted to a vernacular town variety; this is illustrated in the family on the right hand in G2 where Georges, Jean, and their families settled in town and adopted a "town-colored" variety (whereas Xavier, Joseph, and their families stayed in their small town where some of their direct descendants still remain); 2. social mobility gradually increased; this again is illustrated in the family on the right hand where the members of generation (G3) all lived in town and had moved upwards on the social scale, a process later continued by their children. By 1945 Alsace was French again and social mobility implied the use of French. We can now define two new factors of focusing: moving from land to town, climbing up the social scale and adopting new sociolinguistic norms. But a third factor must be added: the representations in favor of French as the new focusing center associated both with the desirability of town-dwelling (and the undesirability of being a peasant) and with the desirability of going up in the social scale.

Finally, complementing the deep social changes that we have described, partly as their symptom and partly as their cause, education with its necessity and attraction became an increasingly important additional focusing factor after World War I for the spread of spoken French, mediated by schools and by the already highly focused written form (Tabouret-Keller 1988: 101 – 104).

From the middle of the nineteenth century to the end of our century the content of people's language performance has changed (Figure 3). People in (G1) were multilingual in a general framework of di- or tri-glossia: Marie (top right hand side) had Alsatian as her daily vernacular but read and wrote French and German fluently, her husband from the Palatinate spoke a Rhenish dialectal form, not much different from Alsatian, and read and wrote German. The following generation (G2) who had its education in German between 1870 and 1918 is a good case to illustrate the Fergusonian diglossic model, with their daily Alsatian dialect and a very limited use of the German Hochsprache (with the exception of Anna, who before her marriage went as a paid companion to a Geneva French-speaking family, where she became fluent in French, a language that she afterwards was always able to speak fluently but not to read well). The following generation (G3) is no longer bilingual and diglossic but tri-lingual and tri-glossic: Alsatian, French, and German (Hochdeutsch), I have already discussed the case of Xavier and his wife Madeleine.

With the next generations, (G4) and (G5) and certainly those who will follow, the linguistic content of what is still being called "bilingualism", "bilinguality", and "diglossia" has changed. Social mobility is still increasing but it means now that young people are able to change their professions and their jobs; geographical mobility has increased; people migrate within their country to get jobs or to get better jobs (the case of

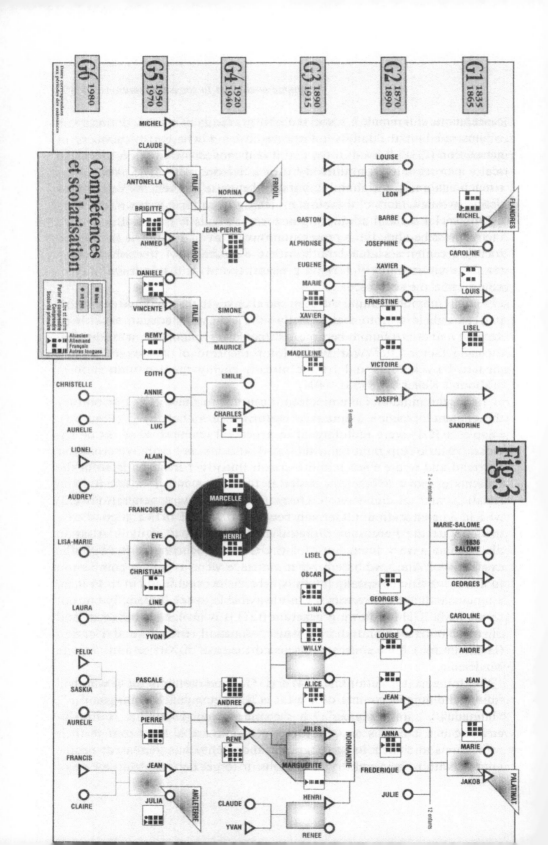

Fig.3

René in G4 or of his son Jean in G5), people emigrate out of their country for the same reasons (the case of Jean-Pierre in G4 or of his son-in-law Ahmed in G5) or for private reasons, for example, to establish a family (the case of Julia in G5). Young people travel easily all over the world, to study or just to visit and in this way get acquainted with other languages and cultures. Therefore "bilingualism", "bilinguality", and "diglossia" no longer refer to a specific, local contact situation like the one we had in Alsace in the nineteenth century, including just Alsatian, French, and German; they refer to a far broader variety and complexity where non-local languages come into the picture: Arabic, English, Italian, etc. (in G5) to which one must add the "foreign languages" taught in schools.

Concluding remarks

The term focusing covers a complexity of processes:

1. on the one hand focusing refers to membership identification to a group or a community of people: language in speech and communication as a mode of expression or behavior is one of the most powerful means of identification

2. on the other hand focusing refers to the effects and consequences of a set of agencies that support social integration processes. People may not wish this integration: in the case of my province as in most minority regions in Europe the choice of the language of literacy is not open nor is the choice of the language(s) one must master in order to get a job. The result of such situations is a complex identity: in a survey made several years ago in Alsace, pupils twelve to fourteen years old said that they were sure of their Alsatian identity but that they no longer spoke the language (Ladin 1982: 185). It remains to be explained why it is so essential for people to be able to assert unity in their social identities.

Note

1. Computer graphics for Figures 1, 2 and 3 by Sylvie Pelletier.

References

Chambers, J. K. — Peter Trudgill
1980   *Dialectology* (Cambridge Textbooks in Linguistics) (Cambridge: Cambridge University Press).

Gardner-Chloros, Penelope
1991   *Language selection and switching in Strasbourg* (Language Contact Series) (London: Oxford University Press).

Hamers, Josiane F. — Michel Blanc
1983   *Bilingualité et bilinguisme* (Bruxelles: Pierre Mardaga).

Ladin, Wolfgang
1982   *Der elsässische Dialekt — museumsreif? Analyse einer Umfrage* (Strasbourg: SALDE).

Le Page, Robert B. — Andrée Tabouret-Keller
1985   *Acts of identity. Creole-based approaches to language and ethnicity* (Cambridge: Cambridge University Press).

Standing Conference of Local and Regional Authorities of Europe
1988   *Resolution 192 (1988) on regional and minority languages in Europe* (Strasbourg: Council of Europe).

Tabouret-Keller, Andrée
1985   "Classification des langues et hierarchisation des langues en Alsace", *Le français en Alsace* (Bulletin de la Faculté des Lettres de Mulhouse, Fasc. IX)) (Paris — Genève: Champion-Slatkine), 11 – 17.

1986   "The case of French", *Abstracts of the proceedings of the workshop of the International Group for the Study of Language Standardisation and the Vernacularisation of Literacy* (York University: Dept of Language), 4 – 7.

1990   "Continuité et discontinuité de la transmission de l'emploi de l'alsacien dans deux familles alliées", *Plurilinguisme* 1.

Tabouret-Keller, Andrée — Robert B. Le Page
1986   "The mother-tongue metaphor", *Grazer Linguistische Studien* 27: 249 – 260.

Dialect typology and social structure

Peter Trudgill

The issue I want to address, in a very preliminary way, is the question of to what extent it is possible to link the typology of language varieties to the typology of societies. That is: do different types of society produce different types of language structure; and do they produce different types of linguistic change?

Of course, these are not new questions, and they are also questions which linguists have, quite rightly, treated with a certain amount of suspicion in the past, because of their links with notions to do with "primitive" languages and "primitive" societies. However, we are now able to consider such issues without making the same type of error (see Dixon, n. d.). I want, therefore, to start to tackle this issue by concentrating in this paper on possible differences between smaller, isolated, tightly-knit speech communities and larger, more central, more loosely-knit societies.

I begin by taking the Scandinavian languages as an example. If we suppose that, say, 1,200 years ago, the ancestor of the modern Scandinavian languages was a relatively unified language, then we can point to the fact that, twelve centuries later, some of these languages, for example, Norwegian and Faroese, have ended up typologically rather different from one another. Within the Indo-European language family, Faroese is sometimes described, not entirely accurately, as a "conservative" or "archaic" variety, while Norwegian is said to be relatively "innovating". Insofar as this is an accurate characterisation, it is true especially of morphology (and might be even more true of Icelandic versus Danish). As we shall see, it is not necessarily true of phonology.

When we talk of "conservative" and "innovating", of course, this means that Norwegian and Faroese, having descended from a common ancestor, Old Norse, today differ considerably from one another, to the point where they are not mutually intelligible, because of changes which have taken place in the last 1,000 years, with more of these changes having taken place in Norwegian than in Faroese. Many of the changes that have taken place, moreover, have led to a typological split, with Norwegian, for instance, having less inflectional morphology than Faroese. Consider, just by way of illustration, one example each of Faroese versus Norwegian adjectival and verbal morphology.

'narrow' (adj.)

Faroese		Norwegian
smala	f. acc. s.; wk. masc. acc. /dat. s.;	smal masc./fem. s.
	wk. fem. nom. s.; neut. nom. / acc. s.	smale pl.; wk.
smalan	masc. acc. s.	smalt neut. s.
smalar	acc. pl.	
smalari	fem. dat. s.	
smali	wk. masc. nom. s.	
smalir	masc. nom. pl.	
smalt	neut. nom. /acc. s.	
smalur	masc. nom. s.	
smøl	fem. nom. s.; neut. pl.	
smølu	wk. fem. acc. s.; wk. fem. acc. /dat. pl.	
smølum	masc./neut. dat. s.; dat. pl.	

'to throw'

Faroese		Norwegian	
kasta	pr. pl.	kaster	pres.
kasti	pr. s. 1	kastet	pst.; pst. part.
kastaði	pst. s.		
kastaðu	pst. pl.		
kastar	pr. s. 2, 3		

This particular adjective has eleven forms and two stems in Faroese, with three forms and one stem in Norwegian, while the Faroese verb has five finite forms to the Norwegian two.

Why has this typological split occurred? Does this development have a social, or partially social, explanation? Can the sociolinguist in general say anything useful about typological issues? There are certainly some relevant areas where sociolinguists have made a contribution. For example, it is widely agreed that languages whose speakers have frequent contact with speakers of other varieties change faster than varieties whose speakers do not. This would be one explanation for the "conservatism" of Faroese. The Faroes have certainly been a more isolated community than Norway since their settlement, and especially in earlier centuries were very much cut off from the outside world. Even today they are relatively remote, located as they are in the North Atlantic ocean 600 kilometres west of Norway and 430 kilometres southeast of Iceland.

But what about the typological split? What about the nature of the linguistic changes that have taken place? How is it that Norwegian has ended up by being typologically different from both Faroese and Old Norse? In considering this issue we can note that changes which typically take place in high language-contact situations have been rather well studied in sociolinguistics – and Norwegian is a relatively high-contact language compared to Faroese. Our investigation of lingua francas, pidgins, creoles, and other high-contact language varieties have led us to expect developments such as change from analytic to synthetic structure, reduction in redundancy, and increases in regularity in these situations. As is very well known, changes of this type are attested in the histories of the Indo-European languages of Western Europe, as well as in the Semitic languages and elsewhere. In comparing continental Scandinavian with Old Norse, English with Old English, French with Latin, we find features such as reduction in overt case-marking and an increase in prepositional usage; reduction in conjugations, declensions, and inflections; loss of the dual number; increase in periphrastic verb forms; more restrictions on word order; and so on.

All changes of this type can be described by the technical term of simplification. I have argued elsewhere (Trudgill 1986) that much of this simplification is due to the imperfect learning that takes place during contact-induced pidginisation. At this point, however, we should note that, as Thomason – Kaufman (1988: 27) have pointed out, it is by no means always the case that contact leads to simplification. It can equally well lead to complication. The reason for this is clear. If we ask of the imperfect learning that occurs in language contact situations: imperfect learning by who?, the answer is fairly apparently: imperfect learning by non-native adults and post-adolescents. Everything we know about young children indicates that in general they are such good language learners that they normally learn perfectly any language variety that they have sufficient exposure to. Imperfect learning, and thus simplification, does not result from non-native language learning as such but from adult non-native language learning.

There is no total consensus about language-learning abilities in the literature, but the view from sociolinguistics (see, for example, Labov

1972) is that children acquire new dialects and languages more or less perfectly up to the age of about eight, and that there is no chance of them learning a language variety perfectly after the age of about fourteen. What happens between eight and fourteen will depend very much on the circumstances and on the individual. This view is held in spite of the fact that particularly complex phonological rules of a new dialect may not be totally mastered in complete detail even by very young children (see Payne 1980; Trudgill 1986). The view from scholars of second-language acquisition, on the other hand, is more disparate (see Krashen 1981), but I myself would want to support those who accept to a greater or lesser degree Lenneberg's critical period hypothesis (Lenneberg 1967). Although it must be the case that sociological and sociopsychological factors are partly responsible for the relatively poor language-learning abilities of adults in natural acquisition situations, it is also apparent that developmental factors must play a vital role.

This critical period, or developmental threshold, therefore has to play an important part in our understanding of language contact phenomena. As I have argued elsewhere (Trudgill 1989), the implication is that simplification will occur in sociolinguistic contact situations only to the extent that adult second-language learning is concerned, as notably in the development of, say, West African Pidgin English. Where contact means permanent or long-term contacts between communities involving children, on the other hand, not only will simplification tend not to occur, but complication may also result, such as the introduction of click consonants into Zulu and Xhosa from Khoisan languages (see Thomason—Kaufman 1988: 132—133). It must always therefore be a mistake to expect that language contact will lead to simplification without first investigating whether or not it is predominantly contact between adults that one is dealing with.

The same thing would appear to be just as true of dialect contact as of language contact. In Trudgill (1986) I examined developments which typically occur in situations of high contact between mutually-intelligible varieties, concentrating on dialect-mixture and new-dialect formation. Dialect contact, it appears, also leads to simplification, as has been observed by a number of scholars. Jakobson, for instance, noted that dialects which serve a relatively wide socio-spatial function tend to have simpler systems than dialects with a more restricted function (Jakobson 1929). And Labov has pointed out that, in contact situations, phonological mergers spread at the expense of contrasts. In dialect contact generally, we encounter a process of koinéisation, in which levelling and simplification both play a role. By levelling we mean the loss of minority, or marked, variants present in the dialect-mixture in favour of majority, or unmarked, forms also present. By simplification is meant the growth of new forms that were not actually present in the initial mixture but developed out of interaction between forms that were present. These interdialect forms are more regular than their predecessors. Explanations for why koinéisation takes the form it does are not necessarily staightforward, but it seems likely that the greater learnability of regular forms is an important factor. Part of the explanation must again be the inability of post-adolescents to acquire new language varieties perfectly, together with the particular difficulties caused for them by irregularity, as far as learnability is concerned.

In our search for links between social and linguistic typology, then, we have found one connection: simplification occurs in certain contact situations as a result of imperfect learning by adults and post-adolescents. We thus have at least one rather close link between a particular social phenomenon − social contact − and type of linguistic change, and therefore language and dialect typology. Speech communities having frequent contacts of certain types with other societies are relatively more likely to produce languages and dialects which demonstrate simplification, the most extreme cases typologically being pidgins and creoles.

In fact, however, the position is a good deal more complex than this, as a comparison of Faroese and Norwegian shows. In the rest of this paper, I want to note, firstly, that concentrating on simplification alone is relatively unhelpful in aiding our understanding of what has been happening to Faroese in the last 1,000 years or so. Faroese might not have undergone as many changes over the centuries as Norwegian, but many changes have certainly occurred. So how are we able to explain the nature of these changes, and what can we say about the relationship, if any, between the nature of Faroese society and the structure of the Faroese language? Secondly, I also want to note that morphology is obviously not the only linguistic level that should be considered. Thirdly, it will also be important to appreciate that simplification is a cover term for a number of different types of linguistic change, not all of which can with equal confidence be ascribed to imperfect learning. And, finally, we will note that imperfect learning is by no means the only difficulty encountered by adult non-native speakers.

Efficient communication is sometimes said to result from achieving an equilibrium between the needs of the speaker and the needs of the listener (see Martinet 1962). The speaker wants to communicate quickly or at least with little effort, while the listener needs enough information to process the message accurately. In contact situations, I would like to suggest, this balance is disturbed, or at least complicated, by the needs of the non-native learner as both speaker and listener. Let us consider some of the linguistic devices and practices which make things less or more difficult for non-native speakers and listeners at different linguistic levels.

At the level of phonetics, obvious candidates for consideration as a potential obstacle for non-native speakers are fast-speech phenomena such as assimilation and elision. Fast-speech phenomena make things easier for the native speaker: the same message can be got across more quickly and with less articulatory effort. As far as the equilibrium is concerned, fast-speech phenomena do not seem to make things more difficult for the native listener, in normal conditions. (In non-normal situations, such as broadcasting, they do have to be reduced.) Notice, however, that fast-speech phenomena make life much more difficult for the non-native listener, by reducing the amount of phonetic information available for processing. Paradoxically enough, however, fast-speech phenomena also make things more difficult for the non-native speaker because they constitute an extra set of things to learn and remember, as well as an extra set of things to remember to do while speaking. English speakers often observe of, say, highly educated Swedes that "they speak English better than we do". This most often means that the Swedes in question do not use many fast-speech processes. Why do skilled non-native speakers not use as many fast-speech phenomena as native speakers? The answer is obviously that they do not use them because they are unable to do so.

One of the things which often happens in linguistic change is that fast-speech phenomena become institutionalised, i. e., they become slow-speech phenomena as well. If it is true that non-native speakers have problems with such processes, then we would expect this institutionalisation to happen less often in high-contact situations. This expectation is certainly confirmed at least by pidgins, which have very few stylistic differences in phonology, especially in their early stages (Mühlhäusler 1986).

Another example can be taken from the level of discourse. An obvious example of a discourse phenomenon which makes things difficult for non-native speakers has links to the work of Basil Bernstein. Non-native speakers have great difficulty with native speakers when the latter speak in restricted code (Bernstein 1971). Speakers of restricted code give relatively little background information, and take a fund of shared knowledge for granted. Bernstein's important insight was to note that speakers who are relatively unused to communicating with interlocutors from outside their own social networks are more likely to use restricted code than speakers who are used to communicating with interlocutors with whom they share relatively little background information, who are therefore more aware of the need not to take too much common knowledge for granted.

Non-native speakers are typically outsiders and will therefore tend to find restricted code a problem, because insufficient information is provided for them. They are presented with a comprehension difficulty caused by a lack of data, just as they are with fast speech processes. Restricted code, on the other hand, makes things easier for the insider and for the native speaker because it is quicker, since more can be taken for granted. It is very important, however, to notice that restricted code will work much better, and therefore presumably be more common, in some types of community than in others. The typological point is that restricted code is much more likely to occur, and will be easier to comprehend even for native speakers, where it occurs in small, tightly-knit, close-network types of community which have large amounts of shared knowledge.

This may not have any implications for language structure as such, in spite of what Bernstein may have thought at one time, but it does connect to the point above about fast-speech phenomena, where we also talked of insufficient information causing difficulties for outsiders. It also leads us to recognise the important point that social-network structure may tell us as much about linguistic developments and structures in low-contact languages like Faroese as imperfect learning does about high-contact languages like Norwegian. As we have observed, fast-speech phenomena may become institutionalised because they make things easier for the native speaker. But this is not just less likely to happen in high-contact situations. It is also more likely to happen in small, tightly knit, perhaps isolated, communities which have large amounts of shared information and where individual personalities are known to all, than in larger communities or communities with looser network ties. In more tightly-knit societies, we can say, the communication equilibrium may tilt over in favour of the speaker. We therefore need to bring into our typology of societies not only how many external contacts members of a speech community have with speakers of other varieties, but also how large the community is − or its component parts are − and how tightly-knit it is in network terms.

If we now return to Faroese vs. Norwegian, the question is: can we say that the differences between these two languages are predictable in terms of differences between Faroese and Norwegian society, considering not only social and linguistic contact, but also community size and network structure? If what we have been hypothesizing is correct, we would expect Faroese (as opposed to Norwegian) to be relatively more characterised by linguistic features and changes that:

1) make things more difficult for the non-native speaker;
2) are more likely to occur or survive in tight social networks; and
3) make things easier for the native speaker.

A number of features suggest themselves as candidates in these categories. As we shall see, many of them occur in more than one category. The following is a selection, concentrating on phonology and morphology.

1. Difficulties for non-native speakers

There are two major types of phenomena that are likely to cause difficulty for the non-native speaker. The first consists of those which cause difficulty of learning and remembering.

An obvious candidate of this type is morphological irregularity. Morphological irregularity, like other types of irregularity, obviously increases problems associated with memory load. Although small children seem to cope with problems of irregularity quite quickly, it causes considerable difficulties for adult language learners, who for the most part have to resort to rote-learning in order to master the details. Morphological irregularity, moreover, is a feature that is more prominent in Faroese than Norwegian. As we have seen, Faroese also has more morphology altogether than Norwegian.

Another similarly problematical feature is high paradigmatic redundancy. This requires some explanation. It is often said that pidginisation leads to reduction in redundancy in language, the implication being that redundancy causes difficulties for non-natives. This is too simple a view. We have to note that redundancy is of two main types. Syntagmatic redundancy involves the repetition of information syntagmatically, as in (gender and number) concord and agreement. Paradigmatic redundancy, on the other hand, involves redundancy in phenomena such as grammatical gender, and different conjugations and declensions. This distinction is important because the two types are affected differently in various types of sociolinguistic situation. In language-death situations, for instance, there is evidence that syntagmatic redundancy is lost before paradigmatic redundancy. In the Arvanitika (Albanian) spoken in the Attica and Boeotia areas of Greece, for example, language shift and loss are occurring (see Trudgill 1983: 155ff.). The language, however, does not demonstrate any loss of paradigmatic redundancy. The three genders remain distinct, as do the different declensions and conjugations. But a number of instances of loss of syntagmatic redundancy are apparent if one compares the speech of older, more fluent speakers with that of younger speakers. For instance, future verb forms such as /do tə jap/ 'I shall give', where /do/ is the future marker and /tə/ the (redundant) subordinator, have become /do jap/, etc., in all but very elderly speech.

For non-native speakers, however, it is paradigmatic redundancy that causes the greatest learning difficulty — witness the amount of effort traditionally devoted in second-language learning situations to the mastery of genders, declensions, and conjugations. It is therefore no surprise to note that Faroese has considerable amounts of paradigmatic redundancy, particularly as compared to Norwegian. We will return below to the notion of syntagmatic redundancy.

The second major source of problems for non-native learners consists of features which lead to difficulty of comprehension.

For a non-native speaker trying to understand a foreign language, a number of phenomena will cause difficulties. We have already mentioned the problems caused by fast-speech phenomena because of the reduction in the amount of phonetic information available for processing by non-natives.

At the morphological level, difficulties will be caused by low morphological transparency, where there is a low degree of correspondence between a grammatical category and its expression (see Haiman 1980; Bauer 1988: 189 − 191). (Difficulties caused for nonnatives by opacity are easier to demonstrate at the level of lexical transparency: the non-native learner will have more difficulty learning and comprehending the English word *dentist* than the transparent German equivalent *Zahnarzt*). Low morphological transparency is of course typical of inflecting or fusional languages (as opposed to agglutinating and isolating languages); and Faroese is a language which is a great deal more fusional than most other northwest European languages. Braunmüller (1984) has, moreover, argued that morphological opacity is a typical characteristic of "small languages", such as Faroese.

Interestingly, difficulties will presumably also be caused for non-natives' comprehension by a low degree of syntagmatic redundancy. It is much easier to comprehend speakers if grammatical information is repeated: a pronoun and a person ending on the verb, for example, give the listener two chances to process and comprehend a message correctly. It is therefore important to observe that we cannot say that Faroese demonstrates a low degree of syntagmatic redundancy — an apparent counterexample to our thesis. We will return to this issue shortly.

2. Features in tightly knit communities

The second type of feature we want to look at consists of those that we might suppose to be more likely to occur in smaller and perhaps more isolated tightly knit social networks. We have already discussed fast-speech processes, at the level of phonetics, and restricted code, at the level of discourse, as probable candidates.

We can now further suggest a high degree of irregularity, including morphological irregularity, as a candidate. This will lead us, however, to introduce a further socially-based explanatory factor into the picture, in addition to the factor of shared information/ease for speakers that we mentioned above. The additonal explanatory factor is as follows. In smaller, tighter communities, I would want to argue, it is easier for the community to enforce and reinforce the learning and use of irregularities by children and adolescents (see Andersen 1988). Sociolinguistic research into the influence of social network structure on linguistic change (Milroy 1980; Bortoni 1985) has revealed that the dense, multiplex networks typical of relatively closed, stable, non-fluid communities are more likely to lead to conformity in linguistic behaviour and to the maintenance of group norms as well as the carrying through of ongoing linguistic changes. We can suppose that similar processes will be at work in the maintenance of linguistic complexity, particularly where there are frequent inter-generational interactions.

The same will probably also be true of the maintenance of paradigmatic redundancy. As we have already seen, Faroese demonstrates more irregularity, and more paradigmatic redundancy, than Norwegian.

At the phonological level, there is some indication that smaller communities may be more likely to produce certain sorts of sound change, and to favour certain types of phonological structure. While small isolated communities might be more resistant to change, when changes do occur, they might also be able, because of their network structures, to push through, enforce, and sustain changes of a less "natural" phonological type that would never make it in larger, more fluid societies (see Bailey 1982). There might also be more scope for the influence of particular individuals and "language missionaries" (see Trudgill 1986: 56 – 57), as is illustrated, for example, in the linguistic history of Tristan da Cunha (see Trudgill forthcoming).

In considering this hypothesis, we have to be very careful about our notion of what is "natural" in linguistic change, as it is easy to fall into the trap of supposing that what is unusual is the same as what is unnatural (see Bailey 1982). Certain peripheral dialects of British English, for example, might appear to English specialists at first sight to have produced some somewhat strange sound changes, particularly when compared to changes which have occurred in geographically more central dialects. For instance, linguists tend not to be very surprised about London-based changes such as vocalisation of /l/, loss of /h/, and loss of non-prevocalic /r/:

/milk/	>	/miuk/	'milk'
/hiːp/	>	/iːp/	'heap'
/hwiːl/	>	/wiːu/	'wheel'
/kaːrt/	>	/kaːt/	'cart'

Apparently much more surprising are changes of the type:

| /hwiːl/ | > | /kwiːl/ | 'wheel' | (peripheral areas of the already peripheral Shetland and Orkney islands) |
| /hwiːl/ | > | /fiːl/ | 'wheel' | (Buchan, N. E. Scotland) |

However, it is probable that we tend to regard such changes as strange simply because they are unusual in English. In actual fact, of course, the sound changes seen simply as such are perfectly unsurprising. The reverse can also be true. The apparently totally unmotivated change of /š/ to /rš/ in words such as *wash* in a small area of southwestern England, which is regarded as a little bizarre by many British linguists, is not observed to be at all unusual by many American linguists for the simple reason that this pronunciation is used over thousands of square miles by millions of speakers in the United States, having presumably been transported from England to North America. It nevertheless remains, at least in my view, a phonological oddity. Subject to this caveat, however, it does still seem that isolated communities may be genuinely more likely to produce changes that could be labelled, in Henning Andersen's words, as "slightly unusual" (Andersen 1988).

In the same paper, Andersen also argues that peripheral communities are more likely to see the development of elaborate phonetic norms and the proliferation of low-level pronunciation rules. Milroy (1982) has also argued that standard varieties are more likely to demonstrate allophonic simplicity than vernacular varieties, citing the Belfast vernacular as having considerable allophonic complexity in its realisation of certain vowels, vis-à-vis the middle-class norm. Thus, while in middle-class speech, /a/ as in *bat*, etc., is realised as [a], in working class speech it has allophones in different phonological contexts which range from [ɛ] through [æ], [a], and [ɑ] to [ɔ]. Note especially that much of this complexity is not of an assimilatory type, with, for example, front [ɛ] occurring as the realisation of /a/ before velar consonants. Milroy ascribes this in part to the tendency of standard varieties to impose invariance, but it may equally be due to the ability of the tightly networked working-class Belfast community to sustain allophonic complexity.

As far as "slightly unusual" phonetic changes are concerned, Andersen discusses the historically unconnected but surely non-fortuitous development of parasitic consonants out of diphthongs in several isolated areas of Europe in a number of languages including Romansch, Provençal, Danish, German, and Flemish, along with the absence of such changes in metropolitan varieties. The isolated German dialect of Waldeck in Hesse, for example, has *biksen* (cf. *beißen*) 'to bite'; *fukst* (cf. *Faust*) 'fist'; *tsikt* (cf. *Zeit*) 'time'; and so on. This particular sound change does strike many historical linguists as unusual, and does appear to be confined to small communities in geographically remote and/or peripheral areas.

As far as our comparison of Faroese and Norwegian is concerned, it is probably true to say that most linguists would agree that sound changes which have occurred in Norwegian in recent centuries have been rather more natural and expected, and rather less complex, than many of those which have occurred in Faroese. For example, the vowel shift undergone by many varieties of Norwegian such that /a:/ > /o:/ > /u:/ > /ü:/ strikes no linguist as at all strange. On the other hand, Faroese changes such as the "Verschärfung" whereby forms developed such as /kigv/ from earlier /ku:/ 'cow', and /nudž/ from earlier /ny:/ 'new'; and diphthongisations such as /i:/ > /uy/ as in /luyk/ from earlier /li:k/ 'like' are intuitively felt by many historical linguists to be rather unusual. Equally, Arnason (1988: 61) writes that "to give a simple and reliable picture of the history of Faroese vocalism is difficult, partly because the development seems to have been so complicated"; while Küspert (1988: 197) says that "the development of vowels in stressed syllables from Old Norse to modern Faroese is clearly a complex and opaque one" (my translation).

3. Ease for native speakers

Finally, we come to features which we might suppose would make language use easier for native speakers. We suggested above that in communities such as the Faroes we might expect to see the communicative equilibrium tip over in favour of the speaker as opposed to the hearer. Among features which might therefore be more likely to occur in such communities there are obvious candidates at the phonetic level. We have already noted fast speech phenomena.

At the morphological level, one could guess that one good candidate for inclusion in this category would be loss of syntagmatic redundancy. As we have already seen, a low degree of syntagmatic redundancy makes things more difficult for the inexpert listener. In at least certain high-contact situations, therefore, syntagmatic redundancy may be expected to increase. For example, Joseph (1983), in his book on the Balkan infinitive, has argued that language contact in the Balkans has been the cause not only of the spread of the loss of the infinitive, but also of the origination of this development. He notes that the use of forms such as Greek

θέλω να γράψω

where first-person present-tense singular is marked on both verbs — a good example of syntagmatic redundancy — will be easier for non-natives to process than forms such as

I want to write

where this information is given only once. He further argues that the Balkan-type finite forms arose and spread, at least in part, because of sensitivity on the part of native speakers in contact situations to the comprehension difficulties of non-native listeners.

Correspondingly, we might also expect a reduction in syntagmatic redundancy in small isolated languages, on the grounds that this will make things easier for the speaker, who is thereby saved the bother of repeating information. The Scandinavian evidence, however, suggests that this is probably not the case. As we have already noted, Faroese cannot be said to demonstrate a low degree of syntagmatic redundancy vis-à-vis Norwegian. On the contrary, there is plenty of syntagmatic redundancy in Faroese, such as adjectival agreement, and rather more than there is in Norwegian. As Barnes (1977) has pointed out, it is true that there is a tendency in modern colloquial Faroese for the dative -*i* morpheme to be omitted from nouns governed by a preposition. This is a change which would appear to make speech production easier for speakers (and, incidentally, make language learning, although not comprehension, easier for non-native listeners). But generally speaking, our hypothesis does not hold water at this point.

The preservation of syntagmatic redundancy in Faroese and other small languages — as opposed to its origination — must therefore be explained in terms of the other factor which at this point conflicts with the ease-for-native-speakers factor — that is, the ability of small, tightly knit communities to ensure the transmission from generation to generation of relatively complex linguistic structures. This supposition is supported by evidence from language-death situations where, as communities disintegrate and network ties loosen, syntagmatic redundancy is also reduced, as in Arvanitika (Trudgill 1983), as we saw above. We do not, therefore, reject the principle concerning native-speaker ease, but we note that, at least at the morphological level, it is probably less powerful than the network-reinforcement factor.

Conclusion

There is some evidence to suggest, then, that it may not be an entirely futile exercise to look for links between social and linguistic structure. The above discussion, moreover, also leads us to make the following point. Language contact is widely and rightly regarded as a highly interesting phenomenon. Our discussion, however, also indicates that language isolation is equally interesting and maybe more challenging for the historical linguist. We can explain changes in high-contact dialects and languages in terms of imperfect learning by adults, interaction between systems, and so on. Perhaps an even more interesting question, however, is: how are we to explain, in sociolinguistic terms, developments that occur in isolated languages and dialects?

If these varieties do genuinely tend to have certain linguistic characteristics in common that are not shared with koinés and other high contact varieties, then obviously the very preliminary discussion in the present paper goes only a very small way towards answering this question. Note, however, that if we want to pursue such issues and explanations further, we had better hurry. Faroese itself is alive and very well, but a very large proportion of the world's isolated languages and dialects may not be with us much longer. Indeed, it could be that, because of demographic and communications developments in the modern world, languages with complicated inflectional morphology and large amounts of irregularity, and dialects with complex and unusual phonetic developments, may increasingly become a thing of the past, as external contacts increase and societies become more fluid. Labov's forthcoming book is subtitled "The use of the present to explain the past". Increasingly, however, the present is going to become less like the past in demographic and social network terms. There may also therefore be differences in the direction of linguistic development and in the distribution of linguistic structures.

Consider the morphological level. It is often said that languages go through a morphological cycle (see Bynon 1977: 265) in which fusional languages lose their morphology, perhaps through phonetic erosion, and gradually become isolating. They later, however, acquire further morphology as phonological and other processes turn independent lexical items into clitics and then into bound morphemes. It is true that Chinese is said currently to be acquiring a certain amount of morphology, and that Comrie (1980) has described the relatively recent development of postpositions into suffixes and then into case-endings in Finnic. Many other cases could no doubt be cited. As we look around the world's languages, however, there are currently very few signs indeed of isolating or even agglutinating languages turning into fully-fledged complex fusional languages of the classical Indo-European type. It is not entirely inconceivable that − for social rather than for internal linguistic reasons − such languages will never develop again.

References

Andersen, Henning
 1988   "Center and periphery: adoption, diffusion and spread", in: Jacek
       Fisiak (ed.), *Historical dialectology* (Berlin: Mouton de Gruyter),
       39−83.

Arnason, Kristjan
1980   *Quantity in historical phonology* (Cambridge: Cambridge University Press).

Bailey, Charles-James
1982   *On the yin and yang nature of language* (Ann Arbor: Karoma).

Barnes, Michael P.
1977   "Case and the preposition *við* in Faroese", *Sjötiu ritgerðir helgaðar J. Benediktssyni*, 39 – 71.

Bauer, Laurie
1988   *Introducing linguistic morphology* (Edinburgh: Edinburgh University Press).

Bernstein, Basil
1971   *Class, codes and control, Vol. 1* (London: Routledge & Kegan Paul).

Bortoni, Stella
1985   *The urbanisation of rural dialect speakers* (Cambridge: Cambridge University Press).

Braunmüller, Kurt
1984   "Morphologische Undurchsichtigkeit — ein Charakteristikum kleiner Sprachen", *Kopenhagener Beiträge zur Germanistischen Linguistik* 22 [1985]: 48 – 68.

Bynon, Theodora
1977   *Historical linguistics* (Cambridge: Cambridge University Press).

Comrie, Bernard
1980   "Morphology and word order reconstruction: problems and prospects", in: Jacek Fisiak (ed.), *Historical morphology* (The Hague: Mouton).

Dixon, Robert
n. d.   "Are some languages better than others?" Unpublished manuscript.

Haiman, John
1980   "The iconicity of grammar", *Language* 53: 515 – 540.

Jakobson, Roman
1929   "Remarques sur l'évolution phonologique du russe comparée à celle des autres langues slaves", *Travaux du Cercle Linguistique de Prague* 2.

Joseph, Brian
1983   *The synchrony and diachrony of the Balkan infinitive* (Cambridge: Cambridge University Press).

Krashen, Steven
1981   *Second language acquisition and second language learning* (Oxford: Pergamon).

Küspert, Klaus-Christian
1988   *Vokalsysteme in Westnordischen* (Tübingen: Niemeyer).

Labov, William
1972   *Sociolinguistic patterns* (Oxford: Blackwell).
in press   *Studies in linguistic change* (Oxford: Blackwell).
Lenneberg, Eric
1967   *Biological foundations of language* (New York: Wiley).
Lockwood, William
1977   *An introduction to modern Faroese* (Tórshavn: Føroya Skúlabóka-
               grunnur).
Martinet, André
1962   *A functional view of language* (Oxford: Oxford University Press).
Milroy, James
1982   "Phonological 'normalisation' and the shape of speech commu-
               nities", in: Suzanne Romaine (ed.), *Sociolinguistic variation in
               speech communities* (London: Edward Arnold), 35—47.
Milroy, Lesley
1980   *Language and social networks* (Oxford: Blackwell).
Mühlhäusler, Peter
1986   *Pidgin and creole linguistics* (Oxford: Blackwell).
Payne, Arvilla
1980   "Factors controlling the acquisition of the Philadelphia dialect by
               out-of-state children", in: William Labov (ed.), *Locating language
               in time and space* (London: Academic Press), 143—178.
Thomason, Sarah—Terrence Kaufman
1988   *Language contact, creolization and genetic linguistics* (Berkeley:
               University of California Press).
Trudgill, Peter
1983   *On dialect* (Oxford: Blackwell).
1986   *Dialects in contact* (Oxford: Blackwell).
1989   "Interlanguage, interdialect and typological change", in: S. Gass
               et al. (eds.), *Variation in second language acquisition: psycholin-
               guistic issues* (Clevedon: Multilingual Matters), 243—253.
forthcoming *Language in isolation.*

Borrowing and non-borrowing in Walapai

Werner Winter

The study of foreign items added to the lexicon of a language can contribute substantially to knowledge about the history of this language and of its speakers. Such study is a legitimate concern of linguistics anywhere; in the case of languages unrecorded until very recently, however, the importance of loanwords as a source of historical information tends to increase considerably.

For the reconstruction of the unrecorded history of a language and its speakers, it is imperative that the immediate source of a loanword (and not some remote ultimate origin) be determined. It is only the immediate contact that counts, not a previous exposure to foreign influence which the source language may have undergone. Thus, whether words transferred from English to a language X are of Anglo-Saxon origin or not is of no concern for the history of X — it is only the contact English — X that counts (cf. Winter 1971: 110, 114 — 115).

It is unusual for a loan transfer to affect only isolated entities; it rather seems to be the rule that clusters of items assignable to specific semantic fields are taken over. This reflects the fact that it is not just words that are borrowed, but usually also the things, skills, and notions designated by these words in the source language, and these things, skills, or notions tend to be part of natural groups or divisible into such groups. If the name and the thing, etc., are both borrowed, then observing borrowing as a linguistic phenomenon will give access to insights into borrowing as a more general cultural event or cluster of events.

There is no compelling need for the transfer of a foreign designation when an element or a feature of a foreign culture is adopted. The designation may be borrowed, but appear in a native guise; for such a loan translation to come into existence, it is, however, necessary that enough of a bilingualism be found to make the translation of the foreign term possible. In the absence of such a bilingualism, or for other reasons, the foreign designation may not be transferred at all, but a native term may be used to name the thing, skill, or notion taken over. This purely native solution may be achieved in various ways: the range of application of a native designation may be extended, a native designation may cease to be used for its original native object of reference, or native means may be used to create new native terms — usually by way of coining neologisms with fully understandable constituents referring to what appears to be taken to be the set of relevant properties of the item or event to be named.

1. In the following remarks, I propose to discuss aspects of the lexicon of a little-known Amerindian language with which I was able to work over a period of more than twenty years, starting in 1956; I was fortunate in having a chance to work with a number of highly-qualified elderly native speakers, some of whom were in their eighties and nineties even in the 1950s. In this way, it was possible to record properties of past stages in the development of the language, a fact which proved important particularly in the area to be discussed here.

Walapai (Hualapai) 'people of the pines', a language of the Yuman group, is spoken by members of a tribe located in the northwestern part of Arizona. The reservation of close to a million acres (4,000 km^2) of semi-arid land comprises a substantial part of the original homeland of the bands now united in one tribe; however, in the south and west, prior to the establishment of the reservation, white settlers and ranchers took over land formerly used by the Walapais. At present, there are more than 1,000 members on the tribal rolls; a large percentage of these people is not fluent in Walapai.

In assembling the data to be analyzed here, I refrained from including what was in the 1950s and 1960s everyday usage of the then younger generation. The reason behind this is that, for most of these people, English has to be considered the dominant, Walapai, the recessive language. This means, for one thing, that English words can no longer be expected to cluster in a significant way; equally important seems to be the fact that words of English origin appear to be fully synonymous with native terms so that the two can be used interchangeably, while loanwords proper may be viewed as preferably filling a semantic or stylistic slot not occupied by a native word (though of course even these loanwords are subject to replacement by paraphrase).

My data thus derive from forms given to me by older people, either in response to the elicitation of vocabulary or in unchanneled discourse, be it in normal dialogue or in stories (traditional or spontaneously formulated) told and in songs recited. Information obtained from fully competent younger speakers was not entirely disregarded, but used essentially only as a source of information for the study of productive word-formation processes and thus was of importance mainly for an evaluation of the respective weight of calques vs. truly native coinages.

My texts (now available at the Yuman Archives at the University of California at San Diego, La Jolla, California) include, as just stated, traditional tales as well as oral histories. The former tend to reflect life of a time prior to exposure to Hispanic and Anglo culture and thus are intrinsically unlikely to make recourse to borrowed words necessary. As a matter of fact, the main body of the mythical tales I was able to record contains, as far as my notes indicate, only one English common noun, viz., /layn/ for 'mountain lion', which the narrator immediately changed to the Walapai equivalent, *nmit*, thereby apparently indicating that the loanword was somehow not properly used. English place-names can be found, but rather as glosses rendering native terms to make them more intelligible to the outsider present when the tale was narrated.

As texts produced on the spur of the moment, life histories are clearly in a different category. Yet even here the position of English is marginal. For the oldest person telling his story, Kate Crozier, who was said, in 1956, to be one hundred years old (and in fact he cannot have been much younger than that), and who reported much more of encounters with white soldiers and ranchers than of personal experiences with old-time traditional life, there is hardly any impact of the English language, except when reference is made to individuals, places, or dates (one cannot be certain whether the occasional use of an English term, such as *prospector* alongside native *wihwál* or *cowboy* beside Walapai *wàksikəwí:c* is not a concession to the white interviewer, whom he at times addresses directly). All in all, it can be said that over the years of his long life, Kate Crozier became completely familiar with the activities typical of the frontier, but the English language, which he did learn, left his Walapai essentially unaffected. (An approximate rendering of the story of Kate Crozier's life is now to be found in Hinton — Watahomigie 1984: 65 – 96.)

2. The English loanwords I recorded are an odd lot indeed. The list includes, apart from *layn* mentioned earlier, two words for 'cat', *pos* and *kíri, kófi* for 'coffee', *hankəc* for 'handkerchief', *monkə* for 'monkey', [c'ánma] for 'Chinese' (and 'Japanese'), and *sìkswí:ci* for 'seventy-five cents'. The last two items will be discussed later on; the others do not invite special comment except that most of them are terms relating to aspects of the everyday life of white families. They certainly do not form a neatly definable semantic set.

A generalization seems possible: loanwords from English were extremely rare in Walapai as used by speakers born in the second half of the nineteenth century. This observation applies to speakers who were, at the time when recordings were made, without exception bilingual in Walapai and at least that variant of English which one might want to call "Walapai English" and of which I published some sample texts (Winter 1963). I will return to this point later on.

3. Words whose Spanish origin seems obvious are considerably more common. My list includes *ʔəru:θ* 'rice', *ʔa:s* 'ace', *cil* 'chili', *haləvuro* 'burro (donkey)', *haltəmiñ* 'Sunday; week', *kanelo* 'sheep', *kapitan* 'captain', *karet* or *katet* 'cart', *kaθve* or *kovθa* 'coffee', *mulo* 'mule', *pap* 'potato', *səva:to* 'goat', *soltaw* 'soldier', *tərha:r* 'work'.

Some semantic groupings can immediately be proposed: domestic animals unknown in Arizona in pre-Columbian times; food and drink; military terminology; and of course the generalized term for 'work', ubiquitous in the Spanish — Amerindian contact areas of the Southwest and Far West. The groupings can be extended in interesting ways, but a very important question should be asked first: It is likely that these words, which are certainly of Spanish origin, were taken over directly from Spanish-speaking people but can they be loanwords from Spanish in the proper, narrow sense?

From what we know about the pre-Anglo history of Northern Arizona, we have to conclude that the answer can only be in the negative: there were not enough contacts between the middle of the sixteenth and the end of the nineteenth century to make a direct transfer probable. The next question follows immediately: Can we determine a source, or sources, closer to Spanish-speaking areas, yet still located near enough to Walapai territory, or in known contact with speakers of Walapai, to facilitate a linguistic transfer?

Two channels of transmission appear likely: one up the Colorado River, the other from New Mexico by way of the Hopis (a third one, from the south, is less probable because of what is reported about a history of hostilities between Walapais and Yavapais).

4. When one inspects *Hopi domains* (Voegelin — Voegelin 1957), one notes that the Walapai terms for 'sheep' and 'goat' agree with the Hopi words for 'sheep' and 'male goat' even to the point of showing preservation of final -*o*. More important, however, is the fact that the agreement extends to the term for 'cow', Walapai *waksi?*: Hopi *wá:qasi* which must be a Hopi adaptation of Spanish *vaca(s)*. Transfer of a Hopi term for a fruit and a fruit tree introduced by the Spaniards is found in the word for 'peach', Walapai *θəpal*: Hopi *sipála*.

5. Mohave, on the other hand, shows even more agreement with Walapai in items traceable to Spanish. 'Chili', 'coffee', 'rice', 'soldier', 'week', 'work' have closely matching forms. Mohave *thivat* (/θivat/; in citing Mohave forms, I follow the practical orthography used in Munro — Brown 1976), the term for 'goat', cannot be the source of Walapai *səva:to* because of the onset *θ*- and the absence of -*o* in Mohave; on the other hand, /θ/ is, as Leanne Hinton has shown, precisely what one would expect to find in an early borrowing from Hopi in Walapai (cf. the word for 'peach'). It may very tentatively be suggested that an old loanword with initial *θ*- was borrowed from Walapai by Mohave before it was replaced, in Walapai, by a more recent loanword from Hopi, a loanword adopted too late to undergo the replacement of pre-Walapai **s*- by *θ*-.

If Mohave *hanidal* 'government' is indeed, as Pamela Munro (Munro — Brown 1976: 35) suggests, a development from Spanish *general*, then one may possibly take the occurrence of Mohave /ð/ as an indication that the River-Yuman change of Proto-Yuman **y* to /ð/ was late at least in this language — the distance between *r* and *ð* seems too great to make a replacement by the latter sound likely. Be that as it may, it seems highly probable that Walapai *haniθal* (with substitution of /θ/ for -*ð*-) is a loanword from Mohave; if so, it appears likely that Walapai *soltaw* 'soldier' was also taken over from Mohave as here, too, we would be dealing with basically military terminology (the same argument would apply to Walapai *kapitan* 'captain').

6. While, up to this point, comments on loans from Mohave have had to be characterized as at best likely or probable, we can be absolutely certain about some forms from a different semantic field. The Walapai terms for 'quarter' and 'half-dollar' contain the Mohave numerals 'two' and 'four', respectively: Walapai *mihvik* or *mifik* reflects Mohave *me havik* 'two bits' and does not contain Walapai *hwak* 'two'; Walapai *micəmpáp* 'four bits' agrees with Mohave *me chumpap* and does not show Walapai *hùpá* 'four'. The word for 'dime', on the other hand, has Walapai 'one' in *mìsi:t*, corresponding to Mohave *me ?asent*.

While these observations suffice to prove borrowing from Mohave, it should be asked whether Mohave *me* can be explained.

The answer to this question seems clear. Mohave -*me* (with an obligatory possessive prefix) means 'foot, feet'. One may assume that a speaker of Mohave, a language which had neither an /f/ nor a /b/, would assign the labial of *bit* to the same sound class as the labiodental of *feet* and thus could provide an "etymology" for *bit* which enabled him to find a loan translation. Speakers of Walapai, in their turn, could then identify Mohave *me* as the word for 'foot' and render it by its Walapai counterpart *ʔmiʔ*.

7. With one exception to be discussed shortly, the entire system of expressions for small amounts of money in Walapai appear to derive from Mohave: The word for 'nickel' is Walapai *hol*, Mohave *hool*; the latter derives from Spanish *jola*, used in the north and northwest of Mexico for a small coin (cf. Santamaria 1959: 642). Corresponding to Mohave *hool ʔakwath* 'yellow jola' we find in Walapai not **hòlqʷáθ* as one would expect, but *hòlhʷát* 'red jola' or *hòlkwál rap* 'little flat red jola' for 'one cent' (in Yavapai, we have 'small yellow war bonnet', clearly a reference to the Indian-head penny). The use of 'one bit' for 'dime', encountered also in Yavapai, has already been mentioned, as has that of Walapai *sìkswì:ci*, obviously a replica of English *six bits*, for 'seventy-five cents'. It is noteworthy that this is the first term discussed here which does not refer to a single United States coin; this may explain its having come into existence independently of other *bit* terms. In Mohave, 'seventy-five cents' also remained outside the *bit* system, but with quite different results: here a loanword from Spanish survived, viz., Mohave *serialk*: Spanish *seis reales* (cf. Munro − Brown 1976: 75).

The availability of a coin may be taken to have been the cause for the adoption of the expression '(one) peso' for 'one dollar' in both Mohave and Walapai: Mohave has *ʔumpees*; for Walapai, I recorded *ʔumpés* for the one-dollar piece, *pes* as a general term for both 'dollar' and 'money' (alongside *ʔumpés* and *ʔəmpés*); I do not think that Walapai *pes* has to be viewed as taken from a different chain of transmission.

8. Among words of at least ultimately Spanish provenience, I mentioned Walapai *ʔa:s* 'ace', This form is matched by Mohave *ʔas*. The agreement between Mohave and Walapai extends to other names for cards and suits of cards: Mohave *ʔaree*, Walapai *réya* 'king'; Mohave *kaavay*, Walapai *kaváya* 'queen'; Mohave *soot*, Walapai *sóta* 'jack'; Mohave *vasta*, Walapai *vá:sta* 'clubs'; Mohave *ʔaspav*, Walapai *spáða* 'spades'; Mohave *koop*, Walapai *kópa* 'hearts'; Mohave *ʔaʔoor*, Walapai *ʔəʔóra* 'diamonds'. The substitution of *-v-* for [ð] in Mohave *ʔaspav* is curious in view of the fact that a voiced interdental fricative is well established in this language; it occurs, however, only in pre-stress position, and phonotactic constraints may have taken precedence over considerations of phonetic similarity. In some cases, the Walapai form is closer to Spanish than its Mohave counterpart, as, e. g., in Mohave *ʔaree*: Walapai *réya*: Spanish *rey* 'king'; the reason may be that my informant, knowing some Spanish, re-Hispanized, as it were, Walapai items (he also gave alternative forms for some of the card names, viz., *los* ~ *dos* 'two', *sé:sa* ~ *seys* 'six', *syéta* ~ *siete* 'seven'). It seems best to ascribe his use of a voiced interdental fricative in the word for 'spades' to this cause — which would not preclude the assumption of a borrowing of card names from Mohave into Walapai.

9. It thus appears that a good case can be made for terms of ultimately Spanish origin having been brought into Walapai not directly, but by way of other Indian languages, viz., Hopi or Mohave. In some instances, such as Walapai *mulo* 'mule', we seem, however, to lack evidence for an intermediate link between Spanish and Walapai; here the general argument that there is no support for an assumption of early contacts with speakers of Spanish has to be brought to bear unless one wants to consider Walapai *mulo* a very recent loanword.

In the case of the 'bit' words, Mohave mediation has to be recognized even for a term of English provenience. The same may hold true for Walapai *c'ánma*, Mohave *chanama* 'Chinese'. Pamela Munro (Munro – Brown 1976: 28) derives the Mohave word from English *Chinaman*, which seems perfectly reasonable. In any case, the term gives the impression of being a fairly early loan from English, and it is highly probable that the Mohaves, living downstream from the Walapais, encountered Chinese sooner than their more easterly neighbors. Thus we are probably well advised in excluding *c'ánma* from the list of items borrowed by speakers of Walapai directly from English.

10. It is widely assumed that Amerindian languages in general make wide use of descriptive terms, that is, of constructs whose parts taken together provide a composite reflection of crucial aspects of the meaning of the term. In its central native vocabulary, Walapai shows only limited recourse to this, as it were, analytic approach; it seems to have been wiedespread not in common nouns, but only in names such as designations of topographical entities. Thus, 'Peach Springs' is called *hà:ktəkwí:va* 'cottonwoods that stand in a row'; 'butte' is rendered by *wì:kəʔil* 'rock-RELATIVE-pointed (large)'; 'mesa', if large, is *wì:kwilkwil* 'rock-level(large)-level(large)', if small, *wì:kwirkwir* 'rock-level(small)-level(small)'. In other semantic domains, descriptive terms are found only occasionally; examples are: *hmàñyá:kiʔ* 'child-lie-INSTRUMENT' = 'cradleboard', *yuñəhay* 'eye-POSSESSIVE-liquid' = 'tears', *θəmpòcyalq* 'bee-excrement' = 'honey'.

Though of limited application, the technique of creating descriptive terms can be considered as having been well established in pre-contact Walapai. It was precisely this technique which could be made use of to cope linguistically with a large influx of new notions from the culture of English-speaking Americans, short of taking over a great number of English words.

11. A short list of rather randomly selected items will serve to illustrate the results of such an avoidance strategy:

'broom'	*wàsəciyiʔ*	(house-MANUAL-stroke-INSTRU-MENT)
'door'	*wàsəʔámiʔ*	(house-MANUAL-close-INSTRU-MENT)
'fence, corral'	*ì:səvkó*	(wood-MANUAL-CLOSE-put)
'lantern'	*ʔòʔúliʔ*	(fire-burn-INSTRUMENT)
'Monday'	*wàsták*	(house-MANUAL-open)
'policeman'	*pàkhér*	(man-RELATIVE-rope in)
'refrigerator'	*kwètəmúniʔ*	(thing-FACTITIVE-cold-INSTRU-MENT)
'telephone'	*k'wàlkwá:wcoʔ*	(metal tool-LOCATIVE-talk-PLU-RAL-INSTRUMENT)
'tramp'	*hàykùmcáy*	(non-Indian-hungry)

None of the Walapai terms given reflects the form of its English equivalent, not even when a certain level of synchronic intra-English analysis would have been possible, as in the case of 'policeman'; thus, for the creation of the new Walapai words, no bilingual competence was required. The independence of Walapai is perhaps most obvious with 'Monday': to an outsider, the decomposition of the notion of 'Monday' into 'house-opening time' makes sense only once he realizes that the reference is to a store and its being closed on Sunday and opened again on Monday.

12. On the other hand, occasionally an English configuration is reflected: Walapai *pà:pmyúl* (potato-sweet) can hardly be entirely independent of English *sweet potatoes* (unless a Mohave combination containing the Spanish loanword *paap* and the native form *maduuly* 'sweet' was nativized in Walapai in a development parallel to that discussed in section 6). Whether the Walapai expression for 'daddy longlegs', *ní:smpàrkəkyúl* (spider-leg-RELATIVE-long), is to be connected with the English term qua form cannot be decided; as 'daddy longlegs' certainly refers to an entity in the environment totally unconnected with Anglo culture, the odds seem to be in favor of partly parallel, yet independent, development in both languages. Likewise, the complex verb form *smà:píkyu* (sleep-die-SAME SUBJECT-be) 'he is drowsy' is not to be taken as a calque on *he is dying to sleep* in spite of the overt similarity of the two constructions as far as their constituent lexemes are concerned.

13. The technique of creating new words through a combination of elements existing in the language, the free and competent use of this technique continued to exist even at a time when it was no longer needed as an avoidance strategy. It was interesting to observe that, when we were involved in the dictionary work, my own attention was focused on collecting old lexical material, not the least because it could be used in work on comparative reconstruction; at the same time, the Walapais active in the Bilingual Education Program would return from interviews with elderly speakers of the language, announcing with great excitement that they had been given new words. These then turned out to be true neologisms, such as a term for 'sewing machine', and no one could possibly tell whether such nonce formations would stand a chance of becoming accepted by the community at large (to the extent that it was still using the native language). The most likely fate of such a neologism was that it might be adopted by some members of the group if it could easily be analyzed and understood, but if it had to compete with another new coinage with the same meaning, it might well end up as just one of several expressions in use in the language. Thus, for 'bank' two variants were recorded, viz., *pèspú:coʔ* and *pèskwá:coʔ*. Both of these have the same internal structure (money-put-PLURAL-PLACE), the only difference being that the lexemes referring to 'put' are not identical; both are equally understandable, and which one might win out should depend entirely on nonlinguistic circumstances.

At times, the odds favoring one set of coinages are very high indeed. One particular informant was asked to provide the names of the months of the year. The terms designating something very close to 'month', which were recorded during the first third of this century (cf. Kroeber 1935: 113–114), were no longer known. Thus, an elderly lady provided a list which agreed only in part with the set of terms others had created earlier; this lady's forms, however, were promoted by inclusion in a calendar prepared and distributed by members of the Bilingualism Program. In a way, then, a set of canonical forms came into existence in the 1970s; whether it will remain the one accepted by the community at large remains to be seen.

14. Cases of reassignment of established native terms to new designations are fairly rare. This is not so surprising: a spontaneous analysis of a word on the basis of known constituents is not possible, in particular not if a word is not complex; here all users of a term have to be aware of the semantic reassignment that has taken place, or else communication will break down. Two such cases of successful transfer may be mentioned: the old meanings of *hpuˀ* 'bow' and *ˀpaˀ* 'arrow' were still known when the more modern use of the terms to designate 'gun' and 'bullet', respectively, had become well-established. The ultimate outcome of this state of affairs is that the modern usage will survive (though in antiquarian texts relating old times and customs 'bow' and 'arrow' may be kept at least for a while). It is interesting to note that the so-called 500-word list compiled by members of the Bilingual Education Program included only 'bullet' and not 'arrow'.

15. The evidence presented so far can be summed up in a few words.

In spite of prolonged and intensive contact of speakers of Walapai and speakers of English, the impact of the latter language has been negligible as far as straightforward transfer of vocabulary items is concerned. Loanwords are few and do not cluster in significant ways. Words of Spanish origin, somewhat more numerous to be sure, were brought into Walapai by the mediation of neighboring Amerindian languages (this indirect transfer also included some terms of English provenience). Direct exposure to, and hence direct borrowing from, Spanish is of a fairly recent date.

Evidence for loan translations is available, but again includes only very few unambiguous items.

It is thus appropriate to say that the Walapai response that can be observed was to nonlinguistic aspects of Anglo culture; it was, as it were, a strictly monolingual response in an increasingly bilingual situation.

16. The question of course arises why all this should have happened. We have, on the one hand, the fact that all aspects of material Anglo (or, more generally, Southwestern) culture were accepted without recognizable resistance, and, on the other, an almost total rejection of English even to the point that calques were avoided to the same extent as were straightforward loanwords. An answer to the question raised is to be sought, and − hopefully − found, in an analysis of certain facets of Walapai − English relations during the first few decades of intensive contact between the two groups of speakers.

17. Since before the end of the nineteenth century, an ever-increasing number of Walapai children came to attend government schools for Indians. In these schools, the basic policy was to make the Indian youngsters more able to cope with all aspects of American life by making them fully conversant in English. To achieve this goal, there was a general tendency to suppress the use of the native Indian language and to make the children speak only English in class and on the school premises − the idea of course being that total immersion was the simplest way to make the young Indians acquire a command of English fast and effectively. No attempts were made − certainly not in the case of a small tribe such as the Walapais − to use the native language as a vehicle of instruction, not even in the lower grades. Once secondary schools were attended, the use of the mother tongue was further impeded by the fact that these schools were designed to accommodate students from a variety of tribes, so that English − now quite naturally − became the normal means of communication on and off campus.

18. Once a boarding school was attended, contacts with the family were usually limited to the period of summer vacations. In this way, the youngsters were rather thoroughly separated from their relatives not going to school. They could no longer participate in many normal tribal activities, such as the telling of traditionial stories that took place on long winter evenings − a practice important for the propagation of a more than superficial knowledge of the archaic language of oral literature and for the preservation of this literature itself. When the youngsters came home, they may have seemed somewhat like strangers to those who stayed home, and these in turn may have appeared, in the light of what the children had been taught in school, to be backward people, if not worse. It seems that a very serious conflict had been pre-programmed: the young and what they could convey to those at home could be seen as totally disruptive forces; the parents and the other members of the family and what they stood for could appear to be entirely out of step with the times. As long as the home scene remained stronger, it could attempt to re-Indianize the youngsters, and — not least because of the traditional high status of the older persons — it could succeed in this attempt; as soon, however, as the home scene had become weakened, Indian traditions, no longer appreciated by the young who were steeped in new values, were bound to give way.

It can be said that this is exactly what seems to have happened, and that both periods so characterized are clearly reflected in different patterns of linguistic behavior.

19. The first period, that of prevailing strength of the native Indian culture, seems to have been characterized by an almost total rejection of at least the verbal aspects of white American civilization. No matter which, and how many, English words and phrases the youngsters may have brought home, virtually none of them found acceptance; it seems as though keeping Walapai pure had become a desirable goal, possibly because this purity was a way to stress the special character of the native culture. Contrary to what is found in many movements dedicated to linguistic purism throughout recent history, there seems to have been no rejection of all foreign elements in the language — the concerted effort to keep Walapai as it was did not lead to the elimination of loanwords from other Indian languages, even if they were ultimately of English origin, such as *c'ánma* 'Chinese'; the attempts to protect, as it were, Walapai in its original state were directed only against the English language as taught in the schools.

20. This state of affairs could have prevailed if the strength of the home scene could have been preserved. This, however, was not the case; the old culture was inevitably subject to slow, but constant, attrition.

The youngsters may have gone back to school most unwillingly (and it is known that many did), and they may have tried to resist the destructive effects of the school system on their native culture as well as they could; yet they could also not help seeing the obvious advantages of being able to find a place, if not within, then at least close to, white society by mastering the white man's language. If they reacted in this way, their attitude toward English could not remain — like that of their elders — one of total rejection, and as schooling for all was extended in time and improved in quality, English was bound to become at least as accepted as Walapai.

It did not take long until, at least for some of the younger Walapais, English, though not the mother tongue, took over the role of the dominant language. When these people returned to the reservation, they were disinclined to give up the use of English, and, depending on the specific conditions in a home, English would gradually become a normal means of communication within the family, frequently reducing Walapai to a very marginal status.

21. This development occurred in particular under two not uncommon conditions. Partly as a result of living in boarding schools and of extended contact with Indians from other tribes, the number of marriages with non-Walapais increased; here English was very often the only language common to both partners. The other factor furthering the use of English was one of attitude, not of outward conditioning: Parents who had reached the conclusion that in order to make one's way in the modern world a full command of English was needed, and who had felt handi-capped by the fact that they themselves had not been able to use the language from very early childhood, now wanted to make life easier for their children; therefore, they would make English the language employed exclusively − or at least preferably − in parent-child communication. The children in their turn would use Walapai at best with outsiders and with members of the older generation; in any case, Walapai would take on the status of a marginal language, if these children did indeed learn it at all.

22. It cannot be said that the replacement of Walapai by English as the language used at home and with children was a universal process within the tribe, encompassing all families and all of them at once. Nevertheless, beginning in the 1960s, there seemed to be ample reason to believe that the native Indian language was slowly, but inexorably, on its way out. Oral literature as a creative art had by then long disappeared from the scene; the transmission of oral literature in its traditional form was precariously kept alive by a few aged story-tellers and singers, but there was no evidence that members of the younger generation would continue to practice the art; the knowledge of the more elaborate archaic language on the part of the younger had become passive, if not rudimentary; the Walapai language in active use was now heavily mixed with borrowings from English, and the grammar had been losing some of its complexities, leading, inter alia, to a reduction of syntactic conjoining.

23. It can be said that the chances for survival of a language depend on a variety of conditions. The number of speakers is undoubtedly one factor; in the case of Walapai one could argue that more than one thousand Walapais, were they all to decide to actively use their language, should be sufficient to assure language maintenance for generations. Facts of economic life doubtlessly play a part; but then the introduction of cattle industry to tribal lands taken by itself did little, if anything, to threaten the continued use of Walapai. The degree of integration into a larger community with a different language appears to be of great importance; there can be no question but that the ties of the Walapais with the world around them have become very strong indeed, and their rediscovery of a separate identity has in many ways not been that, but rather a discovery of a new, pan-Indian identity which is of only little help when aspects of a specific tribal culture are to be kept alive or brought back to life.

For a language to survive, the crucial condition, however, seems to be the willingness of the people to maintain its use. It is thus basically a question of attitudes. As the history of the Walapais shows, repression as practiced in schools for the Indians of the day actually seems to have provoked a reaction on the part of tradition-minded Walapais that served to strengthen their language; however, strength was replaced by weakness when the users of the language themselves began to feel that giving preference to English was more meaningful.

24. The 1970s saw a revival of interest in their language on the part of the Walapais themselves. With the help of a long series of United States government grants, work was carried out on the preparation of teaching aids that were to help in reintroducing young Walapais to their language in the school located at Peach Springs, Arizona; last-minute attempts were made to save at least part of the oral literature for future generations of Walapais. This is a very welcome change from the disinterested state of mind so commonly found in the 1960s; whether the salvage operations will succeed cannot be said even half a generation after they were started. To me it seems that what has been decisive in the past will also be decisive in the future: it is the attitude on the part of those who are, or might be, speakers of a minority language that determines its ultimate fate. If the Walapais really want to speak their language (not just study it in some school text), if they, by speaking it at home and among members of the community at large, make command of the language, and not an entry on the tribal rolls resulting in a claim to joint ownership of the land, the true distinguishing mark that determines whether a person is a Walapai or not — if they decide in favor of such an attitude and take the steps necessary to put this attitude to work, then there may be a fair chance of survival for the language.

Such survival would not mean that all registers of the language could be maintained — the archaic language of the tales and, above all, of the songs will never be used again once the last narrators and singers have passed away. There is little likelihood that a puristically shaped Walapai will seem to be a natural means of communication; some admixture of English will probably be accepted. If it survives in this way, modern Walapai will be very different from the language that had begun to fade away even in the 1950s; but in its own right it will be interesting as a language that reflects both the old and the more recent history of the people that use it. For this to happen, however, the crucial condition is that these people retain or rediscover the will to hold on to their language.

25. The small study of borrowing and non-borrowing in Walapai presented here has, I think, helped to focus our attention on forces that determine the history of languages and of the people who use them, not just on Walapai and the Walapais, no matter how interesting they are as a subject of investigation. It has shown how important attitudes, and likes and dislikes, are in shaping the destiny of a small language in Northern Arizona; what happened to it may be special in certain respects, but on a higher level of abstraction it may be taken as nothing but a variant of what is typical of the way in which human language and human life are interconnected: language and its use is central to human beings as individuals and as members of groups, and what happens to the language touches the individual and the group more deeply than many other experiences. If this is the case, language, and also any particular language, deserves to be respected; it should be allowed to be used as the speakers want to use it and not be interfered with. In particular, for the languages of minorities, Robert Hall's old appeal "Leave your language alone!" should be supplemented by another, "Leave other people's languages alone!". If that is done, it will be possible for those who want to, to keep their language alive; that this freedom from outside interference also implies that speakers may decide to give up their language is part of the deal. Linguists may regret this state of affairs, but theirs is to observe and analyze, perhaps to advise, but never to command.

References

Hinton, Leanne – Lucille J. Watahomigie (eds.)
  1984   *Spirit Mountain. An anthology of Yuman story and song* (*Sun Tracks*, 10) (Tucson, Arizona: Sun Tracks / University of Arizona Press).
Kroeber, Alfred L. (ed.)
  1935   *Walapai ethnography* (Memoirs, American Anthropological Association, 42) (Menasha, Wisconsin).
Munro, Pamela – Nellie Brown
  1976   *A Mojave dictionary. Preliminary version* (Los Angeles, California).
Santamaria, Francisco J.
  1955   *Diccionario de mejicanismos* (Méjico: Porrua).
Voegelin, Charles F. – Florence M. Voegelin
  1957   *Hopi domains* (*IJAL* Memoir 14 = *IJAL* 23.2, supplement) (Baltimore, Maryland: Waverly Press).
Winter, Werner
  1963   "Stories and songs of the Walapai", *Plateau* 35.4: 114–122.
  1971   Review of Ernest Klein, *A comprehensive etymological dictionary of the English language, Linguistics* 71: 108–118.

Subject Index

Leiv Egil Breivik
and Ernst Håkon Jahr
(Editors)

Language Change

Contributions to the Study of Its Causes

1989. 15.5 x 23 cm. VIII, 281 pages. Cloth.
ISBN 3 11 011995 1
(Trends in Linguistics. Studies and Monographs 43)

This collection of 11 papers reflects the recent upsurge of interest in historical linguistics, delving into the complex causes not only of phonological change, but of language change in general.

This work draws on the developments and expansion of disciplines such as sociolinguistics, language contact research, communication theory, child language and creole studies, together with innovations in the study of language-internal developments as well as in the study of language universals and linguistic typology.

Data are drawn from a variety of languages and language types but all focus on the causes of language change.

mouton de gruyter

Berlin · New York

Vladimir Ivir
Damir Kalogjera (Editors)

Languages in Contact and Contrast
Essays in Contact Linguistics

1991. XII, 502 pages. Cloth.
ISBN 3 11 012574 9
(Trends in Linguistics. Studies and Monographs 54)

The invited papers in this collection on contact linguistics deal not only with the effects of linguistic borrowing and mutual influence of linguistic systems, but also, in the broader sense of the term, with the bilingual speaker who is the *locus* of language contact.

Both approaches to contact linguistics are represented in this volume, the first exemplified by analytical papers presenting material from several Indo-European languages that cover different aspects of linguistic description, and the latter by examinations of bilingualism and foreign-language acquisition.

The group of theoretically oriented papers examine the rationale of contact and contrastive linguistics, their relationship, their place among the linguistic disciplines, possible models of description, and methodologies.

Also included are papers which take a broader perspective and consider the social and cultural context in which language contact occurs.

mouton de gruyter
Berlin · New York